D1879845

Munshi Premchand

# Munshi Premchand

Gopal Sharma

KALPAZ

**©Author**

All rights reserved. No part of this work may be reproduced, stored, adapted, or transmitted in any form or by any means, electronic, mechanical, photocopying, micro-filming recording or otherwise, or translated in any language, without the prior written permission of the copyright owner and the publisher. The book is sold subject to the condition that it shall not, by way of trade or otherwise, be lent, resold, hired out, or otherwise circulated without the prior publisher's written consent in any form of binding or cover other than that in which it is published.

The views and opinions expressed in this book are author(s) own and the facts reported by them have been verified to the extent possible, and the publishers are not in any way liable for the same.

First Published, 2019

*Published by*

Kalpaz Publications
C-30, Satyawati Nagar,
Delhi – 110052
Ph.: 011-47034999, 9811692060
www.kalpazpublications.com
E-mail: kalpaz@hotmail.com

*Printed at:* G. Print Process, Delhi

**Cataloging in Publication Data—DK**
Courtesy: D.K. Agencies (P) Ltd. <docinfo@dkagencies.com>

**Sharma, Gopal** *(Professor of English)*, **author.**
Munshi Premchand / Gopal Sharma.
pages cm
Includes bibliographical references.
ISBN 9789353240233

1. Premacanda, 1881-1936. 2. Authors, Hindi—20th century—Biography. 3. Authors, Urdu—20th century—Biography. I. Title.

LCC PK2098.S7S53 2019 | DDC 891.4335 23

# Contents

Foreword ---------- 7
Preface ---------- 9
Acknowledgements ---------- 11
Introduction ---------- 13

Chapter - 1: A pen- picture of Premchand ---------- 15

Chapter - 2: Premchand: The Extra-ordinary Ordinary Man ---------- 19

Chapter - 3: Raconteur Premchand ---------- 51

Chapter - 4: The Engaged Intellectual Premchand ---------- 133

Chapter - 5: Premchand and his contemporaries ---------- 209

Chapter - 6: Wrapping up ---------- 239

*Appendix - I: The Nature and Purpose of Literature* ---------- 241

*Appendix - II: A Hole in Premchand's Shoe* ---------- 249

*Select References* ---------- 253

*Index* ---------- 255

# Foreword

"It is impossible to arrive at any kind of assessment of modern Indian literature without taking full account of Premchand" says Shamsur Rahman Faruqi very aptly when he presents complete short stories in English translation by M. Asaduddin and others and published by Penguin this year. The literary genius called Premchand is the Shakespeare of Indian fiction and has always influenced a large part of our thinking. In fact, Munshi Premchand (1880-1936) is one of the most important writers of the Hindi- Urdu fiction and a complete book encompassing his life and works is required urgently as there is hardly any such book available in the English language. This book fits the bill as it tells the reader not only about the person Premchand but also gives a critical review of his work.

Premchand's stories and novels give a life-like picture of village life. He used his pen to great effect for social reform. He married a child-widow when it was considered a sin. Early in his career he took up the government job of a school teacher but resigned when Gandhiji asked Indians to contribute to the freedom movement.He changed his name and became "Premchand" after one of his books was found to be inflammatory by the British regime. When he was asked why he didn't write anything about him, he very gently replied, "What greatness do I have to tell anything about. I am ordinary. My life is as ordinary as of anyone suffereing now." He opined that good literature is judged by the sharpness of its perception which stirs our feelings and thoughts into motion. He died of penury at the age of 56 leaving his work behind.Given the exigencies of our times, there can be no better way to celebrate Premchand's legacy than to remember his words.

This is a very simple and ordinary narration of such an extra-ordinary man. The book in your hand goes beyond this and tells us about the extraordinary ordinary life of the maker of Indian literature and discusses in depth about him and his work.

I commend Professor Gopal Sharma and his work and wish him good luck in his pursuit. There are very few scholars who have been serving the Hindi Language through English. He is one of them. Dr Sharma had already written on Nelson Mandela, Narendra Modi and Ram Nath Kovind and now that he writes his second book on Premchand, I would like to conclude by quoting here a recent tweet of President Ram Nath Kovind on the occasion of the 138$^{th}$ birth anniversary of Munshi Premchand, "Remembering Munshi Premchand on his birth anniversary.A fine writer and novelist, his poignant stories centred on farmers, the poor and the extraordinary emotions of ordinary people" What the President said very succinctly and others have been saying in great detail is to support to enrich us and to engage us in following the footsteps of the great such as Premchand. This book is also a salutary tribute to him indeed!

**Dr. S.V.S.S. Narayana Raju,**

Professor and Head, Department of Hindi
School of Social Sciences & Humanities
Central university of Tamil Nadu

# Preface

If you have been reading Premchand, you will know that this preface is just a plausible gesture to begin with. But I write in the hope that for at least some of the readers of this volume Premchand is new; and therefore take it for granted that, for the moment, an introduction can be made.

Everybody in India reads at least one of Premchand's stories at school, but most people do not know much about him. The students in the Hindi-heartland read his biography, but others hardly get a chance to know that he was born to a Kayastha family in 1880 in village Lamhi and lived an ordinary life of a school teacher who resigned fom his governemt job at the age of 41 with two young children when Gandhiji called the people for non-cooperation. He was the most successful Hindi and Urdu writer of his day who earned his livelihood mainly by writing and tried to establish a few journals and a printing press. Though he was not a poor writer, he believed in simple living and led an ordinary life that has contributed to the image of Premchand as the quintessentially poor Hindi writer. In fact, he is a "classic" Hindi- Urdu writer of the early twentieth century in the real sense of the term who is a realist, humanist, secularist, social reformer, feminist, educationist, politically engaged etc. And by reading of his novels and stories one will discover a world where the life was an everlasting struggle. His magnum opus *Godan* is termed "the epic of village life"and Premchand is called *Kalam ka sipahi* who used to write not just to earn his livelihood but also to inform and reform the readers.

Premchand is no more yet he is there in his writings. He is also in this text. This book is written to familiarize the readers with the genius of an extra-ordinary writer and to open up his work to new readers and new readings of his text. It is surprising that only a part of his rich and abundant writing is available in English translation. Most of his novels, stories, essays, editorials, letters, reviews and views remain untranslated and the world still is unaware of his literary contribution. Little do we know about this soldier with the pen who was once busy shaping the nation with his writing and is relevant today because India with all her development and material glory still remain tied with a number of traditional, conventional and old values.

The preface is a necessary gesture of homage and parricide, for the book makes a claim of authority or origin which is both true and false. I know that the preface harbors a lie. Dear readers! Don't take me too seriously in the preface. What is true is the text that follows.

**— Gopal Sharma**

# Acknowledgements

This book has evolved over sometime and I have received much support and incurred many debts of gratitude along the way. To begin, I must thank my colleagues at Arba Minch University and its Department of Post Graduate Studies in Ethiopia, who allowed me time and space to be a writer of a book on Premchand alongside my daily job as an instructor teaching English as a foreign language. In this respect, I am particularly grateful to the former head of the department Ato Manguday Mercho who risked his reputation in this regard. Later, the young and dynamic head of the department Ato Degwale Mekonnen too continued the support extended by his predecessor.

In India, I have a very stable and decades old support base of Hindi scholars based in Hyderabad and elsewhere. Central Institute of English and Foreign Languages (CIEFL) which is now renamed English and Foreign Languages University (EFLU) has been my mentor as the first Vice Chancellor of the university Prof. Shivendra Kishore Verma showed me how to balance between English and Hindi and Prof. K. Subramanian (Know Your English fame) who taught me the first lesson of writing effectively. The newly formed School of Literary Studies (2009) and its first head Prof. Venkateshwar Mannar, and present head Dr Shaym Rao Rathod, both have been very generous and kind in guiding and spearheading my endeavours with equal zeal and enthusiasm. Similarly Dakshin Bharat Hindi Prachar Sabha (An Institution of National Importance) and its Post Graduate Research Wing (Hyderabad) with such stalwarts as Prof. Dilip Singh and Prof. Rishabh Deo Sharma have been a source of strength and inspiration. Dr Neeraja G. and her colleagues have all been immensely helpful.

Similarly Dr Devraj of Mahatma Gandhi Antarrashtriya Hindi Vishwavidyalaya (a central university), Wardha has been always available and ready to correct me with his wisdom. Central University of Tamilnadu (CUTN) and Dr Sirivuri Narayanaraju, a friend of long-standing who graced the book with his prudent preface and foreword is worthy of praise and acknowledgement. The vast Hindi fraternity of Hyderabad, particularly of University of Hyderabad, Osmania University, Maulana Azad National Urdu University, and Dr B. R. Ambedkar Open University have been a source of persistent pursuit in the realm of language, literature and teaching. I owe a sense of gratitude for all those who have been strengthening the cause of Hindi in this part of India and spare their time, money and energy by attending conferences, seminars, and gatherings. Persons like Dr Ahilya Mishra, Mr L. N. Agarwal and Mrs Pavitra Agarwal, Dr Ansari, Dr. Shushma Devi, Dr. D. Vidyadhar, Dr Rajesh Agarwal and their ilk are around me and our mutual admiration is the talk of the town. Dr Kavita Vachaknavi (USA) will be happy and contended to go through this book and I recollect those formative years of mine when we had plans and ambitions to move the earth. I take this opportunity to thank my family of five namely Dr Shashi Sharma, Ankur Sharma and his wife Akshitara Singh, and Anshul Sharma. Thank you one and all.

# Introduction

Munshi Premchand, widely extolled as the greatest Hindi fiction writer of the early twentieth century, wrote a dozon novels and more than three hundred short stories in his so-called short span of uneventful life. His range and diversity are limitless and he is matchless in his depiction of village life. His characters are both comic and tragic and they belong to all ages. Now that many of his stories and novels are available in English, it is heartening to see a critical appraisal of his life and works by one of the well-known Premchand scholars.

Prof. Namwar Singh calls Premchand "the unique epic-chronicler (*Maha-granthkar*) of our struggle for freedom" and one who was "like a true artist, concerned first and foremost with human beings and the daily ordinary lives they lived." Premchand was interested in idealistic realism or ideal-oriented realism (*adarshonmukh yatharthwad*) to depict life through his novels and short stories. "Premchand did not write novels and short stories merely for the entertainment of the readers, or to satisfy the curiosity of men and women for stories with problems of sex and love. He had a high idea of art. It was a medium of experience for his ideas on some of the social, political, and economic problems of our life. His novels embody, therefore, social purpose and social criticism; and they are based on fundamental social problems [Madan 1946: 145]."

This book presents the entire gamut and oeuvre of Premchand for the education and delight of the English speaking world. Prof. Sharma is of the view that Premchand's life was exra-ordinary, though he always termed it as ordinary. He lived in an age when nothing ordinary happened. For readers unfamiliar with his stories and novels, this book is an introduction. For those who had already read him a bit will find here a critical review of Premchand. I thank Dr Gopal Sharma and the publisher of this volume who packed so much in a slim volume. Every one of us can receive Premchand in abundance on every page of the book. This is the first time I ever read such a unique preface and the concluding chapter about any subject. The less said the better, let me say, let us not read Premchand just as a novelist and short story writer but a committed writer and thinker of his age and times. This book is a text to be kept along as a handbook in the voyage of discovering and rediscovering Premchand.

**Dr. Shyam Rao Rathod**
Associate Professor and Head,
Department of Hindi, School of Literary Studies
The English and Foreign Languages University
Hyderabad

# Chapter - 1

# A pen- picture of Premchand

Munshi Premchand was born during the days when Indian National Congress was being shaped into an institution. To be precise, he was born on July 31, 1880 as Dhanpatrai in a little hamlet of Lamhi village four miles from Banaras on the road to Aazamgarh. His father was .... But wait, hang on.

In India, the name Premchand is known to every literate person. In the Hindi heartland, stories of Premchand (*Premchand ki kahaniya*) are read not only by students in schools but also by those who want to read fiction in Hindi. Like all great creative artists, Munshi Premchand has proved that his appeal transcends time. As an imaginative mediator and a committed writer, writes Harish Trivedi, Premchand helped steer modern Hindi fiction away from exotic romances and exemplary tales laden with moral didacticism towards more realistic modes of narrative representation. He is the most sought after writer even after nearly a century of his demise. "*The Hindu*" very succinctly underlined this fact in the following of quoted line *"Premchand is India...If you haven't read Premchand; you have missed out on a lot."* Robert Oscar Swan opines that "a study of Premchand is the logical point to begin the study of modern Hindi literature." Premchand is not only in the line of Tulsidas and Kabirdas, he is rolled into one. He is the modern day Vedvyasa and his *Mahabharata* is the epic novel *Godan.* "His influence on later generations has been so great that without a proper reevaluation of his literature we would fail to understand the whole character of modern Hindi literature after him" (Akira Takahashi).

During his life time there were scholars who waxed eloquent on his genius. Dr Hazari Prasad Dwivedi (1907-1979) wrote the following *sloka (1935)* to praise him:

*Premchandarsya chandrasya n kadapi samabhuvo*
*Aik purnkalo nityam aparastu yada kada*

There can be no comparison between Premchandra and Chandra.

For the one is always in his full glory while the other waxes and wanes.

And similarly it was said:

> By your writings Hindi has been enriched and Hindi speakers have been enabled to hold their heads high in the world-when we show *Rangbhoomi* or *Karmabhoomi* to a stranger (i.e. Someone from another language) it is as if we ask him with quiet pride - Have you anything to match this! (Qtd in Rai, 1962, p.338)

Now that Premchand is available in translation and the Oxford India Premchand is there with its omnibus edition, the world of Premchand is accessable to the readers in English and the readers of English. Francesca Orsini labels Premchand as a"classic"writer of the early twentieth century who comes packaged with all the right definitions: realist, humanist, secularist, social reformer, politically engaged, etc. Alok Rai, his grandson, says that Premchand's apparent "organicity", the way in which he came to crystallize and symbolize an entire zone of social consciousness in the decades from the 1910s to the 1930s, makes a remarkable story of self- fashioning as an intellectual and a teller of tales.

In keeping with its tradition of honouring noted personalities from across the globe, Google dedicated a special '*doodle*' to one of the most famous Hindi writers in India. *On 31 July 2016 on* Premchand's 136$^{th}$ birth anniversary Google brought out a doddle in Premchand's honour and noted on its website *"Today's homepage celebrates a man who filled many pages (of a different kind) with words that would forever change India's literary landscape... His last and most famous novel, Godaan (1936) inspired today's doodle which shows Premchand (sometimes referred to as "Upanyas Samrat," or, "emperor among novelists") bringing his signature working-class characters to life. On what would have been his 136th birthday, the illustration pays tribute to the multitude of important stories he told."* The doodle featured an illustration of Premchand, with a pen and paper, ready to write. His figure was surrounded by a typical scene from an Indian village, inspired by one of his most-revered works, *Godaan/ Godan/ Gaudan / The Gift of a Cow*.

Premchand is popularly known as Munshi Premchand (Munshi being an honorary prefix). He started getting name and fame for his fiction and portrayal of the life and time when India was struggling under the British yolk and trying to get total independence. The Era of Premchand falls roughly in between 1918-1936.

What Thomas Hardy is to the English literature and Leo Tolstoy for Russia, Munshi Premchand is to the Hindi literature. Shakespeare is all imagination, drama and history but Premchand is a practitioner of realism or *"idealistic realism"*. Premchand's greatness lies in the fact that he transcends the constraints of vision and conception characterizing Balzac, the author of *The Peasants* and Tolstoy, the mouthpiece of rural Russia of his time. Premchand wrote in Urdu and Hindi and to read him in a third language (English) is a new experience. He is in the line of such celebrated authors as Samuel Beckett, Vladimir Nabokov and Milan Kundera who wrote in two languages. He is one of the most celebrated writers of the Indian subcontinent, and is regarded as one of the foremost Hindustani writers of the early twentieth century.

This *"lean man of medium height with a happy face and eyes full of tenderness arising out of suffering, predominantly white haired, thick moustache, dressed in a sherwani and a chust pyjama, his longish hair jostling out of the Gandhi cap"* was a man of flesh and blood who even acted in a film based on a story written by him. His laughter was contagious: bambook was the nick-name given to him by his bosom friends. Had you seen him even once you would have been surprised at his deep knowledge of art, derived possibly from the reading of world literature. With a touch of an individuality of his own, he lived; he wrote and died when he was just 56 years of age.

The story of this extraordinary man according to him *is drab and dull, nothing extraordinary* and yet we wish to read his biography again and again. There are critics who try to prove that he is not a poor *aam aadmi* but a well to do crafty *Kayasth*, yet readers feign to ignore these claims. For his readers, he is not only a mouthpiece of the wretched of the earth but also one among them.

Born Dhanpat Rai Srivastav, he began writing under the pen name "Nawab Rai", and subsequently switched to other names. The world, however, knows him by a different name-**Premchand** and he has been referred to as the "*Upanyas Samrat*" ("*Emperor among Novelists*") by some Hindi writers and *Kalam ka sipahi* ("*His pen moved as fast as the spade of a laborer*") by others. He voiced the aspirations of the people of rural India in the early part of the twentieth century during the Gandhian era, and projected himself as a writer with substance. His works include more than a dozen novels, around 300 short stories, several essays, a few plays and translations of a number of foreign literary works into Hindi and Urdu, books for children, articles, editorials, forewords, letters, lectures and personal communications... His books are in public domain now and if you want to read him, you can. He is just a click away.

You are going to read Premchand's biography in a short while from now. His wife wrote an account of his life in "*Premchand: Ghar Mein*" and his son too wrote a biography but Premchand himself wrote none. In fact his life is scattered all around his books and the characters he created are partly his own self. There are only a few people left who saw Premchand in flesh and blood and it is very difficult to locate them now. But don't worry, you can still see lots of photographs of him online and there is a very fine portrait of him on the cover of this book.

What is a photograph?

It is just a captured visual image of a present time in the past- of a person who is now actually dead but is present everywhere. Even in this book - Premchand is on the cover and you can also discover him on every page too!

# Chapter - 2

# Premchand: The Extra-ordinary Ordinary Man

## Birth and parentage

Premchand has described his life as *"flat, level and plain where we occasionally find pits".* He says that there is nothing dramatic and extraordinary in his life with no mounds and gentlemen might not find any excitement in it and will be greatly disappointed. He writes:

> My life is a level plain. There are pits here and there but no cliffs, mountains, jungles, deep ravines, or desert wastes. Those good people who have a taste for mountaineering will be disappointed.

Premchand didn't write his autobiography but there is a biography written by Madan Gopal – *Munshi Premchand: A literary Biography* (1964). His son Amrit Rai too wrote a biography: *Kalam ka sipahi* (1962) and his wife Shivrani Devi too penned a book length account *Premchand: ghar mein* (1944). Amritrai starts his father's biography "*Kalam ka Sipahi'* with three anecdotes and the statement "*Koi visheshta jo nahin hai usmen*." The reminiscences of a large number of Premchand's friends and contemporaries as recorded in the Premchand memorial numbers, of *Hans* and *Zamana*, and the writings of other scholars published from time to time can be a good source for one who wishes to venture in search of Premchand's footsteps in the field of Indian literature of the early twentieth century. Premchand himself seems to have given hints about his life in several of his stories. This information can be used to reconstruct an interesting biography. Majority of scholars find in him a person with meager means of livelihood who was trying to somehow live a reasonably average life. There are a few experts who find in him a well to do kayastha eager to make money by writing and publishing. In short, we are largely dependent on the material which is partly authentic and partly narrative.

It is quite possible to frame or present Premchand's biography solely based on his work. His work is an extension of his life and you can read him well in his work. Hansraj "Rehbar" (1913-1994) wrote an unauthorized biography of Premchand by selecting, copying and pasting passages from his work along with brief account of his real life. This is no small wonder that the book by him is not only entertaining but also free from serious errors.

Premchand was born on 31 July 1880 in Lamhi, a village located near Varanasi (Banaras). His grandfather Gursahai Rai was a patwari (village accountant), and his father Ajaib Lal was a post office clerk. His mother was Anandi Devi of Karauni village. Premchand was the fourth child of Ajaib Lal and Anandi; the first two were girls who died as infants, and the third one was a girl named Suggi. His parents named him Dhanpat Rai ("the master of wealth"), while his uncle (Tauji), Mahabir, a rich landowner, nicknamed him "Nawab" ("Prince"). "Nawab Rai" was the first pen name chosen by Premchand.

Amritrai, Premchand's son in his essay *Vans Bel,* published in November 1960 in *Kadambini* narrated the chronological history of his father's forefathers. Gursahailal, a patwari by profession, not only extorted money from the cultivators but also had the reputation of being a drunkard who used to beat his wife mercilessly. Ajaiblal, the third of the four sons of Gursahailal, like his elder brother and through him, took the job of a village postmaster on a salary of ten rupees a month. He helped his younger brother too to become a postmaster, and also got two of his relations fixed up as postmen. He was quite different from his father and believed in human values, universal religion and honesty. He was more like his mother and never ill-treated his wife as his father used to treat his mother. Anandi Devi too was an affable woman who was able to read and write Kaithi, a dialect of her time.

## Childhood

Premchand, like his father, was fair-complexioned and physically a feeble one. It is said that he was a fairly intelligent child and also a little mischievous, as most children of his age are. He too must have had his share of pranks. As an infant he lived at many places because his father used to get frequent transfers. When he was just around three years of age, he lived and visited Banda, Badalganj, Azamgarh, Basti, Gorakhpur, Kanpur, Allahabad and Lucknow.

One incident of his childhood is said to be very funny and innocuous. He imitated a barber and nearly shaved off the ear-lobe of another child in an attempt of giving him a haircut. He used the edge of a bamboo chip as a razor blade and did attempt this ingenious act. He was reprimanded and asked not to act like that in future.

When you read "Qazaki" which is based on the memories of those early innocent days, you find the story of a postal runner and his love for a child. It will certainly remind you Tagore's great story "Kabuliwalla" in which a Kabuliwala and a little girl Mini make the readers cry. When Premchand's father was posted at Jamnia, in Azamgarh Tehsil, there was a postal runner (courier), Qazaki by name, who was very fond of this cute child. The little one was pampered by Qazaki as he used to give the child a ride a day on his back. The child too enjoyed this horse ride...

## Education

When he was 7 years of age, he began his education at a *madarsa* in Lalpur near Lamhi. He learnt Urdu and Persian from a maulvi in the *madarsa*. You can get a glimpse of his early schooling in the story entitled *"Chori" (*Theft). His love for gullli Danda and Kite flying can be seen in stories "*Gulli Danda*" and "*Bade Bhai Saheb*". He loved to eat sugar cane, gur, and sweetened peas / ground nuts. He too used to play truant and bunk the school to watch the constables' parade, madari's display and the arrival and departure of the trains. He used to visit a garden just to get an opportunity to water the plants.

Premchand was not a stout and healthy lad. He was a sickly child. His mother used to take extra care of him as he was the first son born after three daughters (*Tehtar*), and as the superstition was he too brought bad luck for both, first to the mother and later to the father. When he was 8, his mother died after a long illness. His grandmother, who took the responsibility of raising him, died soon after. Premchand felt isolated, as his elder sister had already been married, and his father was always busy with work. Premchand often used to visit the house of a schoolmate and listen to the recitation of *Tilism –i-Hosh Ruba* (the mammoth and everlasting tale of romance in seventeen volumes, each one of at least 2,000 pages of super-royal size). But his unrestricted freedom was short-lived.

His father remarried. She brought her younger brother Vijay Bahadur along with her. Premchand received little affection from his step-mother. The step-mother later became a recurring theme in Premchand's works. A recurring theme in his stories is his childhood days. For example, in the story *Chori* (Theft) his childhood is depicted with the colours of innocence. This is a story in which he tells us how he along with his cousin steals a rupee from his house and one wonders to read the autobiographical vein -"O Childhood! It is impossible to forget you. That decrepit mud-house, the straw-bed, bare-body, bare-footed wandering in the fields, climbing mango trees- I recollect all this very vividly, the wearing of locally -made shoes, gave then more joy than a pair of flex shoes today. Hot Juice of raw mangoes was more pleasurable than rose-syrup now, gram and unripe berries sweeter than grapes and the finest sweets." In the novel Karmbhumi Amarkant says, "Childhood is the time when one needs abundant love and care. If the plant is watered in the beginning, the roots of it will remain intact and strong for life. If proper nourishment is denied the life becomes dry. My mother died when I was hardly seven –eight years of age and since then my soil couldn't get the sustenance it requires."

Gulli Danda and kite flying were his favorite games in his childhood and he later wrote stories based on this sports. He couldn't play every time, the rest of the hours he read.

When his father was posted to Jamniya in the mid-1890s, Premchand enrolled at the Mission High School in class eighth. He now had two more brothers Gulabrai and Mahtabrai (Chhutak). The young lad had no one of his own. The mother- the step-mother was a callous one. Father was indifferent. Brothers were step-brothers and unmindful. It is said that the young Premchand started smoking and used to enjoy juicy tales of youth at the unripe age of thirteen. He was very fond of Ramlila, kite-flying, gulli danda and reading Urdu romance and novels. He used to visit a book seller's shop and borrowed books to read. The book seller used to sell schools guides and keys and the young lad helped him in doing so in return of getting the books of his choice to read.

As said earlier after his mother's death, Premchand sought solace in fiction, and developed a fascination for books. He heard the stories from the Persian-language fantasy epic *Tilism-e-Hoshruba* at a tobaconist's shop. He took the job of selling books for a book wholesaler, thus getting the opportunity to read a lot of books. He studied English in a missionary school and studied several works of fiction including George W. Reynolds's eight-volume The *Mysteries of the Court of London*. Maulana Sharar, Pandit Ratan Nath Sarshar, Mirza Rusva, and Maulvi Mohammed Ali of Hardoi were the popular novelists of the period and he used to read them again and again. At Gorakhpur, he composed his first literary work which was never published. It was a farce on a bachelor, who falls in love with a low-caste woman. The character was based on Premchand's uncle, who used to scold him for being obsessed with reading fiction; the farce was probably written as revenge. At the age of thirteen he did this pen-pushing act to tease (or teach?) an uncle. At the age of fourteen he wrote another skit: *Honhar Birvan ke Chikne Chikne Pat*. And his first novel was written when he was just nineteen!

His father stayed in Gorakhpur for four years and Premchand was able to clear class eighth examination as a student of mission school. He hardly studied course books and passed the examination with pass marks only.

When his father got his transfer from Gorakhpur to Jamnia and the nearest school was Colegiate High School at Benaras, he had to join it as a day scholar in class 9th. The childhood was leaving him and as a teenage boy reading romances and books of adventure, he was like an adult in understanding the ways of the world.

## First Marriage

In 1895, he was married at the age of fifteen. He was studying in the 9th grade then. In fact, he was preparing for the annual examinations. The match was arranged by his maternal step-grandfather. The girl was from a rich landlord family. He found this bride quarrelsome, ill-mannered, ugly and immature. Her face was covered with small-pox marks. One of her shoulders was higher than the other, and she limped too. It seemed she was also older in age. When Premchand saw her face, he was crest-fallen. In a word she was a cartoon. (We don't know the truth- the real truth about her physical appearance and beauty. Even we are not dead sure if she was alive when Premchand married again. Mrs Shivrani Devi Premchand narrates an incident when Premchand's first wife's brother came to visit him. During his last days Premchand admitted that She was alive for many years after their marriage. There is no where any mention of her death at any time. )

Premchand's father died in 1897 after a prolonged illness. He couldn't sit for the final examination. At home he was always harassed by the complaints of his wife and his stepmother, and his ambitions- of taking an M. A. degree and of becoming a lawyer turned into a pipe-dream. It was, as he wrote, "like wanting to climb the Everest with one's feet bound with chains wrought, not in iron but, in the heaviest-known metal." He managed to pass the matriculation exam with second division (below 60% marks) the next year. The students with first division only were given fee concession at the Queen's College. So Premchand sought admission at the Central Hindu College. It was a new college and was started the same year. But he was unsuccessful because of his poor arithmetic skills. Thus, he had to discontinue his studies. (He tried to pass Intermediate examinations but failed twice. He could pass it only when Mathematics became an optional subject. Premchand offered English, Persian, Modern History and Logic, and got through the examination in Second Division in 1916, when he was thirty-six-18 years after Matriculation.)

Premchand then obtained an assignment to coach an advocate's son in Benares at a monthly salary of five rupees. He used to live in a mud-cell over the advocate's stables, and used to send 60% of his earnings back home. Premchand read a lot during these days too. He used to read the literary novels such as *Fasana-i-Azad, Chandrakanla Santati* and Urdu translations of Bankim Chandra Chatterjee's novels.

## Teaching Assignments

After racking up several debts, in 1899, he once went to a book shop to sell one of his collected books. It was a mathematics book. There, he met the headmaster of a missionary school at Chunar, who offered him a job as a teacher at a monthly salary of Rs. 18. Premchand accepted the job. Vijay Bahadur, his step mother's youger brother also went along with him. Vijay Bahadur remained with him wherever Premchand went for work. He was a good help and company as he was just four five years younger to him.

You can have a glimpse of Premchand's life as a school teacher in a short story entitled *Holi ki Chhutti*. This is what the protagonist says: "After my Matriculation, I got a teacher's post in a primary school, situated about eleven miles from my home. The headmaster of my school was obsessed with the idea of making school children read during holidays also. The annual examinations were due in April, but as early as January he would raise a hue and cry. The assistant teachers were exempted from taking night classes, but they would not be allowed leave. Somvati Amavas came and went. Shivaratri too came and went. (But no leave to go home which I had not visited for months). I, therefore, decided that during the forthcoming; Holi vacation, I must go home even if it cost me my job. A week before Holi, which fell on March 20, 1 gave an ultimatum to the headmaster that I would be proceeding on leave on the evening of March 19. The headmaster tried to explain that I was still young, and that it was difficult in these days to get a job, and still more difficult to retain it. Examinations are due in April, and if the school is closed for three or four days, how many boys would get through? Wouldn't a whole year's labor be wasted? Take my advice. Don't go home during these holidays, but go there during any of the holidays after the examinations, e.g. during the Easter holidays. I promise I would not stop you even by a day.' But I was adamant. Neither the headmaster's lecture nor his threats produced any effect on me. When the school closed on March 19, I quietly proceeded home, even without bidding goodbye to the headmaster. For, if I had gone to take leave, he would have stopped me from going home on one pretext or another-totaling up the fees in the register, calculating average attendance, correcting the exercise books of students, etc. as if this was the last act before I proceeded on life's last journey."

Premchand did not remain in this school for a long time. His attitude was such towards work and establishment that he was terminated and dismissed.

In 1900, on July 2, Premchand secured a job as an assistant teacher at the Government District School, Bahraich, at a monthly salary of Rs. 20. Three months later on 21 September, he was transferred to the District School in Pratapgarh, where he stayed in an administrator's bungalow and tutored his son. He was hardly twenty years of age then and passed his time happily and fruitfully. He was not a lad of thirteen years when he wrote a story based on the ill deeds of a relative. He was able to read with a critical eye now and was in a mood to write something significant. He was able to see the weaknesses of Hindu soceity and was also attracted towards the work of Arya Samaj. The glimpse of his life there can be seen in his story "*Chamatkar*". He worked in Pratapgarh adequately for about two years and succeeded in making arrangements for two years teacher's training at the Central Training College, Allahabad.

In April 1904, Premchand passed his "permanent Junior English Teacher's Examination" in the first division. He also passed the special vernacular examination, in Urdu as well as in Hindi, of Allahabad University. In 1905, Dhanpat Rai was relocated to Allahabad from Pratapgarh for training, and subsequently posted at Kanpur. A fellow teacher-trainee presents a pen portrait of Premchand: Of medium height, he was a thin and lean man. His grip, however, was strong and if he "stretched out his fingers, it was not easy to bend them. He was dressed simply: an achkan or an open-necked longish coat, and pyjamas. His headgear was usually a turban or a cap. He was not at all given to show or artificiality. His voice was of a high pitch. Although he was not the one to take things lying down, he was well behaved, a "true gentleman."

His work and conduct was so good that he was called back after nearly 8 months and was appointed the headmaster of the Model School attached to the Normal School, Allahabad. He was just 25 then and he did his duty according to the utmost satisfaction of the superiors. But within three months he was transferred at the royal salary of Rs. 25 in May 1905. He was sent there, on promotion, as Eighth Master in the District School at Kanpur. Premchand stayed in Kanpur for around four years, from May 1905 to June 1909. There he met Daya Narain Nigam, the editor of the magazine *Zamana*, in which he later published several articles and stories.

## Writing

Premchand visited his village Lamhi during the summer vacation, but did not find the stay enjoyable because of a number of reasons. He did not find the weather conducive for writing. He faced domestic troubles due to quarrels between his wife and his step-mother. Premchand scolded his wife several times whenever she tried to attempt suicide or created a violent scene. Ultimately she went to her father's house, and Premchand showed no interest in bringing her back. In one of the letters to Nigam he wrote, "I shall live without a wife. If the cat takes mercy and leaves the hen, it surely can live, even without its feathers." We are not sure about the date of Premchand's separation from his first wife. Premchand himself in a letter in 1935 says that his first wife "died" in 1904. It is certain that there was no love left between them and she was as good as dead for him for a long time.

In 1905, inspired by the nationalist movement, Premchand published an article in *Zamana* on the Indian National Congress leader Gopal Krishna Gokhale. He criticized Gokhale's methods for achieving political freedom, and instead recommended adoption of more extremist measures adopted by Lokmanya Bal Gangadhar Tilak.

Premchand's first published story was *Duniya Ka Sabse Anmol Ratan* ("The Most Precious Jewel in the World"), which appeared in *Zamana* in 1907. According to this story, the most precious "jewel"was the last drop of blood necessary to attain independence. The story begins as per Urdu tradition in an Islamic setting at a forlorn place but ends in a Hindu Rajput patriotic fervor influenced by the Indian independence movement. *"Sheikh-i-Makhmoor"* is another story with a similar theme. It is the story of Masoud, the scion of a royal family who is in hiding and espouses the cause of his subjects now being oppressed by a foreign ruler. He is a brave man, and dons the fakir's robes and is known as Sheikh-i-Makhmoor. When the king of the defeated kingdom dies he tells his son to protect the people "This country is yours. This crown is yours. These subjects are also yours. Protect them and if you fail. Give the responsibility to your son and die."

Dhanpat Rai first wrote under the pseudonym *"Nawab Rai"*. His first short novella was *Asrar e Ma'abid* (*Devasthan Rahasya* in Hindi, "*The Secrets of God's Abode*" or literally *The Secrets of the Sanctum Sanctorum*). It explores corruption among the temple priests and their sexual exploitation of poor women. The Brahmin temple priests are engaged in sexual activities with the young Hindu widows who visit the temple in pretext of religious worship. The novel was published in a series in the Benares-based Urdu weekly *Awaz-e-Khalk* from 8 October 1903 to February 1905. On October 8$^{th}$ his first work was published and exactly after completing 33 years in the service of literature he died on October 8$^{th}$. Siegfried Schulz states that "his inexperience is quite evident in his first novel, which is not well-organized, lacks a good plot and features stereotyped characters." Prakash Chandra Gupta calls it an "immature work", which shows a tendency to "see life only white or black". "It is written in the sprightly, pert and even internally rhyming Urdu prose style, which was generally current at the time and which Premchand had derived basically from his favorite Sarshar" opines Harish Trivedi. The language is heavily loaded with Arabic and Persian words as if the writer wants to show off his knowledge and has the last laugh. "Well, I said to myself—let me write a language that will show them ...'

After a pause he added, 'After all; I am the son of a kayastha, am I not!' (Rai 1982: 347)

## Remarriage

In 1909, Premchand married a child widow, Shivrani Devi. Her father, Munshi Deviprasad, was a kayastha zamindar in Fatehpur district of the U. P. state. In 1905, he wrote a booklet *Kayastha Bal Vidhva Uddharak Pustika* (a booklet on the welfare of the kayastha child widows), in which he advertised for Shivrani's remarriage. Premchand read this book and responded. The marriage was considered to be revolutionary at that time, and Premchand faced a lot of social opposition. After his death, Shivrani Devi wrote a book entitled *Premchand Ghar Mein* ("Premchand at Home "). Jyoti Atwal (2007) says that Shivrani Devi's *"Premchand Ghar Mein"* (1944) is written "with an aim not to simply glorify Premchand but also to reintroduce his character and personality through accounts of his personal life." Shivrani Devi claimed that no other person had the right to evaluate the humanism of Premchand as much as she did because they were travelers of the same boat and had been together through bad and good times. She wrote that she had been truthful and honest while putting down her experiences, although she put them down as and when she could recall events. *Premchand*: *Ghar Mein* is a memoir and is about Premchand as a doting husband and conveys a strong sense of autobiography. Banarasi Das Chaturvedi in his essay on Premchand entitled *'Some Aspects of Premchand's Personality'*, projects Premchand as "a loving husband who was always anxious to take Mrs. Premchand with him when he went out of Benaras". Chaturvedi wrote a foreward for Shivrani's book where he called her *"ek mahila yodhha"* (a female warrior) due to her dogged assertiveness over certain socio-political issues. Shivrani Devi wrote a few stories about women's plight and went to jail during freedom movement. She inspired him to resign his job and persuaded him to work and write more aggressively for the ongoing freedom movement under the leadership of Mahatma Gandhi. Once she retorted about Premchand, *"Hamin si hain jo inke ghar ka intejam kar leti hain."*(It is me alone that can manage this man's household.") That is why Premchand called her a "militant woman."

It is to be noted that there is a lot of confusion about Premchand's first marriage and remarriage. Madan Gopal says that the year of separation of Premchand from his first wife is 1906 and his remarriage is 1909. Mrs Shivrani Premchand in her book says that "Falgun mein meri shadi hui aur chaitra mein aap sub deputy inspector ho gaye" (p. 14). There is no date and year. As Premchand became a Sub-Deputy Inspector in June or July 1909, it would appear that Premchand's second marriage to Shivrani Devi took place in 1909.

It could be added that she narrated an event of 1914 when they were at Basti where Premchand's first wife's brother came one day to meet him and she saw him talking about his ill-fated sister. Then Shivrani Devi realized that his first wife was still alive (p.33). At that time Premchand was the father of a daughter Kamala who was two years of age. Mrs Shivrani Devi wrote a letter to his first wife and requested her to come and join them but she declined to come unless he himself came and took her along.

## First Novel

Premchand's wife Shivrani Devi said that her husband's first novel was *Kishna* and it was published from Allahabad and his second, *Prema,* later called *Vibhav,* in the year of her marriage. Premchand's second son, Amritrai, said that he had been told that his father's first novel was *Shyama* which was a criticism of British rule in India. (*Shyama* may be a distortion of "Suvama"). Daya Narain Nigam, Premchand's closest friend, said that Premchand's first novel in Urdu was *Hum-Khurma-o-Hum Savab* which was published in 1907 by Babu Mahadev Prasad Verma, Aminabad, Lucknow, and printed at Hindustani Press, Lucknow, and that the first novel in Hindi was *Pratigya,* written in 1906. Jageshwar Nath Verma "Betaab" said that Premchand's first novel in Urdu was *Pratapchandra* and also that his first novel in Hindi was *Prema.* Peareylal "Shakir" said that *Hum Khurma-o-Hum Savab,* and its Hindi version, *Prema,* were first published in 1905 and his second novel *Kishna* was published from Banaras in 1908. It is also claimed that in 1907 Premchand's short novel *Kishna* was published by the Medical Hall Press of Benares. This 142-page work satirises women's fondness for jewellery is now lost. Literary critic Nobat Rai reviewed and criticised the work in *Zamana*, calling it a mockery of the women's conditions.

A novel written in the earliest days seems to have been *Pratapchandra* but the whereabouts of the novel are unknown. Premchand's second short novel *Hamkhurma-o-Hamsavab* (*Prema* in Hindi), published in 1907 was penned under the name "*Babu Nawab Rai Banarsi*". The sub-title of Prema, "The marriage of two friends (girls): gripping, instructive and original novel," can give the reader an idea of the theme of the novel. It explores the issue of widow remairriage in the contemporary conservative society. The protagonist Amrit Rai overcomes social opposition to marry the young widow Poorna, giving up his rich and beautiful fiancé Prema. According to Prakash Chandra Gupta, "while containing seeds of his future greatness in many ways, the novel is still youthful and lacks the discipline which full maturity brings".

Premchand's next novel, Kishna, was published in the "Indian social reforms series," in 1907 and was claimed as a novel with an "excellent plot by the arresting pen of Navabrai." Naqqad Lucknavi, A reviewer of the book, praised the novel in the Zamana of October-November 1907 by saying, "This novel relates to social reform. Its author is the famous essayist of Zamana, Munshi Navabrai Banarasi who has excellent command over the art of writing novels. He has caricatured the great love of women for ornaments. In other words, this is the life story of a woman who is not merely in love with ornaments but has it as an obsession..." The story of Kishna is retold in a better style by Premchand in *Gaban*.

## Soz-e-Vatan

During April–August 1907, Premchand's story *Roothi Rani* was published in serial form in *Zamana*. Also in 1907, the publishers of *Zamana* published Premchand's first short story collection, titled *Soz-e-Watan (The Dirge/lament of the Nation)*. The collection, which was later banned, contained stories which sought to inspire the Indians in their struggle for political freedom. The five stories in the collection are Duniya ka sabse Anmol Ratan, Sheikh-i-Makhmoor, Yehi Mera Vatan Hai, Sila-i-Maatam and Ishq-e-Duniya aur Hubbe Vatan. In the preface to the book, Navabrai said: "The literature of a nation reflects the march of time. The ideas which move it and the emotions that are echoed in their hearts are reflected in prose and verse, like your own image in a mirror...Such books are needed by the country badly in order to impress the imprint of patriotism on the coming generations."The *Saraswati* magazine of Allahabad, which did not take notice of Premchand's *Prema* and *Kishna*, mentioned this book in its column of book reviews for December 1908. "The book Soz-i-Vatan," it said, "is in Urdu, and has five stories relating to patriotism. The stories are recreational and full of message. A reading of these stories makes a deep imprint of love for the country. Such stories are badly needed these days."

## From Nawab Rai to Premchand

In 1909, Premchand was transferred to Mahoba, and later posted to Hamirpur as the Sub-deputy Inspector of Schools. Around this time, *Soz-e-Watan* was noticed by the British Government officials, who banned it terming the work as a seditious one. The British collector of the Hamirpur District ordered a raid on Premchand's house, where around five hundred copies of *Soz-e-Watan* were burnt. Subsequently, Dhanpat Rai had to change his pseudonym from "Nawab Rai" to "Premchand".

Premchand and Shivrani Devi had three children. Kamla was born in Mahoba. Shripatrai was born in Gorakhpur in August 1918 and another son Mannu was also born in Gorakhpur who died prematurely. Amritrai was born in August 1922. Father was very fond of his children and devoted some time every day to play with them.

His next short story entitled *Gunah ka Agni Kund* was published in Zamana of March 1910. The name of the writer was not "Navabrai" but an "Afsana Kuhan." The identity of the person writing under the name of "Premchand" was revealed to the readers of Urdu journal *Zamana* as follows, "Are the readers of *Zamana* aware of the fact that 'Premchand' is only a pen-name, adopted by our old and esteemed friend Dhanpatrai, B. A., because of certain special reasons? Old readers of the journal would perhaps remember that its earliest issues carried interesting and absorbing literary pieces by him. We have no hesitation in revealing now that 'Navabrai' and 'Premchand' are the two names of one and the same person-Dhanpatrai." The pen-name "Premchand," which later got countrywide fame, appears for the first time on his story *Bade Ghar ki Beti* published in *Zamana* of December 1910.

Premchand as a sub-deputy inspector of schools at the age of 32 years looked vivacious and full of zest for life. But he was not healthy due to his indifferent eating habits. He used to eat "Arvi" which didn't suit him well. He used to get attack of dysentery because he didn't know what to eat and what to avoid. By June 1913, his health was weak again and during those days his wife delivered a baby-girl. She was given the name "Kamala" (She was married to one Vasudev Prasad of Sagar).

## From Urdu to Hindi

In 1914, Premchand started writing in Hindi. Hindi and Urdu can be considered two different registers of a single language Hindustani. Hindi draws much of its vocabulary from Sanskrit and Urdu is more influenced by Persian and Arabic. By this time, he was already reputed as a fiction writer in Urdu. Sumit Sarkar, Harish Trivedi, Amrit Rai and his biographer Madan Gopal noted that the switch was prompted by the difficulty of finding publishers in Urdu. At first he published in Hindi journals some of his stories that were originally published in Urdu and then during 1918–19, he rewrote and published, first in Hindi, his sixth novel under the title *Sevasadan* while its original Urdu version *Bazar-e-Husn* lay unpublished for another four years due to the lack of a publisher. His first Hindi story *Saut* was published in the magazine *Saraswati* in December 1915 and his first short story collection *Sapta Saroj* was published in June 1917.

In September 1915, Premchand wrote a letter to his friend and editor of *Zamana* "*Urdu mein ab gujar nahi hai... urdunavisi mein kis Hindu ko faiz hua jo mujhe ho jayega*." The Urdu writers other than Muslims were few and were derided by them as *bu- e- kachori*. First novel he wrote as Dhanpat Rai, second as Navab Rai and the last one as Premchand. In 1915 he arrived in Hindi with his story "Saut". It should be noted that neither the contemporary readers nor critics welcomed "Prema" which was a transcreation of Premchand's Urdu novel. The readers didn't read it wholeheartedly as the novel couldn't get a reprint when Kishori Lal Goswami, Brij Nandan Sahay and Mehta Lazza Ram Sharma's novels were being reprinted. Pt. Bal Krishna Bhatt wrote a sharp review and advised the proprietor of Indian Press not to publish such novels ( Hindi Pradeep, July 1907). You can understand that Premchand's arrival in Hindi was not such a warm welcome one and smooth then because his type of writing was not understood by the common readers of the day. But Premchand knew that he had a different tale to tell and within a span of five years he became the most sought after writer because once they read him in *Sapt Saroj* and *Sevasadan* they wanted his type of stories and novels. It was a refreshing change indeed!

In August 1916, Premchand was transferred to Gorakhpur on a promotion. He became the Assistant Master at the Normal High School, Gorakhpur. At Gorakhpur he developed friendship with the bookseller Buddhi Lal, who allowed him to borrow novels for reading, in exchange for selling examination oriented guide books at the school. Premchand was an enthusiastic reader of classics of other languages, and translated several of these works in Hindi.

## Sevasadan

By 1919, Premchand's novel Sevasadan was published in Hindi. It was originally written in Urdu under the title *Bazaar-e-Husn*, but was published in Hindi first by a Calcutta-based publisher, who offered Premchand Rs. 450 for his work. The Urdu Publisher of Lahore published the novel later in 1924, paying Premchand a pittance of Rs.250. The novel tells the story of an unhappy housewife, who first becomes a courtesan, and then manages an orphanage for the young daughters of the courtesans. It was well received by the critics, and helped Premchand gain wider recognition.

In 1919, Premchand obtained a BA degree from Allahabad. He had tried unsuccessfully for the post of lecturer in Urdu at Osmania University, and of headmaster of the D. A. V. School at Kanpur. In a letter, he once wrote "Let me go my own way. My life's aim is to become the headmaster of a privately-run (as against government-run) school, to edit some good paper which should espouse the cause of the peasants and laborers, and be of some service to the people." How could he get a place in Osmania University where Allama Iqbal, the great Urdu poet couldn't get employment as a lecturer in the department of philosophy?

## Resignation

On 8 February 1921, he attended a meeting in Gorakhpur, where Mahatma Gandhi asked people to resign from government jobs as part of the non-cooperation movement. Premchand, although physically unwell and had two kids and a pregnant wife to support, thought about it for 5 days and decided, with the consent of his wife, to resign from his government job. This incident is described in detail by Shivrani Devi in *Premchand Gar Mein* as follows: "After the Jallianwala Bagh massacre, it was natural that everyone's heart was inflamed with rage. Perhaps it was in my heart too! Next day I prepared myself for all the troubles that were to come after quitting the government service. ... When I said that we have to together put an end to this inhumanity; the policies of the government are beyond the limits of tolerance, he (Premchand) laughed and said - 'Before putting an end to others think of your own end... think it over, later do not tell me that you suffered and made me suffer too! There will be many troubles ahead; you may have to go without food.' I replied- 'I have thought it over!'

A story which is entitled *Lal Fita (Red Tape)* written during those days reveals the state of his mind. In the story the protagonist Har Bilas, a teacher, tenders his resignation with these words "Sir, it is my belief that God's will is reflected in the conduct of human affairs. His laws are based on truth, mercy and justice. For the last fifteen years, I have served the government and carried out my duties with the fullest loyalty and devotion. It is possible that on some occasions some of the superiors were not fully satisfied because I have never taken it upon myself to carry out their personal wishes. Whenever there was a conflict between the orders of the superior officer and law I followed the path of law. I have always understood government service as the best medium to serve the people and the country. The orders conveyed through Circular No.... dated ... however, are against my conscience and against my principles. They interfere, in my view, with truth and justice. I am unable to implement them. These orders are an obstacle in the way of the country's independence and constitute an attack on its political awakening. In the circumstances, for me to continue my relationship with the government would be a disservice to the country and to the nation. Along with other rights, the subjects have also the right to wage a political struggle. And as the government is determined to snatch away this right, I, as an Indian, am unable to serve the government. I request, therefore, that I be relieved of my post as soon as possible."

After quitting his job, Premchand left Gorakhpur for Benaras on 18 March 1921 and decided to focus on his literary career.

## Saraswati Press

In 1923, he established a printing press and publishing house in Benares, christened "Saraswati Press". During those days his wife delivered another baby-girl on March 3, 1924 who died in June. The year 1924 saw the publication of Premchand's *Rangabhumi*, which has a blind beggar called Surdas as its tragic hero. Schulz mentions that in *Rangabhumi*, Premchand comes across as a "superb social chronicler", and although the novel contains some "structural flaws" and "too many authorial explanations", it shows a "marked progress" in Premchand's writing style. According to Schulz, it was in *Nirmala* (1925) and *Pratigya* (1927) that Premchand found his way to "a balanced, realistic level" that surpasses his earlier works and manages to "hold his readers in tutelage". *Nirmala*, a novel dealing with the dowry system in India, was first serialized in the magazine Chand between November 1925 and November 1926, before being published as a novel. *Pratigya* ("The Vow") dealt with the subject of widow and widower remarriage.

In 1928, Premchand's novel *Gaban* ("Embezzlement"), focusing on the middle class' greed, was published. In March 1930, Premchand launched a literary-political weekly magazine *Hans*, aimed at inspiring the Indians to mobilize against the British rule. The magazine, noted for its politically provocative views, failed to make a profit. Premchand then took over and edited another magazine called *Jagaran*, which too ran at a loss.

In 1931, Premchand moved to Kanpur as a headmaster in the Marwari School, but had to leave because of differences with the college administration. You can see the glimpses of his differences with Kashi Nath, the manager of the school, in the story *"Prerna"*. He then returned to Benares, and became the editor of *Maryada* magazine. In 1932, he published another novel titled *Karmabhumi*. He briefly served as the in charge of the high school section of Kashi Vidyapeeth, an institution of repute. After the school's closure or his resignation due to differences with the management, he became the editor of the *Madhuri* magazine in Lucknow.

In 1932, Pandit Banarsidas Chaturvedi asked him how much money he had made from writing. "Please don't embarrass me" he replied," first books were sold to publishers; the Hindi Pustak Agency gave me three thousand rupees for Seva-Sadan, Premashram, Sapt-Saroj and Sangram. A few others brought me a couple of hundred. Shri Dularelal paid Rs 1,200 for Rangabhumi. Kayakalp, A Story of Freedom, Prem-Pratima and Pratigya I published myself, and these have brought in about Rs 600 so far. I should say that I received about Rs 15 a month from my writings; even this amount is a generous figure. Hack work and translation: not more than Rs 2,000."

It is true that Premchand struggled. But it is not right to label him as a poor man struggling to get two morsels of food everyday. For example Indra Nath Madan (1946: 21) writes "His father was an ill-paid clerk who rose to the position of a petty master of a petty post office, getting forty rupees a month. Mrs. Premchand has recorded a number of incidents which reveal the extreme poverty of his family. Considering relatively low prices of those days and the existense of the populace living at the verge of starvation around him, we cannot say that forty rupees a month was a small sum of money and we cannot help feeling surprise at the expression, "the extreme poverty of his family."He too earned a lot of money throughout his life and was able to give considerable dowry at the time of his daughter's marriage. His sons studied in boarding schools and he used to buy ornaments for his wife. We should not forget that he could afford both the time and money for reading and writing throughout his life. The story of hardships he had to go through is a kind of retrospection of a successful person who likes to exaggerate them in order to stress the importance of his achievement. Kamal Kishore Goenka presented the copies of his bank account details to shatter this myth but an average Hindi student thinks that he was a poor man.

## Mumbai Filmdom

Premchand arrived in Mumbai on 31 May 1934 to try his luck in the Hindi film industry. He had accepted a script writing job for the production house Ajanta Cinetone, hoping that the yearly salary of Rs. 8000 would help him overcome his financial troubles. He stayed at Dadar, and wrote the script for the film *Mazdoor* ("The Labourer"). The film, directed by Mohan Bhawnani, depicted the poor conditions on the labour class. Premchand himself did a cameo as the leader of laborers in the film. Some influential businessmen managed to get a stay on its release in Mumbai. The film was released in Lahore and Delhi, but was banned again after it inspired the mill workers to stand up against the owners.

Ironically, the film inspired the workers of his loss-making press in Benares to launch a strike, after they were not paid their salaries. By 1934–35, Premchand's Saraswati Press was under a heavy debt of Rs. 4000, and Premchand was forced to discontinue the publication of *Jagaran*. Meanwhile, Premchand was beginning to dislike the non-literary commercial environment of the Mumbai film industry, and wanted to return to Benares. During this time and his subsequent stay in Bombay, he saw only one film and this was the only one he had ever seen! At times he felt annoyed with himself for having left the idyllic peace of Banaras. The world of Bombay was entirely different from that of Banaras. Dhunnu, his son, failed in the examination and his poor performance pained Premchand. As he had signed a one-year contract with the production house, he was undecided. He ultimately left Mumbai on 4 April 1935, before the completion of one year. Himanshu Roy, the founder of Bombay Talkies, tried to convince Premchand to stay back, but did not succeed.

"It is becoming difficult for me to write stories for the cinema," wrote Premchand in a letter to Jainendra Kumar three days after his return to Bombay. "What is needed here is stories that can be staged and be easy for the artistes. Even when a story is good, so long as suitable actors are not available for staging them, who will play the roles? I don't expect the need for miracles. My two stories submitted to them are simple stories. The director is all in all in the film industry. The writer may be the master of the pen but this empire is that of the director. The writer can have no say. Indeed, it is only when the writer accepts the sovereignty of the producer that he can stay on here."

## Later Premchand

The biography of Premchand *"Kalam ka Sipahi"* starts with an anecdote as follows: Mr Chandrahasan, a Hindi-acolyte from South India reached Banaras to meet Premchand. He got his address and reached at his doorsteps in the evening. He stayed outside for a while and made some clatter-chatter too to register his presence. But when no one came outside, he peeped inside the house and saw a man with remarkably thick mustache who was sting on the floor and writing intently. The arrivant thought that the man must be Premchand's scribe. He paced a little further and asked the man, "I want to meet Premchandji." The man looked up the arrivant with eager eyes and placed his pen in the inkstand, and then with a hearty laugh, "Will you meet him standing like this? Please be seated and meet him."Nobody could recognize him at the first meeting because *"koi visheshta jo nahin thi unmein"* (Rai, 1962, 2). This simple attired man became a legend in his later life. He was acknowledged as a man of letters.

After leaving Bombay on April 4, 1935, Premchand went to meet his daughter and son and reached Lamhi on April 24. He wanted to settle in Allahabad where his sons Sripat Rai and Amrit Rai were studying. He also planned to publish *Hans* from there. However, owing to his poor financial condition and ill-health, he had to hand over *Hans* to the Indian Literary Counsel and move to Benares.

## Godan

The time Premchand spent at the film land, the time he devoted in translation and the time he was engaged in printing and publishing loss-making magazines was a sheer waste of time. It slowed down the writing of his magnum opus "*Godan*". This 600 page long novel took a lot of time to get completed. He began writing it in 1932 and was not able to complete it till November 1934. It was with him during his stay in Mumbai. He must have completed it after his return from Mumbai. Even the printing of the novel was delayed and the novel could see the light of the day in June 1936 only, just a few months before his untimely death. Premchand wrote in 1934 during his Godan days 'I believe in social evolution ... Revolution is the failure of saner methods'. He was neither a Marxist nor a Gandhian. His hero is Hori, an out and out Premchand of his time.

Premchand wrote up to his last breath. Apart from his essay on *Mahajani Sabhyata*, Premchand was writing a novel titled *Mangalsutra* (He could write about 70 pages only). This novel is the story of a writer "Mahatma" Dev Kumar, his wife Shaivya, his elder son Sant Kumar, a lawyer, and his wife Pushpa, his younger son Sadhu kumar, and a married daughter Pankaja. The novel, a veiled biography of Premchand, might have been one of his best had he finished it. The Gandhi in him had gone to sleep for a while and now Premchand was a new soldier with a pen that was a syringe and a sword.

In 1936, Premchand was elected as the first President of the Progressive Writers' Association. The address given by him at the occasion of its first conference at Lucknow was later published as *"Sahitya Ka Uddeshya" (The Nature and Purpose of literatutre)* where he presented the manifesto of his creed as follows: In olden times, religion held the reins of society... Now, literature has taken this task upon itself...It is the duty of literature to champion and advocate the cause of whoever may be oppressed, exploited and deprived-whether it is an individual or a community. Only that kind of literature will be assessed as true by us which has high thinking, a sense of independence, the essence of beauty, the soul of creativity, the illumination of the truths of life-which causes agitation in us and movement and does not send us to sleep ; for to sleep any more would be a sign of death." For him "the writer is the path-finder of the nation. His heart brims with affection. In his heart there is no place for fanaticism or bigotry. Who are the people that fight the war psychosis? They are the writers." He was one such writer himself.

AIPWA meeting is a confluence of the socialistic trends as Cappola calls it, " from which the socialist realist movement of India flowed, a movement which, next to Mahatma Gandhi, produced what is probably the most powerful literary effect upon Indian creative writing during the first three quarters of the twentieth century.

Premchand was a writer who inspired other writers also. He used to think that the young writers who come to him for guidance must be carefully cultivated and groomed. His doors were always open for such budding writers. Sudershan was one such story teller who became a friend. Premchand wrote a foreword to his book *Baharistan.* Poet Balakrishna Sharma "Naveen" who had been his colleague in the Marwari Vidyalaya at Kanpur was a friend. Essayists like Ramvriksha Benipuri and Shivpujan Sahai, and novelist Jainendra Kumar Jain were like friends than followers to him. While at Gorakhpur, he came to know Raghupati Sahai "Firaq" who was studying at the Muir Central College Allahabad. They used to meet daily and the friendship grew into partnership in publishing business also. Firaq had a complaint too. In fact, he didn't like Premchand's neutral and dispassionate response to Urdu poetry.

Premchand was worried about the future of *Hans,* and his wife and children. "My aspirations," he wrote to B. D. Chaturvedi, "are few, and foremost among them is that we should be successful in our struggle for independence. I no longer aspire for wealth or fame. I expect very little even from my two sons. In fact, all that I expect of them is that they should be honest, truthful, and resolute. I would hate my children hankering after wealth, and luxuries and become sycophants. I also do not wish to retire from active life. My needs are few, extremely simple food and very ordinary clothes. I do not aspire for a motor car or a huge mansion to live in. I do, of course, wish to write a few top class books. But the object in writing them is also the attainment of the goal of independence."

His health continuously deteriorated. At the age of 56, he used to look frail and fragile. He was sick and a fatal gastric ulcer made his stomach bloated. His "dark-circled eyes, peering from abysms, sunken dry cheeks"made him really frightful to look at. But his skinny fingers continued writing. He wrote a tearful obituary to Gorky and went to attend a prayer meeting where he couldn't reach comfortably and collapsed. His address was read by someone else. Jainendra Kumar was present when he became sick and feeble. On the last day of his life the ultimate conversation he had with Jainendra Kumar is as follows.

"In this condition, Jainendra, people think of God, I also have been advised to do likewise, but I haven't yet been able to persuade myself to bother Him..."

"... Ideals won't do."

"...But ideals..." said Jainedra.

"...Don't argue..." Premchand said finally and went into a coma.

He died on 8 October 1936, after several days of sickness. Madan Gopal, his biographer, ends the story of his life with these words- "The light that had lit millions of hearts in all parts of India had gone out. The life of the master storyteller who had given joy and happiness to countless people, who had carried on a ceaseless campaign for political freedom and social reform, who had given a voice to the dumb and mute dwellers of rural India, who had elevated human existence, had become a story, and his name a legend."

## Premchand's Progeny

Premchand's sons followed the footprints of their father. Sripat Rai (Dhunnu) edited and presented him. He took care of Sarasvati Press and started a journal *"Kahani"*. Amrit Rai (Bannu) wrote Premchand's biography and edited several collections of Premchand's work and continued editing *Hans*. *Kalam Ka Sipahi* got him Sahitya Akademi award in 1971. His novel *Beej* (1952) is also worth mentioning. Few people know that Amrit Rai married Sudha Chauhan who was the daughter of Subhadra Kumari Chauhan, the famed poetess who wrote *"khub ladi mardani vo to Jhansi vali rani thi"* and

Sudha Chauhan too wrote her mother's biography *"Mila Tej se Tej"*. Premchand's grandson Alok Rai was a Professor at IIT (Delhi) and his book *"Hindi Nationalism"* is an exciting work indeed. He translated "Nirmala" into English. Both, father and son wrote in English. But Premchand is Premchand and his sons and grandsons were just his shadows. The son of Premchand's daughter Kamla is Dr Prabodh Kumar Srivastava. He had been very active in getting *Premchand Ghar Mein* republished and was a friend and follower of Muktibodh. (You may be interested to know that the retired professor of Anthropology Prabodh Kumar Srivastava was in the news for inspiring his domestic helper Baby Halder to write her autobiography and she wrote a best selling one "*Aalo Andhaari*" [A life less ordinary, 2006].)

## Bambook

Scholars fail to remember that this voracious reader and budding novelist during his youth was called "Bambook" by his friends. You must have heard the word *Dambuk* or *Banduk* but he was *Bambook*. If you want me to translate it, I would say it means a *gas balloon*. He joined the laughing club which held a laughing session on a daily basis. His full throated peals of laughter were his mark and signature. Even though he lived in penury for most of his life, he was carefree. An incident is recorded by his biographer when his abundant laughter is earmarked as follows: Once in the house of a neighbor of Nigam, a gramophone record of Bert Shepherd's laughing song entitled "I sat in a corner," was being played. For some time Premchand restrained himself, but then burst out. "I will join him in laughter," he said and gave peals after peals of laughter in harmony with the singer, other friends joining him, or rather were provoked into joining him. He was indeed a great one to laugh. We are told by his friends that if he laughed, cobwebs vibrated. If he laughed while passing through the market place, the attention of every shopkeeper would be drawn towards him. And he did not need any particular occasion to laugh..."

"When he laughed", according to Mirza Mohammed Hassan Askari, who met him at the residence of Maulana Zafrul Mulk, "he did not stint . . . 1 found him always amiable, always smiling. In fact, I used to tease him for never showing anger."

"Don't you ever get angry? Not even at home?" And he would laugh at that too.'

Alas! We see him in the photographs only as a serious person. One who could laugh with us, at us and at himself too is no more!

Premchand was aware of his nick-name. He didn't fail to encash this name which he got in 1905 in the company of his friends during his Kanpur days. He used this in some of the hilarious pieces he wrote for *"Jamana"*. For instance the funny and humourous essays *"Tange vale Ki Bad"* (September, 1926) and *"Shadi ki Vajah"* (March, 1927) were published in the magazine with the name of the author "Bambook".

I wish to include a couplet (doha) written by Mannan Dwivedi who sent it along with a basket of fish after seeing Premchand buying fish from the fish-market.

> *Dheemar ne fashyo abhi deen heen safreen*
> *Premchand Bhojan Karen vidya buddhi praveen*

When Premchand came home and read out the couplet he laughed heartily. When Dwivediji came to visit him again, Premchand welcomed him with his signature laughter and promised him to write a poem in return of his verses.

## Love life

Young Premchand used to read romances and romantic tales in the Urdu language since childhood. He kept the company of friends who were also like him. His stepmother was callous and careless. His father was busy in his work. The maulvis who taught him and the schools he joined in were not able to direct and discipline him well. This unrestricted freedom was not healthy for a growing mind. Madan Gopal gives the following hint about his fling with a married woman:

> The stepmother's influence on Premchand was unhealthy. The young wife of an old man, she would discuss intimate details of married life with the landlady, an Ahir widow, within Premchand's hearing. The boy would listen attentively, and, at the tender age

of thirteen, "knew certain facts of life which would normally ruin a young man's life." He also took to smoking-secretly. (1964: 16)

What about love and love-affairs? Premchand says, ""I have had no love affairs. Life was so engrossing and bread-winning was such a tough job that it left no scope for romances. There were some petty affairs of a very universal type, and I cannot call them love affairs." (Gopal 1964:58)

Do you think that there could be something else between a man and a woman except "petty affairs of a very universal type"? *Premchand in Love* can be a romantic movie indeed! Don't insist me to reveal more, we should go through the slight hint given by Mrs Premchand in her book.

> *Aap Bole: Acchcha aik aur chori suno, Maine apni pahli stri ke jeevan kal mein hi aik aur stri rakh chodi thi. Tumhare aane par bhi mera us stri se sambandh tha.*
>
> Main Boli: Mujhe malum hai.
>
> Yah sunkar ve meri aur dekhne lage... (1944, 356)

Do you want me to translate it? The philosophical revelation below is an extract from *Godan* which can reveal a part of his thinking about love, marriage and sex:

> The dawn of married life is rosy with an intoxicating desire whose golden rays illumine the horizons of the soul. Then comes the scorching heat of noon, when whirlwinds blow and the earth begins to tremble. The golden shelter of desire melts away. Stark reality emerges. After that comes restful evening, cool and peaceful, when, like weary travellers, we discuss the day's journey with a detachment as though seated on some high mountain top removed from the clamour below.

If we extend the discussion a little further and reach out for his views about love, sex and marriage, we come across Gobar and Jhuniya of *Godan* and their love at the time of drought. There is selfless love for which he could live and die; love not fulfilled like a glowworm's but slow and steady like the flame of an earthen lamp. Crafty Jhunya very coyly asks Gobar, "to get all he has to give all. You will have to be mine. And then if I see you begging before others, I'll give you up for ever." She wishes and wants –

> To pass my days with one man is the pleasure of my life. The men spoil their wives. If a husband runs after women, it's natural for his wife to exchange glances with other men... Can you keep a wife under lock and key and play the fool yourself? What do you do openly she'll do secretly.

Then there is a kind of love relationship between Matadin and Selia which is based on fulfilling sexual desires. She says, "Give up the Pandit, let him starve me, beat me, kill me. I can't leave him. I prefer death to becoming someone else's woman."

The love between husband and wife and the husband's extra-marital affair is also interestingly presented by Premchand in Godan. Mr. and Mrs. Khanna and the role of the butterfly Malati is another shade of love. Mehta looks every inch a philosopher and is known for his intellect and wisdom and Malti is "vivacious, lavishly made up, witty, forward and well up in the ways of men, fond of good things in life, coquettish –in short very modern." Premchand comments very intelligently:

> If a man richly takes on the qualities of a woman he becomes a mahatma. But if a woman imbibes the qualities of a man she becomes evil. A man is really attracted only towards a woman who possesses the essential attributes of a woman.

Just one more example form a short story to pinpoint the views of the writer. Miss Padma is presented as an educated liberated woman and through her Premchand indicates about love, sex, live-in-relationship and single motherhood.

> Padma was not averse to luxury, she hated dependence, hated the idea of marriage. When you can enjoy life being indepdnent, why not? To her, morality didn't come in the way of pleasure, which was bodily requirement for her. The requirement can be met if you can find the right shop.

And last but not the least, Shivrani Devi mentions in her book "*Premchand : Ghar mein*" that she was not on cordial terms with his stepmother, a domineering, fussy woman, and would go to stay with her father for the best part of each year. One day Premchand refused to give her permission to leave. She flared up. There was a quarrel. He slapped her twice, and left the house, returning towards the evening.

"Why must you flare up?" he asked softly.

"I had no reason!" She replied softly.

"I've nothing in my defence. But you are angry. Not a word since then."

"What should I talk about? I'm in prison; a prisoner has nothing to say. You tried to teach me a lesson. I've learnt."

"No, no lesson, I didn't want to hurt you in the least. It's just that I need you too much to want to see you leave. I want you with me, near me. This is your home. Why don't you make it yours?"

"I know very well I'm not mistress in this house."

"If you go away, it'll all collapse."

"It won't. I just don't like it here. Your chachi loves you well enough; she'll take care of you." "What you call love, is not love, Shivrani, I think 1 know that better than you do."

Shivrani Devi did not go that year to her father's home.

"What you call love, is not love." The statement is loaded with meaning.

Premchand concludes that love resides at home and it is futile to search for it elsewhere, "'Home' evokes many a memories of purity, softness and beauty. Home is a playground of love. Love has achieved this gift after strict meditation."

## Munshi Premchand

Why do we very fondly and indubitably call Premchand as *"Munshi Premchand"?* What is this munshi? Why does Dharmveer write a book on him and gives the title "Samamton *ka munshi*"? As far as I know the word "munshi" is a very common Hindi-Urdu word and it means an accountant (Don't you remember an Amitabh Bachchan film in which he teases Mukri for his mustache? (*Muchchen hon to munshiji jaisi*). Kayashths in North India are those who often take the work of accountancy as their means of livelihood. There used to be a number of munshis in the workplaces. It is also a popular saying that Kayasths are the people who are not dependable. It is believed that they are selfish and half-Hindu and half-Muslim. They eat, drink and do not bother about others. (It is interesting to know that Dr Harivansha Rai Bachchan in his autobiography *"Kya Bhulun Kya yaad karun"* gives details of his caste and tells us about the saying " if you meet a snake and a kayastha on the way, kill the kayastha first as he will never spare you.") Munshiji is also a kind of honorific word for head accountant. Munshi Premchand is "Munshi" not because he was an accountant or a kayashth but he became munshi as Gandhi became Mahatma. Premchand was a school teacher. He became head master and Inspector of schools too but could never become a lecturer or a professor. He applied for the post of a lecturer in Osmania University Hyderabad but was not selected. In those days school masters too used to be called "Munshi or Munshi ji". Kayashths used to be called "munshi" on account of their work. But Premchand never called himself "Munshi Premchand". Though his son Amritrai addresses him as "Munshi" and "Munshiji" in the *(Basti ke Tara Shankar Nashad Munshiji se milne Lucknow pahunche- page 1*) biographical book *"Kalam ka Sipahi."* His readers, critics, admirers and scholars call him "Munshi Premchand" because they think that this prefix is their mark of honor for the novelist. It is also claimed that this prefix has been used for him because of confusion. It so happened that Kanhiya Lal Manik Lal Munshi was also the editor of *Hans* magazine and the names of Premchand and him were inadvertently printed as, *Sampadak: Munshi, Premchand*. As it was, there were two literary stalwarts who were Hans' editors but readers mistook them as one and later they started addressing him as "Munshi Premchand."

To sum up the extra-ordinary story of Premchand's life and his deeds one can say in the words of a reviewer, Ulka Anjaria, a professor working in the Department of English Brandeis University U. S. A., [ in her first book "the study of the mid 20th-century Indian novel and focusing on the the movement of progressive writing that inspired many writers in the lead-up to Indian independence and also in Realism in the Twentieth-Century Indian Novel: Colonial Difference and Literary Form (2012)] that Premchand was a Gandhian and later a socialist, but he was also a fickle son, a hands off father, a flighty husband, a poor struggling writer, a failed publisher, a loyal but easily roused friend, a superb story teller, a democrat, a secularist, and in all an inhabitant of his time." I think P. Lal is a little bit kind and considerate to him in *"Premchand: An Appreciation"* (1980) when he concludes, "Premchand's life and work are full of such apparent contradictions, and the critic must wait for time to sift them before he "places" Premchand. While such contradictions slowly fall into clearer focus, this much may be said with certainty: Premchand is a memorable writer because he has sincerity and style and purpose. But a writer with as much heart as Premchand had should not be ignored, for he may one day baffle the timid critic and announce himself a 'major' writer, instead of one merely readable and instructive." Similarly, *Rakhshanda Jalil writes too, "* Here is the doyen of Hindi literature, rising above the thorny issue of language (Hindi-Urdu-Hindustani) and talking about what concerns, or *should* concern, all writers irrespective of language. He urged writers to discard individual and personal concerns and, instead, speak in a collective voice taking upon themselves public and political roles. Literature, which had hitherto been content to entertain or at best educate, must now, given the exigencies of the times, advance human knowledge and freedom."

# Chapter - 3

# Raconteur Premchand

*"Literature is written by geniuses. Novelists are geniuses."*
**— E. M. Forster (1927)**

When I was in search of a suitable title for this chapter, I was very confused. Premchand wrote novels, stories, dramas, essays, and gave us so much in such a short life that it was really difficult to give all of it a composite name or a title. That is why I was tempted to use a noun as an adjective to form and coin a new word, a new collocation: *Raconteur Premchand.* A raconteur is one who is good at telling stories. India has been really good at telling stories. This is the land of Panchtantra and Pt. Vishnu Sharma. Before Premchand (BP) and After Premchand (AP) are the two conditions and features of Hindi fiction. Premchand Turn is such a turn in Hindi fiction that nobody after him could return to the old ways of *dastaangardi*. It will not be an exercise in futility to first look at the rise of the novel in the West, more importantly in the English speaking world, and then look at its impact on the Indian writers.

Hans Raj "Rahbar", a novelist and short story writer in his earlier book on Premchand entitled *"Premchand: His life and work"(*1957) said as follows:Though not the focus of attraction, Premchand was the finest friend and ranconteur a man could find. He had a knack of putting others at ease..." Therefore Premchand is a ranconteur, conversationalist, narrator, story-teller and novelist of a high order and it is appropriate to give this chapter the title it deserves.

## The Rise of the Novel before Premchand

The novel is generally regarded as having been imported from the West. The first novel of Hindi in the English Style (*Angreji Dhang Ka Pahla upanyas*) is said to be written by Lala Srinivas Das. It is *Pariksha Guru.* According to Ram Chandra Shukla, *Pariksha-Guru,* (The Master Examiner) published in 1882 was a novel which cautioned young men (especially of well-to-do families) against falling into bad company which could trap them into loose morals.

What is this English Style indeed? What is an English novel? M. Abel Chevalley, a French critic in his brilliant little manual "Le *Roman Anglais de Notre Temps*" provides a definition when he says, "a fiction in prose of a certain extent" *(une fiction en prose d'une certain etendue).* This extent should not be less than 50000 words.

Let us first understand the rise of the novel in England to know what this English style is. We must also look into the growth and development of novel in Indian languages. Meenakshi Mukherjee in the introductory remark of her notable editied volume *"Early Novels in India"* says that fictional texts written in different languages from 1860 onwards, later identified as novels, came to be evaluated largely in terms of their closeness to Western Models. (2001: VIII)

No study of Hindi novel or the novels and fiction of Premchand can be carried out well without going through the history of the growth and development of novels in India. It is also noteworthy that the very word *"Upanyas"* is not the only word for it. Even in Europe there is another word"*Romance*". We have *naval Katha* in Gujarati, *Kadambari* in Marathi and *Upanyas* in Bengali. In 1862 Bhudev Mukherji (1827-1894) wrote an article *"Aitihasik Upanyas"* (Historical Novel) in which he used this word first time. Ram Chandra Shukla was of the opinion that the word came into Hindi via Bengali literature. In Hindi we used to write *"Kuch aap biti kuch jag biti*" and "*Devrani Jethani ki kahani*". Sustained narratives were known to the educated Indian as texts in the *itihiasa* or *akhyana* tradition, while the uneducated Indian was served by the *katha* tradition.

The concluding passage in the novelist E. M. Forster's lectures (*The Clark Lectures- Spring 1927, Trinity College, Cambridge*) printed in the form of a worthwhile book *"Aspects of the Novel"* (1927) (which was also read and recommended by Premchand) can be a good starting point to discuss about the rise and development of novel in England, "Human nature is unchangeable, and that it produces in rapid succession prose fictions, when they contain 50000 words or more, are called novels. If we had the power or license to take a wider view, and survey all human and pre-human activity, we might not conclude like this; the crablike movement, the shifting of the passengers, might be visible, and the phrase "the development of the novel" might cease to be a pseudo-scholarly tag or a technical triviality, and become important, because it implied the development of humanity. (246-247)

In England as the earnings of the common men increased, the writers experimented with different literary styles. Henry Fielding who wrote "*Tom Jones*" (1749) was a novelist of the early 18th century. He claimed that he was the founder of a new province of writing where he could make his own laws. Walter Scott wrote historical novels about wars between Scottish clans by collecting Scottish ballads. Samual Richardson wrote *Pamela* in 18th century in the form of letters. It was the first epistolary novel. The publishing market was costly at the beginning. Henry Fielding's *Tom Jones* was sold at three shillings for each of its six volumes – more than a laborer's earnings in a week. In 1836, first novel to be serialized in a magazine was Charles Dickens'(1812-1870) *Pickwick Papers*. The suspense created by such publications reminds us of the TV serials today. In those days novels were one of the first mass-produced items to be sold. The World of the Novel in the 19th century was about ordinary people. It reflected the industrial age of the 19th century, problems created by factories, unemployed poor, homeless people living in workhouses. For example, Charles Dickens' novel *Hard Times* describes the terrible conditions of urban life under capitalism. *Oliver Twist* is a tale of a poor orphan caught up in a world of petty criminals. B. Emile Zola's *Germinal* (1885) is the life of French miners, the gloomy life led by them ends on a note of despair. Thomas Hardy's (1840-1928) novels such as "The *Mayor of Casterbridge*" (1886) brought the vast majority of urban readers closer to the rural community and society.

There were many women writers who explored the world of women, their emotions, identities, experiences and problems. Jane Austen's (1775–1817) novel Pride *and Prejudice* portrays life of women in genteel rural society in the early 19th century England. In *Pride and Prejudice* Mrs. Bennett, the mother of five unmarried daughters had only one obsession — to get her daughters married to rich, well to do men. That is why Pride *and Prejudice* begins with the ironical statement, *"It is a truth universally acknowledged that a single man in possession of a good fortune must be in want of a wife."* Charlotte Bronte's (1816–1855) *Jane Eyre* portrays an independent and assertive girl who protests against hypocrisy and cruelty. The novel shows protest against hypocrisy of elders with startling bluntness, breaking the established norms of society. For instance, the following dialogue is remarkably nothing less than a revolution "People think you a good woman, but you are bad – you are deceitful. I will never call you aunt as long as I live."

George Eliot's (1819–1880), *Mill on the Floss*, is about freedom given by novels to women to express them freely. George Eliot's real name is Mary Ann Evans. She believed that novels gave women unique opportunity to express themselves and every woman could write novels. She says, ""Fiction is a department of literature in which women can alter their kind, fully equal men .... No educational restrictions can shut women from the materials of fiction, and there is no species of art that is so free from rigid requirements."

Novels for the young such as *Treasure Island* (1883) were written by R. L. Stevenson which idealized a new type of powerful, assertive, daring and independent man. These novels were novels of adventure. Rudyard Kipling wrote *Jungle Book* (1894). Colonizers namely the British colonizers were portrayed as heroic and honorable, confronting 'Natives', adapting themselves to strange places, colonizing territories and developing nations. G. A. Henty (1832–1902) wrote novels such as Under *Drake's Flag*. They were historical and adventure novels for boys and depicted the zenith of the British Empire. Helen Hunt Jackson (Ramona - 1884), Sarah Wolsey (*What Katy Did* - 1872) wrote love stories for girls.

Novels were written in Europe which portrayed colonialists as a superior community. Colonized people were seen as primitive, barbaric and less than human. Joseph Conrad (1857–1924) showed the darker side of colonial occupation only in later 20th century. Daniel Defoe's *Robinson Crusoe* (1719) portrayed an adventurer who treated colored people as inferior creatures. He rescued a '*native*' and made him his slave. Colonial rule was portrayed as necessary to civilize the natives, to make them human.

The Art of fiction writing arrived in India during 19th century. Novels in prose were unknown to India till the 19th century. Great epics were largely written in verse form; though in fourth century AD some of the stories were written in Sanskrit prose style such as Panchtantra and Kadambari. To start the discussion about the rise of novel in India, it can be said that the inspiration and model of the novel we got from the West but there were our own tradition and way of narration of folk tales and epics and heroic tales of adventure and romance (*aakhyanas).* There was a great churning for a considerable period of time and with the mingling of it with the literary and social climate it took another shape altogether. Meenakshi Mukherjee (1994) writes in this regard, "In spite of the basic incompatabilities ... the novel in India which began under English tutelage soon began to acquire its own distinctive character...The synthesis of a borrowed literary form and indigenous aesthetics –as well as cultural expectations-in order to determine the extent to which the novel form has undergone mutation in the process. *(Realism amd Reality: The novel and Society in India, p.18).* Similarly Sisir Kumar Das in his authoritative study "History of Indian Literature: 1800– 1910" says that the Western impact on Indian novelists was not unlimited. The Indian mind was not ready to receive anything and everything of their culture. They often resisted and declined to accept them in totality:

> What makes this period unique in our literary history is its continuous conflict between the indigenous and the alien ideals, values and sensibilites. It was not a contact between two authors or two texts, it was a contact between two civilizations in an unfortunate historical circumstance...This love and hate

relationship with the West made the literary contact tortuous and complex." (p. 331)

The art of novel writing was first picked up by the novelists in Marathi and Bengali languages. Baba Padmanji's *Yamuna Paryatan* (1857) is a simple story about the plight of widows. Lakshman Moreshwar Halbe's *Muktamala* (1861) is an imaginary 'romance' with a moral purpose. Hari Narayan Apte (1864-1919) wrote historical novels. His *Ushakala* is still famous and read. Naro Sadashiv Rishud wrote *Manju Ghosha*. It is a novel full of amazing events. In defense of his novel *Manju ghosha*, he wrote, """Because of our attitude to marriage and for several other reasons one finds in the Hindus neither interesting views nor virtues. If we write about things that we experience daily there would be nothing enthralling about them, so that if we set out to write an entertaining book we are forced to take up with the marvelous."

The novelists found the mundane life dull and uninspiring, so they wrote about the marvelous and unknown. The novel in South India, most importantly in Kerala, started with translations of English novels. Chandu Menon (1847-1899) attempted a translation of Benjamin Disraeli's *Henrietta Temple.* He gave it up as he realized English culture might be difficult to grasp by the people of Kerala. Therefore, he wrote a charming and fresh novel in Malayalam and gave it the title *Indulekha* (1889). It is said to be the first modern novel in Malayalam. The heroine Indulekha is portrayed as highly intelligent, artistic and educated in Sanskrit and English. She is very beautiful too. Madhavan, the hero is equally an ideal one. He is a member of the educated class of Nayars. He studies at the University of Madras and is a first-rate Sanskrit scholar. He dresses in western clothes but keeps a long tuft of hair as the Nayar tradition is. They are the representive characters of those who have taken the best of the colonial West without giving up the traditions of their own culture. Chandu Menon projected Indulekha as an ideal before the contemporary women and said:

> Twety years from hence there may be found hundreds of Indulekhas in Malabar who would be able to choose their own husbands for pure and sweet love. My narrative of the love and

courtship of Madhav is intended to show to the young ladies of Malabar how happy they can be if they have the freedom to choose their partners.

Kathanjali, a Kannada magazine, used to publish short stories regularly. *Indirabai* (1899), a Kannada novel, written by Gulawadi Venkata Rao tells the story of women's education, widow's plight and problems created by early marriages of girls. He said that he first thought of translating an English novel into Kannada but when he considered a few such works in English, they did not seem to agree with our Hindu sensibility ( *Hindu Maryada).*

In Andhra Pradesh Kandukuri Viresalingam (1848–1919) too began by translating Oliver Goldsmith's *Vicar of Wakefield* into Telugu. He also abandoned it and wrote *Rajashekhara Charitamu* in 1878 in Telugu.

In Punjab, Bhai Vir Singh (1872-1957) wrote his first novel at the age of 26. The novel *"Sundri"* is also the first novel in Punjabi. He enriched Punjabi literature with a new vision and a new content by presenting two more novels *Bijay Singh* (1900) and *Satvant Kaur* (1900) in quick succession. These three novels make a trilogy dealing with the eighteenth century Sikh history and life.

D. V. Seshaiyangar's verse narrative *Athiyuravadhani* (Self-made Man -1875) is claimed by the author an original Tamil novel delineating pictures of modern Hindu life. But Samuel Vedanayakam Pillai (1826-1889) wrote the first proper novel in Tamil *"Piratapa Mutaliyar Charittiram*" (1879). It is also a didactic novel. One can not judge this novel by the modern standards and should be viewed as "the culmination of the indigenous narrative tradition in the Tamil land and also a forerunner of the massive prose literature that developed in Tamil." The most popular historical novelist in Tamil was R. Krishnamurthy who wrote under the penname *'Kalki'*. He was an active participant in the freedom movement and the editor of the widely read Tamil magazines *Anandavikatan* and *Kalki.* Written in simple language and full of heroism, adventure and suspense, Kalki's novels captivated the Tamil-reading public of an entire generation. One of his well known novels is *Ponniyin Selvan* (1951).

In Bengal, novels were love stories based on historical events. Novels portrayed the romantic relations between men and women, and there were some novels that dealt with the social problems. Bhudev Mukhopadhay's *Anguriya Binimoy* (1857) was the first historical novel written in Bengal. The novel described how Shivaji fought valiantly against Aurangzeb. Bankim Chandra Chattopadhyaya (1838-1894) wrote his first novel *Durgeshnandini* (1865) and started a new trend by portraying ordinary people with the strength and weaknesses of ordinary people. Bankim Chandra's *Anandamath* (1882) is a novel about a Hindu militia that fought Muslims to establish a Hindu kingdom. The song *Vande Mataram* is a national patriotic lyric which is a marching song in the novel. Bankim Chandra's fiction influenced all later nationalists' imagination. He represented the image of the Hindu goddess as "a nurturer" and the "giver of food" to the angry and livid Kali. Rabindranath Tagore (1861–1941) was the great Bengali writer after Bankim Chandra. He started writing historical novels and later wrote novels about family relationships. The themes of his novels were mainly based on the condition of women and nationalism as he understood them. Sarat Chandra Chattopadhyaya (1876–1938) was and still is one of the most popular novelists in Bengal. His portrayal of women is really very sharp and sound. *Devdas* is his immortal creation.

In Odisa the first novel *Saudamani* was penned by Ramashankar Ray (1877-1918). Fakir Mohan Senapati (1843–1918) wrote *Chha Mana Atha Guntha* (1899). It means six acres and twenty two decimals of land. The novel deals with the question of land and its possessions. It was written on a serious theme – land and its possession. The theme of the novel influenced many writers in later years such as Tara Shankar Bandyopadyaya, Takazhi Shivshankar Pillai, Panna Lal Patel, Gopinath Mohanty and Premchand. The protagonist of the novel, Ramchandra Mangaraj, is a cunning and deceitful manager of a landlord. He not only cheats his idle and drunkard landlord, but tries to snatch away the land of poor illiterate people. He swindles Bhagia and Sharia, a childless weaver couple, of their fertile land by trapping them in debt. His novel highlights the problems of the rural people for the first time and makes the urban readers aware of them.

The first novels in Assam were written by missionaries. Two of them were translations of Bengali novels including *Phulmoni* and *Karuna*. In 1888, Assamese students in Kolkata formed the *'Asamya Bhasar Unnatisadhan'*and brought out a journal called *Jonaki*. This journal opened up the opportunities for new authors to develop the art and craft of the novel. Rajanikanta Bardoloi wrote the first major historical novel Manomati (1900). It is set in the Burmase invasion, stories of which the author had probably heard from old soldiers who had fought in the 1819 campaign. It is a tale of two lovers belonging to two hostile families who are separated by the war and finally reunited.

Everyone did not approve of the novel and novel reading. It was accused that the novel had an immoral influence on the readers. Women and children were specially warned to avoid reading novels as their formative minds could be easily corrupted.

> 'Dear children, don't read these novels, don't even touch them. Your life will be ruined. You will suffer disease and ailments. Why did the good Lord make you – to wither away at a tender age and to suffer in disease? To be despised by your brothers, relatives and those around you. No. No. You must become mothers; you must lead happy lives; this is the divine purpose, you, who were born to fulfill this sublime goal, should you ruin your life by going crazy after despicable novels?'
>
> (From *an essay by Thiru Vi. Ka (1927) Translated by A. R. Venkatachalapathy)*

Pt. Vihnu Chandra Sharma read a paper in Hindi Sahitya Sammelan's Calcutta meeting in 1912. The title of the paper was *'Hindi ka hanikar sahitya'* in which he spelt out the following drawbacks of this literary form:

> The first drawback is that they are full of love and sex and the readers start worshipping love as a deity. The result is that after a while the readers become devoid of character, zest for life, health, strength, vigour, vitality and wealth. The second drawback is that reading fiction does not result into success in the mundane and other worldly pursuits. And the third drawback is that it

results into narrow-minded views and downsizing intellectual and rational thinking which might result into a kind of intellectual laziness (*Buddhi ka Sukhiyapan*).

Champa Lal Johari "Sudhakar" wrote another article *"Hindi Sahitya mein Dakaiti*" published in "Indu*" (September 1914)* in which he refuted the charges leveled again the art of fiction. It shows that the critics kept a vigilant eye on this new imported form.

The parents and adults were also very apprehensive about the ill-effects of novels on the formative minds of the children and that was one of the reasons that they were scared of. They didn't want that the young minds should be polluted by obscene suggestive language adopted by certain novelists in depicting female characters. But nobody could say even a single world against Premchand because he never resorted to such depiction of flesh and sexuality. It not only helped him in winning the confidence of the people but the readers were now in a position to discuss and recommend his books to others. Premchand's daughter Kamla Devi said that her father never allowed her to read the books written by G. P. Srivastava and Pandey Bechan Sharma "Ugr". He tore off the book *"Ganga Jamuna*" himself. (Mere Babuji, p.33)

In fact, the women not only read the novels but they started writing also. They started writing novels themselves and it became a way of expressing one self. Perhaps they thought that by writing they could at least control a part of their own lives. Rokeya Hossein (1880–1932), a widow who started a girl's school in Calcutta, wrote two books. *Sultana's Dream* (1905), a fantasy in English which showed a world where women took the place of men and Padmarag which exhorted women to improve their position by their own actions. Hannah Mullens, a Christian missionary wrote *Karuna o Phulmonir Bibaran* (1852).

Novels like *Indirabai* (Kannada), and *Indulekha* (Malayalam) were written by members of the upper-castes and had upper-caste characters. There were some writers who were from other castes too and they portrayed their cause very effectively. For instance, Potheri Kunjambu wrote *Saraswativijayam (1892)* and attacked the others for the oppression suffered by the lower castes, to which he himself belonged. The novel is a direct attack on caste oppression. The novel's hero, an 'untouchable' leaves his village to escape from cruelty of a Brahmin landlord. He converts to Christianity, receives modern education and returns to his village as a judge of a local court. In the meantime, the villagers bring the landlord to his court; they believe the landlord's men had killed the hero. The judge reveals himself and the Nambuthri landlord repents and promises to reform. The novel emphasizes the role of education in uplifting the lower classes.

In Bengal from 1920, a new trend of novel emerged. It portrayed lives of poor peasants and 'low castes'. Advaita Malla Burman (1914-1951) wrote *Titash Ekti Nadir Naam* (1956). It is an epic about a community of fisherfolk – the Mallas, who live by the river. Vaikkom Muhammad Basheer (1908-1996) was a famous writer in Malyalam. He had very little formal education, took part in Salt Satyagraha, travelled all over India, even up to Arabia, worked in ships, lived with sufis and saniyasis and presented a mystifying world to his readers, He wrote about poverty, insanity and life in prisons. These subjects were never the part of Malayalam fiction before. Prof. K. R. Srinivas Iyengar in his scholarly study *"Indian Writing in English"* sums up the early twentieth century fiction scene as follows, "Bankim Chandra's novels were but romances distinctly imitative of Scott, with a historical or mystical slant; Tagore was chiefly interested in the upper and middle classes, Sarat Chandra in the lower middle classes and Munshi Premchand chose his themes from the peasantry and humble folk of Uttar Pradesh. None of them cared to produce realistic or naturalistic fiction after the manner of a Balzac or a Zola."

In Hindi Bhartendu Harishchandra (1850-1884), Bal Krishan Bhatt (1844-1914), Shrinivas Das (1851-1887), Radhakrishan Das (1865-1907) and Radhacharan Goswami (1856-1925) and others tried their hand in writing fiction but were not very successful. Bharatendu Harishchandra, a pioneer of modern Hindi literature did not write a novel himself but encouraged writers to recreate and translate novels from other languages. Radha Charan Goswami translated *"Deep Nirwan"* and *"Sarojini"*; Babu Gadadhar Singh translated *"Kadambari"* and "*Durgeshnandani*"; Pt. Ram Shankar Vyas translated "*Madhumati*" and Babu Radha Krishna Das translated "*Swarn Lata*". The very first proper modern Hindi novel was *Pariksha Guru*. It was written in 1882 by Srinivas Das of Delhi. The novel teaches the young readers the right way to live and expects all 'sensible men' to remain worldly wise and practical and to remain rooted in the values of their own tradition and culture. Pyare chand Mitra (1814-1883) in his novel *Alaler Gharer Dulal* (1858) presented the appalling effects of allowing children to be improperly brought up; similarly Pariksha Guru also ridiculed those Indians who adopted the Western way of life. It was too moralizing in its style and did not become very popular. In fact, like "*Pariksha Guru*" many of the novels took to too much moral instruction for the young minds. In this novel a true friend helps his rich friend to get rid of bad company. Similarly in Bal Krishan Bhatt's "*so ajan aik sujan"(1890)* there is a friend who helps Seth Hiranand's two sons to come out of their evil ways. Radhakrisna Das wrote a novel "*Nissahay Hindu*" (Helpless Hindu) to underline the plight of the children of rich Hindu families who were taking to sensual pleasures. Radha Charan Goswami penned the conflict among the farmers and zamindars long before Premchand. Devaki Nandan Khatri (1861-1913) created a novel reading public. His *Chandrakanta* was a bestseller romance mixed with dazzling fantasy. This novel though written purely for 'pleasure of reading', gave some interesting insights into the fears and desires of its reading public. Devki Nandan Khatri was very successful indeed and his *Chandrakanta Santati* ran in twenty-eight volumes. Twenty volumes of *Bhut Nath* are nothing less than sensation. His novels or "novel experiences" represent the collective imagination of the period after the debacle of 1857. People learnt Hindi to read him. Amrik Kalsi in "*Realism in the Hindi Novel*" (Ph. D. thesis, University of Cambridge, 1975) states that in the history of modern Hindi literature, then, and of the Hindi novel in particular, Chandrakanta and the sub-genre of adventure as well as tilismi novels that it spawned are usually not thought of as literature but considered at best an unfortunate stage in the progress towards the realistic novel represented by the work of Premchand. Rajendra Yadav in a write up entitled "*Dayniy Mahanta ki Dilchasp Dastan*" (An Interesting Story of Pathetic Greatness-1986) argues that the novel corresponds to the collective *imaginaire* of the period after the defeat of 1957 as people accepted the material and social defeat but not the intellectual and spiritual defeat. The celebration of vigilance (*Chaukannapan*) and extraordinary intelligence in *Chandrakanta* can be linked to this.

Kishorilal Goswami (1870-1937) was a novelist of repute who was inspired by Sanskrit literary masterpieces and was an expert in weaving social messages into fiction in line with the English fiction. Acharya Ram Chandra Shukla said that he should be called the first novelist of Hindi literature. He wrote not less than 65 novels. Others also wrote original novels but they were not novelists. Goswani was a novelist in the real sense of the term. He started a monthly magazine "*Upanyas*". But his novels were accused of sexual overtones and his novel " *Chapla*" was considered a blue book. When Premchand entered in the realm of Hindi novel with his "*Sevasadan*" he was treading the path shown by Kishori Lal Goswami and not particularly of Devkinandan Khatri or Gopal Ram Gahmari. Goswami's "*Kusum Kumari*", "*Tara*", "*Anguthi ka Nagina*" and his story "*Indumati*" (1900) were way ahead of Premchand.

We should mention the work of Ayodhya Singh Upadhaya Harioudh also who gave the public *"Theth Hindi ka Thath" (1899)* and *"Adh khila phool" (1907)* when he was asked by Dr Grierson to do so for the sake of Civil Service trainees. Though no writer imitated his style, yet his novels helped in refining Khari Boli.

It is an interesting fact that like the present day viewers of television soaps, serialization of novels allowed readers to relish the suspense. They could discuss the characters of the novel as viewers of TV soaps do today and readers could live for weeks with their stories as viewers do today. From Devki Nandan Khatri to Premchand novels were serialized in magazines before getting them published in book form.it is to be noted that there were not less than five magazines in Hindi that used to publish novels in serialized form to entertain the readers. "*Upanyas Lahri*" (Devki Nandan Khatri), "*Upanyas*" (Kishori Lal Goswami), "*Jasoos*" (Gopal Ram Gahmari), "*Upanyas Bahar"* (Jai Ram Das Gupt), "*Daroga Daftar"* (Ram Lal

Verma) were really famous magazines and readers used to throng to receive their copies.

In Urdu, there were a number of novelists too. Dr. Nazir Ahmed (1836-1912) used to write about Muslim middle class of Delhi and adopted the English novel's techniques. His novel *"Tabatun Nusooh"* is based on an English novel *"Family Instructor"*. Mirza Muhamed Hadi Rusva, who wrote *Umrao Jan Ada,* depicted the life of Lucknow and was considered a notable novelist of his time. This novel is said to be inspired by the English novel *"Rosa Lambert"*. He declared, "Our novels are neither tragedies nor comedies. The heroes neither got killed by swords and spears nor they commit suicide, they are neither separated nor meet endlessly. Our novels should be considered the chronicles of the contemporary social fabric." He was well aware that the old tradition of story-telling was over and the new one was already there to be followed by the novelists of his time. In the opening couplet of his novel *"Umrao Jan Ada"* he said: I too used to remember such wonderful tales of adventure, but now all I can recollect has turned into painful requiems.

*Ham ko bhi kya maze ki danstane yad thin*
*Lekin ab tamhid –e-dard-o matam ho gayin*

There had been two other prominent Urdu novelists before Premchand. Ratan Nath Dar 'Sarshar' (1846–1902), the famous editor of *Avadh Akhbar,* whose *Fasana-i-Azad* was serialised in the journal, and Abdul Halim 'Sharar' (1860–1926). Sarshar was a Hindu Kashmiri Pandit and Sharar was a Muslim. Sarshar used to write about Lucknow of the Nawabs and Sharar preferred to write about the ancient Arabian culture. Premchand appreciated and enjoyed Reynolds and Sarshar both but he was sure about the purpose of a novel. In an article on "Sharar and Sarshar" (1909) he clarifies that the difference between a *fasana* and a *navil* he wrote, is that the latter draws "a clear picture of the period it narrates, it throws light on its customs, habits and behavior and it gives no place to supernatural events, or even if it does, it is with such skill that ordinary readers will consider them to be true."

When we go through the advent, growth and development of novel in India, we find that either a woman or a peasant is there in the centre of a notable novel. Namvar Singh and Makarand Paranjape opine that women are actual figures in history whose material lives need to be documented and if possible ameliorated. Panna Patel in Gujarati, Manik Bandhopadhyaya, Bibhuti Bandhopadhyaya and Tarashankar Bandhopadhyaya in Bengali, Venktesh Nagulkar in Marathi, Shiv Ram Karant in Kannada, T. Shivshankar Pillai and S. K. Pottekat in Malyalam etc are the novelists who prominently keep the farmer and his world in their novels and discussions. There are others like Hadi Ruswa who keep woman at the centre. Fakir Mohan Senapati projected both, the farmer and the woman. Premchand takes up woman in *Sevasadan* and the farmer in *Premashram* and presents both in *Godan*. In early nineteenth century the woman and the farmer were projected more than the middle class. Premchand is an announcement of the maturity of Indian fiction. The combined work of earlier novelist created a platform of reading public and Premchand too was benefitted from it. The readers who were used to read *dastaans* and romances and remained in a state of imagination and slumber started reading the truth of life presented by Premchand. He changed their taste and like a piped piper took them towards the narration in which they could visualize the nation. In this way he was instrumental in leading them towards the real colonial India in which the oppression had to be challenged. He found Gandhi and his mass appeal appealing and converted him into a recurring character of his novels. Not only Gandhi, he took along with him the ideals and ideas of Arya Samaj, teachings of Swami Vivekananda, Marx and Marxism, Socialism and Communism also. In a sense, he was also experimenting with these "isms"and ideals and asking his readers to join the school called life. In an authoritative study " *History of Indian Literature: 1911-1956"* Professor Sisir Kumar Das says, "The Hindi novel was dominated by themes of adventure and romance till the emergence of Premchand who not only established the realistic trend in Hindi but also used the novel as a medium for social change. His novels are characterized by deep social concerns, understanding of the dynamics of Indian rural society and the ability to narrativize the contemporary history" *(*1991, 283).

Kalidas Kapur, a reviewer of Sevasadan, compares the literary scene in Hindi before Premchand to a garden overrun by foreign plants:

> You can find every kind of plants good or bad over here. If you look over there you will see trellises of literary blossoms from the Bengali Bankim and Ravindra, and over there a vine of Saraswatichandra brought over from Gujarat. In other places, there are attempts to plant the historical novels of Hugo and Dumas. Elsewhere a few gentlemen are attempting to decorate the garden with the litter and debris of English literature. And hiding in some corner, a few lovers of literature can be spotted planting the seeds of a true literary service. The hope is that novels like Sevasadan would fertilize the soil well enough that there would be a day when there would be no shortage of Thackerays, Dickenses, Scotts, and Rabindras in Hindi literature. (Qtd in Gopal, 1965, p. 94)

Premchand himself wrote in Sewasadan about the condition of fiction in Indian literature when one of the characters named Aniruddh Singh said:

> It's really a shame that the country that produced priceless epics like the Ramayana, gave birth to wonderful poetry like Sursagar, has to rely on translations for even ordinary novels. In Bengal and Maharastra, where they have a strong tradition of music, they haven't lost their sense of beauty. They still have wonderful imagination and aesthetic sense. I have stopped reading Hindi novels altogether. The translations aside, there is really nothing of worth other than a few plays by Harishchandra and a few things like Chandrakanta Santati. And worse, there are some individuals who have translated a couple of English novels with the help of Bengali and Marathi translators and who think that they are prominent literati in this country. One such man generated a word-for –word translation of Kalidasa's plays, and now he considers himself the Hindi Kalidasa. One scholar translate two books by Mill, not himself, but with the help of Marathi and Gujarati translators, and he thinks that he single-handed revived Hindi literature. I think that all these translations

are ruining Hindi literature. Originality never has a chance to thrive.( Sevasadan 162-163)

Premchand was an avid reader of Urdu-Hindi fiction since his childhood as his not so wonderful early life also gave him enough time to devote on reading novels of all types. When he was a teacher in Chunagarh, Pratapgarh, Allahabad, and Kanpur, he cultivated the art of storytelling and even tried his hand in writing something in imitation of his reading of his contemporaries. His first attempts were greatly influenced by Sarshar's style and language. Even the art of characterization in *Asrar-j-Maabid* (1903-1905) a caricature of the Brahmin priestly class, published under the name of "Dhanpatrai, alias Navabrai Allahabadi" was liberally borrowed from him.

Premchand was a Hindu and it was natural for him to practice to write in Hindi too. He must have also noted that the Urdu literary field was particularly filled with Muslim writers and he was always treated like an outsider. This fact was very succinctly underlined by Graham Bailey in the concluding chapter of his history of Urdu literature: About 250 authors have been mentioned in this work. Apart from Prem Cand ... only eight are Hindus, the rest are Muhammedans. The only famous writers among them are Daya Shankar Nasim, Ratn Nath Sarshar, and Durga Sahae Suroor. Hindu authors of real ability prefer to write in Hindi. (Bailey 1929: 102)

## Premchand Arrives

He was welcomed in the Hindi literary firmament with warmth and friendliness. Though "*Prema*" and "*Kishna*" were not success and criticized; yet after a couple of years his name and fame reached all and sundry. In his 'Preface' to Premchand's first book in Hindi, a collection of seven short stories "*Sapta Saroj*" (Seven Lotuses), Pandit Mannan Dwivedi Gajapuri welcomed his arrival in the most befitting manner as follows : Premchandji occupies a very high place among the Hindu virtuoso of Urdu literature. Your books are shining in the Urdu literary world and the journals and magazines in the Urdu language are all in praise for your stories and novels. It is a matter of joy that mother-tongue Hindi has of late attracted his heart. Premchandji has entered the Temple of Nagari to offer worship and the Mother has adopted this glorious loving son Prem by embracing him to her bosom. Your stories are marvelously great offering for the Hindi world. Hindi magazines are always eager to publish your articles and essays. Some critics say that your stories are comparable to Sahitya Martand Rabindra Babu. It will be futile and unnecessary to write more for such a scholar and famous writer." (1917)

Premchand cultivated, and nurtured the unkempt garden of Hindi fiction like a deft gardener. But we should never forget that what was called an unkempt garden was a garden and it would be nothing but mere verbosity to dismiss all the novelists of Pre-Premchand era. Devki Nandan Khatri, Kishori Lal Goswami and Gopal Ram Gahmari really created a Hindi readership and it was not Premchand alone who brought the so called literary nationalism all of a sudden by translating *Bazaar-e-Husn* into *Sevasadan*. The novelists who fed the readers the diet of fancy and fantasy couldn't be dismissed and shouldn't be erased from memory. After all, it was Khatri who wrote the longest Hindi Novel of the nineteenth century and his "*tilism*" was mesmerizing. How could he be forgotten who wrote that "ordinary language" and firmly said that the "dictionary language" should not be used for writing fiction? (Kisi *daarshnik granth ya patr ki bhasha ke liye kisi bade kosh ko tatolna pade to parwah nahin; parntu saadharan vishayon ke liye bhi kosh tatolna pade to nisandeh dosh ki baat hai. Meri Hindi kis shreni ki hai iska nirdharan main naihin karta, parantu main yah jaanta hun ke padhne ke liye kosh ki talash nahin karni padegi. : Hindi Upanyas ka vikas p. 24-25).* Here is an echo of what Wordsworth said in the Preface of his Lyrical Ballads. Novels like "*Shyama Swapan*" which were written in the manner of Sanskrit romances and in Sanskritized Hindi laden with unreal fantastical miracles and magic were just mentioned by Acharya Ramchandra Shukla and even though Gopal Rai and several others advocated for Pt. Gauri Dutt's novel "*Devrani Jethani Ki Kahani*" (1870) which did use the language of the common folk, it was with Premchand, in the tradition of Khatri and others, we found the use of Hindi –Urdu that was real. Premchand was not a *daastango* in the literal sense of the term but his stories and early novels were greatly inspired with the tradition. There was no aiyyar in "Duniya *ka Sabse anmol Ratan*" but the element of fantastical was present as an aspect of the real.

To present himself differently, Premchand took a difficult path. He took inspiration from the Urdu- Hindi tradition but transformed it as if he was in search of an ideal. There are novels such as *Nirmala* and *Gaban* in which drama is akin to melodrama. In *Sevasadan* fantasy is still at work. *Hridayparivartan* or change of heart is the formula Premchand evolved for himself and he is so much for it that he writes an essay in support of it. It starts evolving from Premashram. Premchand states, "The splendor of a novelist lies in the creation of characters that captivate readers with their good conduct and ideas. A novel whose characters do not have this quality is worthless. (*Upanyakaar ki sabse badi vibhuti aise charitron ki sristi karna hai, jo apne sadvyavhar aur sadvichar se pathak ko mohit kar len. Jis upanyas ke charitron mein yah gun nahin hai, vah do kaudi ka hai.* (Rachna Sanchayan 697). In 1936, at the All-India Progressive Writers' Conference held at Lucknow, Premchand advocated for a turn to realism. "In earlier times we might well have been impressed by fairy tales, ghost stories and accounts of star-crossed lovers but those have little interest for us anymore", and declared, "In order to produce an impression in literature it is necessary for it to be a mirror on life's truths [jeevan ki sachaiyon ka darpan]." The following words from Ralf Fox's book "The Novel and the People" were once quoted by Dr. Mahendra Bhatnagar (1976) to underline Premchand's use of realism as a technique:

> Can a novelist remain indifferent to the problems of the world in which he lives? Can he shut his ears to the clamor of preparing war; his eyes to the state of his country, can he keep his mouth closed when he sees honor around him and life being denied daily in the name of a state pledged to maintain the sanctity of private greed? More and more novelists are beginning to feel that eyes, ears, and voice are, in fact, organs of senses, responsible to the stimulus of the human world, and not mere passive servants of a spiritual world supposed traditionally to be the domain of art.

Premchand did not keep his organs of senses shut. His AIPWA'S speech in 1936 is his vision for realism. It was in conformity with what Acharya Ramchandra Shukla writes in *"Gadhya sahitya ki vartman gati"* while putting his thoughts about novels and stories that our novelists should look engagingly in the present life and time themselves and literature must remain above politics and never dance according to the tunes of the political masters. It is interesting to note that Premch and himself was aware of this danger and forewarning others by saying that the writer is not the truth following the tenets of patriotism and politics, it is the truth that goes before them like a torch. But when we read the speech now by deploying colonial aesthetic norms, we find as called by Michael Denning "simple represetnationalism" and as commented by Ulka Anjaria "naïve". Priyamvada Gopal too says that the realism's political purpose in Premchand's time within the framework of his speech is less a specific aesthetic technique than a philosophy that brings together an affective sense of justice, fairness and harmony. Snehal Shingavi in his celebrated essay *"Premchand and Language: On Translation, Cultural Nationalism, and Irony"*(2016) says that the struggle of Premchand is in a sense about literary publics in North India and the transition from poetry to prose, from romance to realism, from élite to democratic sensibilities, from pleasure to asceticism, and from Urdu to Hindi, all of which are involved in the production of what Rashmi Sadana (2012) calls a *"literary nationality"*. Premchand could domesticate romance and brought realism to the fore in such a way that the charge of obscenity so frequently labelled against novels of his contemporaries has never been inducted against him which made him a darling of the reading public. In fact he contributed immensely to the development of reading public in Hindi.

## Novelist Premchand

The following novels by Premchand (excluding translations) are well-known:

Asrar-i-Maabid, Baazaar-e Husn (Sevasadan), Bevah (Hum Khurma-o-Hum Savab), Chauglm-i-Hasti (Rangabhoomi), Gaban, Godan, Goshai-i-Afiat (Premashram), Jalva-i-Isar (Vardan),

Karmabhoomi (Maidan-i-Amal), Kayakalpa,Kishna, Mangal Sutra, Naakaam (Premashram), Nirmala, Pardai-Majllz (Kayakalpa), Pratigya, Pratapchandra, Prema, Premashram (Gosha-i-Afiat), Rangabhoomi (Chaugan-i-Hasti), Sevasadan (Baazaar-i-Husn).

The above is not a chronological list but an alphabetical one. It is also Urdu Hindi mix. Premchand started writing when he was a teenager. He was hardly 20 when he wrote his first novel *"Devasthan-Rahasya"*, a story of corrupt priests and widows with questionable characters. In the second novel "Prema" the ill-fated life of young widows are presented. Then he wrote to be of some help to the social and political cause and with the Influence of Swami Dayanand, the founder of Arya Samaj he started writing stories of Rajput chivalary and their sacrifice for the motherland. In "Vardan" (The Benediction"), he brings out a character named Balaji who is Vivekananda, Dayanada and Gandhi rolled into one. Premchand is writing for "*Satyarth prakash*" and these little pieces of fiction are also his experiments with truth. In " "*Sevasadan*" the problem of prostitution is in the focus and in *Kayakalp* without even ever reading Kafka he presents a kind of metamorphoses and transformation never found before in Indian fiction. In "*Rangabhumi*" Gandhi and his non-violent movement is all around. Surdas is Gandhi in a garb of socially deprived poor beggar. "*Premashram*" is the national movement. "Nirmala" is a tragic tale of a young girl married to an older man. In "*Pratigya*" the double standards of the society with regard to man and woman are highlighted. Premchand is for Hindu-Muslim unity at any cost. No novel by him is untouched by this challange. In *"Gaban"* he is sarcastic about his own caste and their lure for ornaments. *"Godan"* is the ultimate complete novel which very poignantly presents the pathetic condition of a peasant Hori who dies penniless and cann't afford even a customary Gaudan before his last breath. Premchand's enthusiastic literary contribution for the betterment of society and freedom form the British oppression is recognized by all. His stories, like his novels, are the stories where the reality of life is depicted with a view to underlining the idealism and ultimate goodness of human beings. His work can be easily taken as political, social, economic, religious, moral, and spiritual tract and can be termed "literature with a purpose".

Let us read about the novels in detail and in an orderly manner.

## Sevasadan (1919)

Sevasadan was originally written in Urdu under the title *Bazaar-e-Husn* ("Market of Beauty") but was first published in Hindi from Calcutta as *Sevasadan* ("The House of Service"), in 1919. It was published in Urdu, in 1924, from Lahore. Shyam Sunder Das (1930) in his history describes the Hindi *Sevasadan* Premchand's "first original novel" and Ram Chandra Shukla (1929) too discusses Premchand's stories published around 1916 first. Even the Age of Premchand starts from 1918 that is why it can be said that Premchand arrived in the Hindi scene with the Hindi *Sevasadan*. "While the Urdu title highlights the fall of the heroine, the Hindi title highlights her redemption: It is tempting to see the two titles as widely symptomatic of their respective literary cultures" says one of the scholars. Harish Trivedi too echoes the same sentiments when he writes, "Of Bazar-e-Husn or Sevasadan, the transitional novel, the titles themselves are symptomatic of the shift in Premchand's sensibility. Amorous beauty and the marketplace are highlighted in the Urdu title while in contrast; more austere concepts of home and social service constitute the Hindi title, for a novel which is substantially the same in both versions." The problem of prostitution was there in earlier novels such as "*Pariksha Guru*" and "So *ajan aik sujan*" also. In fact Sevasadan is a novel in the line of such other novels as Kishankanter Uil (1878) by Bankim Chanda, Charitraheen (1913) by Saratchandra, Fasana-e-Mubtala (1885) by Nazin Ahmad and Umrao Jan Ada (1899) by M. H. Ruswa. Premchand went a little deeper than other novelists; he wanted to depict feminity through the figure of a courtesan. He enumerates the various reasons of this evil and gives an indicative solution too. He is not as bitter as Shaw and Galsworthy are but is compassionate enough in showing them a direction. Whereas in "War *and Peace"* the problem is national and is projected with broad implications, Premchand gives it a social and domestic look. In the words of Krupa Shandilya in "The *Widow, the wife and the Courtesan...*" (2016) "The novel expouses a specifically Gandhian nationalist ideology, which opens up space for a new figure – The

Indian woman: rather than the Hindu woman. It opens a nationlist solution to the question of social reform."

With the publication of this novel in Hindi, Premchand was placed among the few *"lonely pioneers"* who sowed the seeds of literature in their "quiet unknown corners". Sevasadan was well received in Saraswati's book column in February 1919 and reviewed favorably in the issue of February 1920 again. In the words of the reviewer: "Hindi literature required a blending of Western techniques with the soul of India so that the centuries old traditions and ideas could be changed. Such a blending is seen in Premchand's work *Sevasadan*. Pulsating with patriotism, love for the lingua franca, Hindu-Muslim unity, etc. Sevasadan shows that the author has unparalleled experience about different problems of Indian life." It will not be exaggeration to say by borrowing the words from Leslie Fiedler that with Premchand "The country and the novel were reborn" in Hindi.

Premchand is not only a novelist; he is an idealist and preacher of good conduct also. There are a number of long debates between various characters on burning topics of the day and it will not be incorrect to call the novel "a novel of ideas."For instance, there is an unending debate among the members of Municipal Board to decide to move the courtesans' quarter out of the city limits. The reader can very evidently feel that the writer is trying to pinpoint the social and cultural differences of the characters with a view to underlining the gap being created by such ominous discussions. You will be reminded of what Amartya Sen says in the first sentence of his book "The *Argumentative Indian*": Prolixity is not alien to us in India. We are able to talk at some length.

Though Premchand takes his readers out of the vitiating atmosphere of Banaras city to the "kutcha mohalla," or its outskirts or the countryside where Sevasadan, the home for the daughters of prostitutes was established, the principal theme in Sevasadan is related to prostitution in the suburban part of Banaras inhabited by absentee landlords. Vasudha Dalmia, Professor of Hindi and Modern South Asian Studies, University of California Berkeley points out that "the title itself, Seva (service) and Sadan (house), suggests the many layered social texture of Varanasi. The move to remove the courtesans from the heart of the city (*Chauk*) can be seen as a metaphor, for a new (North) India, which was seeking to modernise and refashion its image — removing courtesans from its heart and shifting them to the periphery."

> In Sevasadan, the brothel is not visualised as a place where young women suffer; rather it is a place full of comfort and material riches. Premchand goes beyond the material lure; his female protagonist also finds a brothel somewhat "respectable" and "dignified" because men are slavish towards her. Notwithstanding this temporary empowerment psychologically, in the end the brothel proves to be destructive and its "respectability", illusionary. The protagonist finally finds peace in a destitute womens' home. (Quoted in Atwal, p. 1637)

In fact, in the novel brothel or Kotha or Dalmandi or the red-light area where the prostitutes (sex-workers included) conduct their business is a part of the social set up of the city and as said by one of the charcters Padam Singh in the novel that it is the perverse reflection of our life.

> We do not have any right to hate them...It is our sinful desire, our social oppression, our evil customs that have taken the form of the prostitute. The 'Dalmandi' the red light area, is the perverse reflection of our life, our devilish conducts incarnate. On which ground can we hate them?

In Sevasadan the character of Krishna Chandra develops slowly. He is a good man in the beginning but becomes a sinner once he takes money due to reasons beyond his control. He goes to jail and when comes back he is a changed man. He thinks that taking bribe is a sin but he takes because he wants money for his daughter's marriage. This is the root cause of evil. The tree grew into a tree of desires but the fruit of the tree is Sevasadan. In a way the novelist try to project that the fruit of sin or poison can be nectar too. Suman gets married but has to leave her husband and home to live as a courtesan. Her husband becomes a sanyasi, swami Gajanand. Suman too starts Sevasadan to help the daughters of prostitutes. The novel shows as if everyone is in search of mental peace and wants to get rid of his or her sins. Penance is the key word. Everyone has only one way- the way of service. The novelist has a problem – a social evil and he wants to show the way to salvation. He hardly enters the palce called home. Let it be Suman's home, Madan Singh's home, Padam Singh's home, Uma Nath's home or any other home the novelists is not trying to depict the sweet home. His eyes are glued on a social evil and only that part of home is discussed and portrayed where it can be done. All the characters in Sevasadan are eager to penance and none of them even tries to fight. The novelist has a limited purpose. He never goes out of the city. All the characters belong to the middle class.

It is worth mentioning that in none of his major original novels written after Sevasadan, did Premchand return to the life in the cities alone. They deal largely with the life of the people in the villages; the city-dwellers appear only when their work relates to the life in the villages.

*Sevasadan* is translated into English in 2005 by Snehal Shingavi, University of California, Berkeley, and published by OUP. Vasudha Dalmia has written 31 page long and lucid introduction to the book. She says that the translation is a liberal and racy one. Arshia Sattar in a review of the translation states that "Premchand has always used his women characters as the lens through which society is critiqued. A reading of his 'Sevasadan' in English translation almost 90 years after it was written brings home the fact that little has changed: women are still striving to control their own destinies." It is worth noting that *Bazaar-e-Husn* (Courtesans' Quarter) is also translated into English by Amina Azfar and published by OUP, Karachi (Pakistan). What would you say if I tell you that Sevasadan in English is available by paying Rs 750 but you can get Bazar-e- Husn in English by paying just 250 Pakistani rupees? It is also interesting to note that Premchand, though he wrote in Hindi and Urdu, was an avid reader of English fiction. He used to write the plots of his novels in English. His correspondence with many scholars used to be in English. But in the novels and elsewhere he used to stress the need to get rid of English as it was the indication of our mental slaverly. In this novel there is a conversation between two characters in which they are discussing over the issue of "Mental slavery" and a third character (perhaps Premchand's mouthpiece) comes and intervenes by saying, "As long as the educated among us remain under the spell of English, no national language can come into being." After a span of nearly a century we find ourselves still in the spell of English. Therefore, there is no hope for a national language to prosper.

Amartya Sen (The *Argumentative Indian* famed Nobel Prize winner economist) should have read this novel also to see how our fictional characters too argue and debate.

## Vardan (1912)

Sevasadan was a success. Readers and critics both liked the treatment of the problem and the character of Suman. Premchand was encouraged to do something quickly and bring out some quicky. Premchand did the same and gave to the eager readers "*Vardan*" which was the Hindi translation of his Urdu novel *Jalva-i-Isar*. Granth Bhandar of Bombay published it with the author's name as "Premchand" instead of " Nawabrai". Critics found that the book was not as racy and readable as the earlier one. *Saraswati* magazine reviewed the book and declared, "It is not of the standard of Sevasadan. The flow of the plot is not too smooth...the incidents are not as attractive as to arouse the curiosity of the reader...The novel is nevertheless beautiful and only such as Premchand alone could write." Premchand is not a realist in this novel. The beginning and the end both are unrealistic. The novel can be placed among the tradition of nineteenth century novels written in Bhartendu Yug. It is an epistolary novel in character as there are a number of letters exchanged between Virjan and Kamalacharan. These letters not only tells about their relationship but also portray the village life and the surroundings.

It is the story of Pratap and Virjan and it's a kind of Man Mohan Desai masala blockbuster in which Pratap and Virjan thought that they were destined to be together but got separated. Virjan is married to another man called Kamlacharan who is a nincompoop or a foolish and stupid person. (Don't you recollect Bhartendu's social novel *Chandraprabha*?) Virjan and Kamlacharan try to adjust but fail and the latter dies. Virjan tries to lead a normal life and becomes a poetess. In short, Vardan is a story of two star crossed lovers.

Later Pratap reappears transformed as Balaji. Balaji is Gandhi. Balaji is Swami Vivekananda. Balaji is the Vishnu and Balaji is an Avatar. He becomes an ideal character shaped by circumstances. He represents the ideal and idealism of his creator. (Don't you see a glimpse of R. K. Narayan's masterpiece "The Guide" in it?)

## Premashram (1922)

Premashram was written first in Urdu probably between May 1918 and March 1920, as K. K. Goenka suggests in his "Premchand's Craftsmanship in His Novels" (Delhi & Allahabad: Saraswati Press, 1973), pp. 62, 64. The Hindi version, prepared soon afterwards, was published by the Hindi Pustak Agency, Calcutta, either towards the end of 1921 or the beginning of 1922; the Urdu version in 1928 by the Darul-Ishat, Lahore, under the title Gosh-e-Afiat—"*A Peaceful Corner*."

Jallianwala Bagh Massacre was a big blow on the Indian masses by the colonial masters who killed Indians like cattle and there was a huge outcry. Tagore renounced his knighthood but Premchand remained silent. He was taking his B. A. examination then. In his biography "Kalam *ka Sipahi"* Amrit Rai, Premchand's son, writes that the news of the dastardly act reached him but free speech was restricted then and Premchand could only confide with his friend Taj. So he wrote to him, "Thank God Punjab is quiet again!" That was all he said then. But his heart smoldered and his resolve grew stronger to cast off his chains. Rai tells us that the feelings of anger, indignation, and revolt that simmered within him for quite a long time found full expression in Premashram which forced open issues concerning colonial exploitation through long descriptions of forced labor and the molestation of poor peasants and their wives at the hands of rich landlords. His response was literary intervention in the form of this novel.

Pratapgarh, Rae Bareili and Faizabad were the three districts with which Premchand was familiar. During his days, these places became the scene of a great agrarian commotion in the wake of the severe exploitation by the taluqdars and their "inhuman treatment" making their condition totally unbearable. Zamindar's agents, moneylenders, government officials and police also made the life of the poor farmer's more or less like hell. They could hardly get a morsel of food everyday. These problems are the theme of Premchand's novel *"Premashram"* which was provisionally named *Nakaam* (in Urdu) to underline the plight of the weak and down-trodden. Prof. Ramdas Gaur praised Premashram in his foreword to the novel. "Those who have read Bankim Chandra Chatterji's novels in Bengali would agree with us unhesitatingly that, in his portrayal of the characters in Premashram, Premchand has gone far ahead of Bankim Babu. Whereas Bankim is verbose, Premchand has cleverly effected an economy of words-and his method of effecting economy is his own...When the future historians of India write about the unwritten record of the life of Indian peasantry, they will have to give credit for a true, almost photographic, portrayal of their lives to Premchand. Although he is a non-cooperator, he is not a partisan even when portraying the true emotions of those who are his opponents. He is a faithful chronicler of the mental processes of his characters. His characters are not idealists. In fact, he has portrayed truly the lives of the people, poor as well as the rich, the zamindar and the tenant, as also the bureaucrat- in other words, all those who form part of the nation- and their true physical and mental conditions." (Holi, March 1922)

*Premashram* ("The Abode of Love") was planned by Premchand on an epic scale similar to *Middlemarch* and *War and Peace*. In a nutshell, we can say that it is the story of an individual, a family, and a community. The individual is Gyan Shankar, the family is that of the Shankars of Kashi (Benaras), and the community is that of the villagers of Lakhanpur. Premashram is one of the best novels of Premchand in which all the other features and qualities pertaining to readable novels are present, yet "here the originality and Premchand's signature is somewhat missing and slipping from sight" say a few readers and critics. Let us find out.

To Indra Nath Madan Premashram is primarily a social novel because it seeks to arouse the people against the exploitation by the zamindars. Ram Vilas Sharma sees it as a great novel but his emphasis is exclusively on the socio-political aspect, with hardly any reference to the moral and cultural issues involved. Dr Hazari Prasad Dwivedi finds that the novel which claims to be a novel depicting the ideals of brotherhood and love seems to be lacking in spirit. In fact, Premashram is both a social and political novel with cultural and moral overtones. Premchand's moral resoluteness and firm idealism places him in the line of Victorian "sages" such as Carlyle, Ruskin, George Eliot, and Matthew Arnold and the spirit is the reader's reaction which is of amazement and grandness.

Naakaam or in vain, all efforts towards enriching the element of brotherhood and love seems to become *naakaam*. The sound and fury of life becomes like a Shakespearean tale told by an idiot. Is it so? Is it merely a tearful tale of the farmers? Is it a novel in which the peasants and workers fight for their rights in vain?

Let us look at the novel as a sequal of "Sevasadan", the first notable Hindi novel by Premchand. Premashram is the next important one. The change of era which is given so much importance in the first novel is visible in the second. Once Premchand takes up Premasharm, he tries to paint a wider canvas than before. He expands his reach upto the village which is his core area. The charcters in Premashram are more complex and wide. In village there are wily Zamindars, crafty and cunning people. Children are also there who sacrifice themselves at the altar of superstition. In Premashram the novelist goes inside home too. Premashram introduces a widow also.

When we read the novel we fail to locate the purpose of the novel. Is it to show the poor conditions of the farmers? Is it about the struggle between the farmers and zamindars? Who is the hero or protagonist? Is he Premshankar? Govind Narayan Sharma, Acadia University, in a finely crafted research paper on Premsharm compares the craft of Premchand with that of George Eliot and says, "Like the novels of George Eliot, "the organic form" of Premchand's novels consists of "an inner circle (a small group of individuals involved in a moral dilemma) surrounded by an outer circle (the social world within which the dilemma has to be resolved)." The plot of Premashram also moves in two circles. In the inner circle it is the drama of the life of the hero Gyan Shankar and the heroine Gayatri; in the outer circle, of the villagers of Lakhanpur in their struggle against the vested interests, both inside and outside the village( 1978, 42).

The novel opens with a scene in which the farmers of Lakhanpur are engaged in conversation about the colonial rulers and zamindars in which the British are praised but the Indian zamindars are condemned. Even in the end of the novel the novelist shows that the end of zamindari custom brings Ram Raj for them. It looks as if he wants to give us a carbon copy of the village life – pre -zamindari and post –zamindari. The village named Lakhanpur is in the beginning and in the end but the main story begins at Banaras, is developed at Lucknow and Gorakhpur and ends in the flow of the Ganga.

Gyan Shankar is the protagonist of the main narration and in the background of his character Prabhashankar shines. The other characters such as Rai Kamlanand, Gayatri, Irfan Ali, Jwala Singh, Daya Shankar, Dr Priy Nath, and Maya Shankar, all are in a way try to underline the main theme of the novel and in the end the most suitable person Maya Shankar becomes the mouthpiece of all including the novelist when he says as follows:

> Zamindars are not there for enjoying life in pomp and pleasure with the hard earned money of their subjects; construct palatial building in front of their tattered huts; insult their nudity and lack of clothes with their jewel-studded ornamental clothings; offend their plain contentment with plentiful leisure; make fun of their hunger with their passion for delicious cuisines. He is ready to sacrifice his life for his people but is unmindful of his duties towards his subjects. The poor subjects should get rid of such heartless oppressors as early as possible.

Premshankar too puts his views to abolish the institution called Zamindari:

> The responsibility for their poverty rests not with them but with the conditions under which their life is spent . . . and an institution which depends for its existence on the life-blood of the peasants. What justice is this that whiles someone toils and someone else protects him, it is we who collect the money? . . . Land belongs

> to the tiller. The ruler can claim a share for keeping peace and order in the country. No third group can have a place in society.'

Rajas, talukdars and zamindars were the slaves of their desires. Premshankar used to think that the farmers were in such a pitiable condition not because they were lazy, stupid and uneducatedbut because of the unfavouable conditions. They were hard working, spend-thrift, and self-sustained. There needs were few and demands and expectations were meagre. They were experts in making the both ends meet. Premasharm is a tale to present the exploitation of farmers by crafty zamindars in the same manner as Godan is a tale of exploitation of the farmers by wily money-lenders.

Not only Zamindars even the British Government was nothing less than oppressors and exploiters. Suppression was there weapon and as said by one of the characters Sheelmani, Jwala Singh's wife:

> I have seen that during the last world war, the British Government in India raised the so-called 'loans' which in effect were compulsory taxes. Suppression was resorted to and pressure of all types brought to bear upon the poor people to contribute to war loans. Some of them were indeed forced to sell their bullocks and even their ploughs in order to subscribe to the loans. When a person refused to do so he was beaten up or harassed on one flimsy pretext or another. ... As Jwala Singh did not oppress the people and left it to them to subscribe or not, the subscription from his area was lower than those from the others which had given lakhs of rupees. As a result, his superior officers complained against him, and he was demoted. When I saw all this I myself persuaded him to resign.

In one stroke Premchand shows us the change of heart in zamindars and the way they were being inspired by their dutiful wives. Not only this I feel Premchand is trying to project and tell his readers the circumstances that led him also to resign from his job to free himself from the British yoke. (He was also persuaded and supported by his wife Mrs Shivrani Devi.)

The last page of the novel contains the following words spoken by the most dependable farmer named Kadir:

> Look at me. Previously I was a farmer with 20 bigha fields. I had to pay Rs. 100 as tax (lagaan). I used to pay nearly ten –twenty rupees a year in gifts and presents. Now I pay only Rs 20 as lagan. There is no need to spend on gifts and presents. Once it was not possible to bring home the grain from the field. The peons, workers, and others used to force us to sell it according to their demands and rates. Now we keep the grain in our homes and sell as and when we wish. In last two years not less than rupees three-four hundred have been saved. We bought a pair of oxen for one hundred and fifty, got the house repaired, and thatched the courtyard. We replaced all the mud pots and brought copper pots and brass wares. The most important thing is that no one is there to bully us and order us to do forced labour without paying for it. We pay our taxes and return home without a word. Once upon a time, we used to shudder in fear every moment we of our lives. Now we are engrossed in Allah's prayer, otherwise even Namaz used to be a burden of sorts.

Therefore the theme of the novel is to portray the unwantedness and uselessness of the zamindari system. All the characters are there to help the novelist to attain this objective. Is Premshankar's hard work and his ideal of brotherhood futile? Is the novel a novel of negative values? No, it has definitely helped all other characters such as Irfan Ali, Jwala Singh, and Priy Nath to see reason and favour the farmers. But the effect of this ideal is minimal in the main theme of the novel. That is why Premashram is a theme- based novel and the portrayal of characters worth remembering is not the novelist's major aim.

Premchand wants to underline the fact that the path of Ahimsa is the right one. Those farmers of Lakhanpur who took to violence were decimated. Manohar committed suicide in the prison cell. On the other hand those who followed Gandhi and Ahimsa rebuilt the village. Premshankar is Gandhi. Gandhi came back after staying for a long time in S. A., Premshankar too came back from the U. S. A. Premchand devoted his spare time in writing this novel as he was busy then to appear in the B. A. examination. During the time of the year he wrote only one story *"Pashu se Manushya"* and that story is also a part of Premashram.

And yes, we must not forget that there is an implied theme too which is introduced right at the beginning of the novel in the discussion between the illiterate peasants of Lakhanpur. "What is the use of education?" they seem to ask. "In what way is the educated man superior to those who are uneducated? The answer to this question is spread through out the pages of the novel.

## Rangbhumi (1925)

Rangabhoomi (in Urdu *Chaugan-i-Hasti*) was first published in Hindi, though it was written in Urdu first. It is a novel of epic length, nearly 1000 pages and tells the story of his time. Four years after its publication in 1928-29, Premchand was awarded a prize of five hundred rupees by the Hindustani Academy for Rangabhumi. It was the first ever prize to be awarded by the Academy. After reading the novel he was crowned with the unofficial title of *Upanyas Samrat* by his admirers and fans.

The protagonist of the novel is a blind beggar Surdas. He owns a plot of land in a village and an industrialist John Sewak wants to acquire this piece of land to build a cigarette factory. But Surdas does not want to part with this land and intends to construct a dhramshala and a well there so that it is of some use to all after his demise. He is a beggar and a Harijan Dalit by birth. He is a true Gandhian; nay a Gandhi himself. In the making and background of this character there is a blind begger who used to sit everyday in Premchand's ken and secondly there is the nationalist freedom movement spearheaded by the stalwart figure of Gandhiji and also the simmering discontent among the so-called princely states of India. Surdas saves five hundred rupees out of the alms he collects everyday. His life's sole aim is to see the welfare of the village he lives in. John Sevak asks him to sell his plot but he refuses and says that a cigarette factory can be built on his dead body only.

Industrialist John Sevak goes to church every Sunday but he hardly believes in religion. "You may believe in Christ as the Son of

God, or as a superman, but I have no such belief. I respect him only as an ordinary fakir." He believes that to live in this world one must take recourse to business, not religion. On the other hand Surdas is a noble soul. He believes in religion and he forgives Bhairon who burns his hut and steals his lifetime savings, the five hundred rupees he saved to get a dharmshala constructed. When Bhairon's righteous wife Subhagi quietly returns the amount to Surdas, he goes and gives it back to Bhairon. The contrast between these characters is really overpowering.

Rangbhumi should be read as a work of colonial past. There is a character, though minor one, named Virpal Singh. He is a militant freedom fighter. He says that the princely ruler of their city is a puppet in the hands of the British Resident. The ruler, he says, goes abroad to have a good time or accompanies the British Resident for shikar or attends on him. The real ruler in the Indian princely state is the British Resident who wants that there should be chaos. He says "While the accused has a right to be heard, we have none. There is no appellate body for us and there is no law. There are no precedents. Any charge can be levied against us. And any sort of punishment can be imposed on us." On the other hand, the Resident says, "The British policy is to rule India for all times to come. Whether it is the Conservatives in power, or Liberals, Radicals or Labour, Nationalists or Socialists, all are unanimous on this goal of British policy.... The British people have never been known for renunciation or for sacrificing their lives for high principles. Basically, we are all imperialists." In the words of Prakash Chandra Gupta (1968: 33) the strength of the novel lies in its appeal against social justice. The conscience of the community is roused by Suardas against wrongdoing and the oppressors tremble in the face of the people's wrath.

One can see a faint kind of similarity between Vanity Fair and Rangabhomi but Premchand's fair is not the fair of vanity. Instead it is a festival of mankind. It is a stage called life in which the respledent drama is played. This is a rangbhomi in which the actors remind us that a play should be played with the spirit of a play. If you do not play it like a play, you will be out of it.

Surdas is the mouthpiece of Premchand. Surdas treats life as a game and considers that we are all players in a game on the playfield of life and are born to play. Victory or defeat is immaterial. Only one side can win. Defeat is a spur to further continuance of the game. "I have lost, you have won. I couldn't hold out. You are an experienced player. You don't lose breath. I do. My team was divided within. For you to clap on your victory is no part of the credo of a sportsman.... Let us rest a while. We shall try again and, learning from experience, we shall defeat you some day."

You can hear the echo of not only a sportsman here but also a Gandhian who wants to win freedom in a friendly match with the imperialist and colonial British power. If you are reminded of Aamir Khan's *Lagaan* by reading these lines, you are a great reader.

Here are two extracts translated by two different translators: One Englishman and the other an Indian.

## Premchand Rangbhumi: The Arena of Life. Translated by Christopher King, Delhi, OUP, 2010, pp. 1-2

The CITY is a place where rich people live and conduct their business. The area outside the city is a place for their diversion and pleasure. In its middle portion are the schools for their boys and the arenas for their lawsuit addicts, where the poor are throttled in the name of the law. All around the city are settlements of the poor. In Banaras, Pandepur is just such a settlement. Neither the light of the city street lamps, nor the drops of the city sprinklers, nor the flow of the city water supply reaches there. Along the sides of the street are tiny shops of merchants and sweet sellers, and behind them live a number of *ikka* drivers, bullock car drivers, milkmen and labourers. There are also three or four houses of down and out which coller workers, whose desperate condition banished them from the city. Rich among them lives a destitute and blind Chamar, whom people call Surdas. In India there is no need for blind people to have a name, or to have work. Surdas is a ready - made name and begging a ready-made occupation. The nature and virtues these blind people share with their namesake, the blind poet Surdas, are world-famous: a special relish for singing and playing, a special affection in the heart and a special love for the way of devotion and spiritual contemplation, these are their inherent traits. The outward vision is closed and the inner vision open,

> Surdas was extremely feeble- bodied, thin, and simple individual. Perhanps fate had made him just for begging. Every day, leaning on his lathi, he would come and sit on the main road and pray for the welfare of the passers-by: "Oh my benefactor! May God make you prosperous!" This was his refrain, and he repeated it over and over. Perhaps he thought it was a mantra to inspire people to take pity on him. He remained seated in his place when he addressed his prayers to those on foot. But if an *ikka* came along he would run after it, and when it came to a buggi, his feet acquired wings. He considered motor, however, to be beyond the reach of his good wishes. Experience had taught him that motorcars don't pay any heed to what anyone says. From morning to evening he spent his time in wishing others well, nor was he ever absent, even in the cloudiness and cold winds of January or the burning heat and hot winds of June.

## Rangbhoomi: Playground. Translated by Manju Jain, Delhi, Penguin, 2011

A city is a site where the rich live and trade. The area outside it is a space for their recreation and amusement. In the city's centre are located schools for their sons and their arenas for litigantion, where the poor are stangled in the name of justice. On the peripheries of the cit are to be found bastis, settlements of the poor. One such basti is Pandeypur in Banaras. The light of the city lamps don't reach there, nor do drops of water when the city is sprinkled, nor does the flow from the city's water works. There are small shops of hualvais and banias on the roadside, behind which live severa ikka-vala, carters, cowherds, and labourers. There are also a few houses belonging to the depraved rich, which have been banished from the city because of their dilapidated condition. A poor blind chamaar, whom people call Soordas, lives in one of these. Blind men need neither name nor work in India. Soordas is their ready-made name, begging for almstheir ready-made vocation. Theri qualities and temperament are also universally celebrated; special interest in music, exceptional love I the heart, distinctive passion for spirituality and religious devotion are their natural traits. The other vision shut and the inner open. Soordas was extremely frail, weak and simple. Prehaps destiny had created him only to beg for alms. Every day, he would go tapping his stick to sit by the tar road and implore the welfare of the passers-by. "Benefactor! May God make you prosperous" was his constant refrain. Perhaps he thought it a mantra to inspire compassion in people. He would remain seated while invoking blessings upon pedestrians. But if an ikka happened to pass by he would run after it, and his feet grew wings if they were buggies. Victorias, however, he considered to be beyond the scope of his good wishes. Experience had taught him that victorias don't listen to anybody. From morning to evening his time was spent only in invoking blessings. Neither the clouds and winds nor the hot blasts of summer could keep him away.

## Kayakalp (1926)

Kayakalp is a novel to highlight the question of Hindu- Muslim unity. Premchand believes that it is only through unity that this nation will achieve her freedom. One of the characters in the novel proclaims, ""There are some people in both the communities whose prestige and prosperity is dependent on the continuance of tension between the two communities. I sincerely believe that whether you are a Hindu or a Muslim, you should be a truthful and a good man. No single community can have the monopoly of all the good qualities. Not all the Muslims are gods, nor all the Hindus kafirs. Anyone who hates the members of the other community is as far removed from God as possible."

The original draft of Kayakalpa mentions three alternative names for the novel, *Asadhya Sadhana, Maya Swapna and Artanaad*. Premchand's handling of the theme of birth and death and reincarnation makes this novel incomprehensible in parts and therefore the novel is an allegory, a travel in search of the ultimate truth. If you get a chance to read the novel's manuscript you will find the following suggestive ideas written in English by Premchand, "Trials and troubles mould the human character; they make heroes of men; power and authority is the curse of humanity; even the highest fall a victim to power and lose their character. Chakradhar rose morally while struggling for existence; his fall began when he came to power." The making of the novel is based on ideas such as these.

There is a charcter in the novel Khwaja Saheb who says in the beginning "Any Muslim who abducts a Hindu girl would earn sawab equal to a thousand Haj pilgrimages."

But in the end the same Khwaja does not weep at the murder of his son who is killed in the attempt to rape Ahalya; "he did something horrible, something which is inhuman."

He is a changed man when he says, "The excuses to precipitate communal riots at times are so trivial and frivolous as to arouse contempt. While the leader of one group goes to the house of the Collector in the morning to salaam him, the leader of the other goes there in the evening. Both swear by their loyalty to him. It is only through unity that this nation will achieve its liberation."

Another character Yashodanand says in the beginning: "The murder of one Muslim is equal to, even better than, one hundred thousand gaudans."

Later he says,"There are some people in both the communities whose prestige and prosperity is dependent on the continuance of tension between the two communities. I sincerely believe that whether you may be a Hindu or a Muslim, you should be a truthful and a good man. No one community can have the monopoly of all the good qualities. Not all the Muslims are gods, nor all the Hindus kafirs. Anyone who hates the members of the other community is as far removed from God as possible."

Yashodanand's wife also says when Yashodanand was murdered: "I used to tell him not to get involved in these Hindu-Muslim tussles. There is no way out either for the Hindus or the Muslims; the two have to live in this country and to die in this country. Neither can swallow the other. The two should live in unity and peace."

In the spiritual sense the novel Kayakalp is a metaphor or allegory. When someone comes out of his garb and sees himself/herself from an outer plane, he /she realizes that his desires and meanderings are there to look at. These wanderings are kayakalp. All the characters: zamindars, Hindus, Muslims, farmers, rich and poor, men and women are just actors in the general drama of deceit. The world is maya and bondage. Man is on a life-long sojourn and is in search of his real self and liberation. As if from *Rangbhumi* characters reappear with different names and shades for the sake of Kayakalp. This return is reincarnation or rebirth. It is Kayakalp.

It will not be asking for too much if I propose that we must re-read the novel in the backdrop of our ongoing discussion about tolerance.

## Nirmala (1927)

From the beginning of the growth and development of novel as a genre in India we find that women remain a symbol, a metaphor and an allegory for the novelists and to make them free from bondage of different kinds was in a way the expression of their desire to see India free not only from the colonial power but also from the shackles of the society. The first social novel in Hindi "Chandraprabha" was written by Bharatendu Harishchandra. The principal female character of the novel, Chandraprabha, is married to a foolish old man, Dundiraj. Bhartendu wanted to expose the evil consequences of unequal marriages and there was a veiled message for imparting education to girls for their future. Similarly, ***Nirmala*** (*virtuous* or *pure*) is a novel centered on Nirmala, a young girl who is forced to marry a widower of her father's age. She is a "fragile and touching heroine, endearing through her weaknesses as mush as her genuine virtues." Premchand makes the story revolve around the young girl under 18 who suddenly becomes a woman after marrying a man who is much older. The plot unfolds to reveal her husband's suspicion of a relationship between her and his eldest son, a suspicion that leads to the son's death. *Nirmala's* reformist agenda is transparent in its theme which deals with the problem of dowry, incompatible marriages and related issues. The story uses fiction to highlight an era of much needed social reform in 1920s Indian society. *Nirmala* was serialized in 1928 in *Chand*, a women's magazine. The novel has a unity of structure and plot unparalleled by any of his other novel. It should be remembered, says Madan Gopal, that Premchand is not original and new in the story. It is *an old wine in new bottle*. It was first translated in 1988 as *The Second Wife* by David Rubin. Though "Nirmala" means "virtuous" or "pure", David Rubin changed the title into *The Second Wife*. In the translator's introduction he says that the novel is a tale of woman's tragedy, which nevertheless rises above the usual limitations of a *roman a these* in its dramatization of very specific and highly individualized private lives and makes its appeal on a basis of universal human experience that transcends any local peculiarities of customs and culture. Francesca Orsini called it a prime example of Premchand's combination of social realism and drama. Alok Rai, Premchand's grandson, also translated Nirmala into English in 1999 and was termed 'changed in rebirth'. Harish Trivedi says that Alok Rai "renders Nirmala with confident ease and flair and an occasional Indianism; he also provides a sophisticated discussion of the mode of melodrama which Premchand is said to resort to." In the afterword of the novel he says:

> Nirmala is a monster of passivity, someone who destroys through her inability ( and / or refusal : weapons of the weak) to think and to act, to be a person. She destroys the same male world which has made her what she is, by the simple and ruthless expedient of insisting on being that which she has been made into.

Gulzar who directed a TV serial based on the novel believes that the novel is a little outstretched, and has a tendency to repeat many emotions, but also has its diversions and contradictions. A few TV serials such as *Tehreer Munshi Premchand Ki* directed by Gulzar and several Hindi films revolve around this theme.

An Indian reader familiar with the scourge of dowry will keep Nirmala in his heart of hearts. She remains unsoiled-nirmala, though there were social sircumstances to destroy her purity.

## Nirmala: the Second Wife (page 1-2) David Rubin, Orient Paperback

Although there were scores of relatives living in Udaybhanu's household-maternal and paternal uncles, nephews and nieces- we are not concerned with them here. Udaybhanu was a fine lawyer, fortune had smiled upon him, and to give shelter to the impoverished members of his clan was only his filial duty. But our concern is only with his daughters, the elder named Nirmala and the younger Krishna. Until only yesterday both were still playing with dolls. Nirmala was fifteen, Krishna only ten, but in their temperaments and habits there was scarcely any difference. Both were lively, playful and mad about shows and excursions, both married off their dolls with pomp and circumstance, and both constantly shirked their household duties. Their mother kept calling out for them, but unsure about the task they were being summoned to, they would hide themselves on the terrace. They fought with their brothers, scolded the servants and as soon as they heard the sound of music in the street would rush to stand in the doorway. But today, quite suddenly, an event occured which made the elder a grown up while the younger remained only a child: Krihna was her old self, but Nirmala had now become serious, shy, and fond of solitude.

For months now Udaybhan had been negotiating Nirmala's marriage. Today his labour had borne fruit, for he had finalized her alliance with Babu Bhalchandra Sinha's eldest son, Bhuvan Mohan. The groom's father had declared that he didn't care whether Udaybhanu gave a dowry or not. Of course, the members of the marriage party ought to be treated with the customary respect and hospitality, so that there was no occasion for either of the families being held in ridicule.

## Nirmala (Translated by Alok Rai)

Although there were dozens of people in Babu Udayabhanulal's hpusehold-cousins maternal and paternal, sons of brothers, sons of brothers, sons of sisters-there is little reason to concern overselves with them here. He was a good lawyer, the goddess of wealth smiled on his labours, and providing shelter to the less fortunate members of his family was neither more nor less than his duty. We are concerned here only with his two daughters, the older of whom is called Nirmala, the younger Krishna. Till but yesterdayboth were playing with dolls. Nirmala was in her fifteenth year. Krishna in her tenth, yet there was little difference between their temperaments. Both playful, mischievious, full of fun and frolic. Their dolls would playful, mschieveous, full of fun and frolic. Their mother would keep calling away, but the two would stay lurking on the terracr as if unaware altogether as to what the calling might be about, as if unaware altogether as to what the calling might be about. They quarreled with their brothers, scolded the servants, and would dash to the front door at the merest sound of an itinerant musician. But something has happened today, something that has suddenly made the older one that much older, the younger one decidedly younger. Krishna is much the same as ever, but Nirmala has suddenly become somber, bashful, and a seeker of solitude. For the past several months Babu Udayabhanulal has been on the lookout for a husband for Nirmala. Today his labours have been crowned with success. A match has been arranged with the elder son of Babu Bhalchandra Sinha, Bhuwan Mohan Sinha. The groom's father has declared he has no demands whatsoever in the matter of a dowry- Babu Udaybhanulal may choose to give or not give anything, just as he pleases. But the members of the Baraat must be treated with generous hospitality, he insisted, so as to protect both parties from all possible redicule. Babu Udaybhanulal was a lawyer all right, but he didn't know how to accumulate wealth. The question of dowry had been a tough nut for him to crack. Thus his relief knew no bounds when the groom's father declared that the dowry was purely optional. He had been apprehensive about all the debt he would have to incur and even made provisional arrangements with a few moneylenders. His most conservative estimates of the likely cost had been in the region of twenty thousand rupees. He was overjoyed at being relieved of that anxiety.

## Pratigya (1927)

After the resounding success of the serialization of Nirmala, Premchand continued the publication of another novel in the same journal. The novel is again a short one and it is called Pratigya. It is a new version of an earlier novel *Prema* or *Hum Khurma –o- Hum Sal'ab.* Nirmala was published by the Chand Press of Allahabad; Premchand published Pratigya from his own Saraswati Press in Banaras.

Amritrai is a widower. He listens to the lecture of an Arya Samajist Amar Nath and takes a pledge to marry none but a widow. Therefore he refuses to marry Prema, his sister-in-law with whom he has been engaged for three years. He persuades his closest friend, Professor Dan Nath, to marry her. Prema is married to Dan Nath but she continues loving Amritrai. Prema's friend, Purna, the wife of a poor Brahmin clerk, Basant Kumar, becomes a widow. Once Prema's brother Kamlaprasad takes Purna to a deserted house and tries to rape her. She hits him hard and runs to the rescue home built by Amritrai. It is to be noted with regret that Purna becomes the target of Kamlaprasad's lust and overtures because she was too poor to afford basic neccicities of life. She exclaims, "If women get even two meagre meals a day and a coarse cloth to wear, they will protect their chastity unto death." The question of satitva and chastity is paramount for a woman according to Premchand. The suspicion of Dan Nath that there is some relationship between his wife Prema and Amritrai goes away and Amritrai decides to devote his time to the rescue home for the widows.

Sometimes the reader fails to understand the theme of the novel. What does Premchand wish to convey? Is it about the necessity of married life as told by Prof Dan Nath? "I have never thought an unmarried life as an ideal one. How can it be an ideal to be followed? Unnatural thing can never be an ideal." Or is it widow remarriage? In "Prema" the protagonist marries a widow but in Pratigya the poetic justice is not attained.

## Gaban (1931)

Through this novel *Gaban* (literally, *Embezzlement*), Premchand tries to show the falling moral values among lower middle class Indian youth in the era of British India, and to what heights a person can get to, to reach the world of leisure class, and maintain the false image as a rich person. It tells the story of Ramanath, a handsome, pleasure seeking, boastful, but a morally weak person, who tries to make his wife Jalpa happy by gifting her jewelry and ornaments which he can't really afford to buy from his meager salary, and then gets engulfed in a web of debts, which ultimately forces him to commit embezzlement. It is considered Premchand's best work after Godaan. The shadow of Meerut Conspiracy Case (1929) seems to have fallen on the part of the novel. In the words of Harish Trivedi "the hairline fracture in the plot is bound and healed by Premchand's pervasive concern with appearance and reality, with ostentation and simplicity, with social and political justice, and with truth and falsehood."

Christopher R. King who once wrote a book on "*One language, Two Scripts*" (1994) translates this novel and he glaringly misspells the title of the novel as "*Ghaban*". Thus a significant novel which has anti-colonial overtones is marred by awkward and gawky translation and can be placed among the literal translations, not a literary one. Let me give you an excerpt for your reading:

> It was the rainy season, the month of July. Masses of golden clouds were through the sky. A light drizzle was falling intermittently. It was only mid-afternoon but it seemed as if evening had come. In the mango groves girls and their mothers were swinging; three or four on the swings, three or four pushing. Some were singing folk songs, some poetry. In this season, childhood memories awoke in the women. It was as if the soft rain washed away worries from the heart, as if it made even withered minds fresh and green. Everyone was filled with enthusiasm. Green saris echoed the greenery of nature.
>
> Just then a travelling pedlar came and stood near the swings. As soon as he was seen, the swinging stopped and everyone big and small crowded around him. He opened his box and displayed his glittereing sparkling wares. There were ornaments of raw pearls, unfinished lace, and gold and silver bemming, coloured socks, beautiful dolls and dolls' ornaments, and children's tops and rattles. Some took one thing, others another. One big-eyed little girl liked the most beautiful among all those sparkiling

objects- a splendidly coloured chandrahar. “Mummy, “she said, “I will take this neckless.”

The mother asked the pedlar, “How much is this?” Wiping the necklace with a handkerchief, the pedler said, “It cost me twenty annas. The lady can give what she likes.”

“That is very expensive. Its shine will disappear after a very few days.”

Tenderly shaking his head, the pedler said, Beti, in a very few days the child will be married and receive a real chandrahar of her own.”

These warmed-hearted words went straight to the mother’s heard; the neckless was purchased.

The little girl’s joy had no limits; may be even a diamond neckless would not given her as much pleasure. Putting it on, she danced and twirled through the whole village. Among her childish treasures, this crystal neckless was the dearest and most precious.

The girl’s name was Jalpa, her mother’s Manaki.

## Karmbhumi (1932)

Premchand is a novelist with a purpose. He was not writing to entertain the masses or earn name and fame. The purpose of his work was awakening the minds of the people to realize and understand the situation under which India of those days was suffereing. He was with Gandhi and his ideals were very dear to him. But he often disagreed with him too. When he saw that Bhagat Singh and others were hanged and Gandhi didn’t do what he should have done. Premchand was very agitated. In that state of mind he wrote the following letter. “I wanted to attend the Karachi (session). Bhagat Singh’s death by hanging has broken my heart. With what hopes could one go there now? People will hoot down Gandhi and the Congress will pass into the hands of irresponsible extremists, and there will be no place for us. What path we shall pursue is not clear. 1 am crest fallen. The future is bleak. The events in Banaras, Mirzapur and Agra,

1 feel, will encourage the government. But no government could ever commit a greater stupidity. How deep an impact could the government have created, if it had commuted the death sentence (of Bhagat Singh and his comrades) into transportation for life? Its attitude, however, betrays that there has been no change of heart, and that the government is determined to go its irresponsible way."

In the early thirties the political atmosphere of the country was very volatile. There was commotion because of unrest among the Harijans and Muslims. The temple entry movement was gaining momentum. Masses were angry with Zamindars. They were apprehensive about the treatment they were receiveing from the British and were not sure how Gandhiji and others would make their movement successful. The young Indian blood was boiling and wanted to teach the oppressor a lesson. The days of persuation seemed to be over. People were ready to pay any price for independence. They became impatient and rebellious. Premchand sensed this and turned the ire of the people into words. Premchand wrote: cursing their fate, naked, starved and dying like dogs, people continued to till the fields. What choice did they have? Many had migrated to the cities and found employment there. Many others had resorted to wage labour. But there was still no dearth of tenants. In predominantly agricultural country, cultivation is not merely a means of livelihood; it is also a status symbol.

*Karmabhoomi* is set in the Uttar Pradesh of the 1930s. By the beginning of the 20th century, Islam and Hinduism had coexisted in India for over a thousand years. Barring the occasional outbursts of violence, the two religious communities had lived together peacefully and shared strong social bonds except marriage. English education, however, drove a wedge between the communities. India of the early 1930s consisted of a great mass of poor and illiterate people who were exploited by the rich and powerful, irrespective of caste or religion. The author has sympathy for these poor and toiling masses is clearly reflected in his writings. It is against this backdrop that Premchand wrote *Karmabhumi*. An English translation of this novel is attempted by Lalit Srivastava and published by OUP.

The novel introduces participation of women in the freedom movement and also highlights problems such as untouchabilty which is a recurring theme of his great novels beginning from Sevasadan, Rangbhumi and Kayakalp. The novel begins with a severe criticism of education in India. The political situation of the time is also highlighted and even the colonial masters are there to indicate the indignation of the masses towards them. There is an instance which is given as follows:

> Two British Tommies are standing guard for the third tommy who has raped a woman. Amarkant and others are furious. When the tommy comes out, there is a scene. The three Tommies are beaten up and sent to hospital. Says Salim: "These tommies, coming from the poorest families of England, dare do these things because India is enslaved, because they know that the people of this country have been thoroughly demoralized and would bear all that is inflicted on them. We shall have to awaken the people and arouse them to throw off the foreign yoke."

The main character of the novel Amar Kant seems to be inspired from the personality of Pt. Govind Vallabh Pant. But Premchand's real motive is not characterization. Instead he wants to depict human nature in its wider perspective. He is there to present the life of his time, the current political upheaval.

## Godan (1936)

In colonial countries the peasants alone are revolutionary. For they have nothing to lose and everything to gain. The starving peasant, outside the class system, is the first among the exploited to discover that only violence pays. For him there is no compromise, no possible coming to terms.

Franz Fanon: The Wretched of the Earth

Premchand will never attain the heights which are within his reach unless he goes back to his tales of the village life which he has lived, and the Hindu villagers whom he understands. Those tales alone ring true, and only they enable him to express his soul.

T. Graham Bailey: History of Urdu Literature (1928)

Godan (I am going to use any of the spellings of this Hindi word- Godan, Godaan, Gaudan alternatively) is one such tale and the swan song of the *bard of Lamhi. Godaan/Godan or Gaudan* (*The Gift of a Cow*, 1936), Premchand's last completed work is generally accepted as his best novel. It is also considered as one of the finest Hindi novels. Godaan is the best and last completed novel of Premchand. Once Namvar Singh very poetically spoke that in Godan there is a confluence of two separate rivers: Ganga and Yamuna. In the centre of *Sevasadan* the character of woman named Suman is like the holy Ganga. In *Premashram* the centre-place is taken by the peasant. He is like the river Yamuna. Godan is the novel in which Ganga (the woman) and Yamuna (the peasant) merge and unite together. According to Bender, Premchand is "the first major Hindi Novelist" and enjoys a "canonical status in modern India". Critics like Mahendra V. Desai also consider it "the finest of the century" and Sisir da very adroitly comments that Godan is a record of authentic experience and of the suffering and struggle of the Indian rural people and it is now a classic of modern Indian literature. According to Schulz (1981) "Godan is a well-structured and well-balanced novel which amply fulfills the literary requirements postulated by the Western literary standards." One can very easily see that the novel is very much influenced by the novels of Dickens and Godan can be said an Indian copy of *Hard Times*. Another German scholar Günter Grass said that the novel is a wonderful book. Dorothea Dieckmann said that reading Godan means diving into the legendary and still existing contrast between poor and rich, the countryside and the city, need and double standards, tradition and cynicism, a repressive family system and liberty brought forth by luxury. Pin-sharp portraits of low caste peasants, Brahmin village elders, opportunist intellectuals and corrupt landlords are embedded in an elaborate ensemble of exemplary episodes. Kamal Kishore Goenka says that the novel is not about the particular happenings of an age; it is instead a realistic account of the collapse of an agricultural civilization... a moving expression of some deep and solemn anguish piling up bit by bit in the author's mind. Premchand's Godan resembles with Leonard Woolf's "A *village in the Jungle"* (1913)" says Ranjini Obeyesekere. As the Sri Lankan novel records farmers anguish and decay in a village, similarly Godan also presents the pitiable condition of peasants in Indian setting.

The novel is aptly said to be Premchand's gaudan to Hindi and Urdu literature. Look at the last lines of the novel: "But there is no cow in the house; nor is there money for it. There is only twenty annas in the house-the previous day's earnings. Dhaniya brings it, puts it into the hand of the Brahmin and says: "Maharaj, there is no cow in the house, not even a she-calf. Accept these twenty annas; there is nothing left in the house. This then is his gaudan. She faints. Hori dies."

When a reader in English looks for some more information about the novel and directly goes to Wikipedia, he finds the following lines:

> The protagonist, Hori, a poor peasant, desperately longs for a cow, a symbol of wealth and prestige in rural India. In a Faustian twist of fate, Hori gets his cow, but pays for it with his life. After his death, the village priests demand a cow from his widow to bring his soul absolution, and peace (Godaan). The narrative represents the average Indian farmer's existence under colonial rule, with the protagonist facing cultural and feudal exploitation.

But this is not the story in a nutshell. The novel is much more than a villager's struggle to get a cow or gift a cow. There are several parallel sub-plots: the story of Hori and his wife Dhaniya; the story of Hori's son Gobar and his wife Jhuniya who leave the farm in rural UP for an urban life in nearby Lucknow; and the story of the Rai Sahib and his friends in Lucknow. The novel is, in short, an epic length story in the manner of the grand Victorian novels, with about fifteen major characters. In fact, Godaan presents two distinct worlds and their distinction is so wide apart that the twine can never meet. The one world is rural and rustic. It is filled with characters drawn from different backgrounds and who generally live in penury, the other is urban and their people live in luxary. So there are two distinct classes: labour class and pleasure class. Although the two worlds often communicate with each other, yet they seldom see eye to eye. This is a very complicated cosmos in which two worlds co-exist. There is a gap between them which can be best understood by Derridean idea of *differance*.

Hori is the wretched of the earth. He has devoted his entire life to get nothing but two morsels of food for the family. He is God – fearing, superstitious and a slave to traditions and customs. "We have been born to shed our blood, to enrich others, to pay the principal twice over as interest, knowing fully well that the principal is still there to be paid .... In other words, there is no deliverance for us." He thinks that "The peasant is like green· fodder. If he doesn't give presents and the customary bribes, he cannot continue to live in the village." When Sobha asks Hori if they will ever be free from the moneylenders' clutches, Hori says: "There is no hope in this life. We ask neither for a kingdom, nor for a throne, not even for comforts. We want to have coarse meals and coarse clothes -and to live with our honour intact. But even that is denied to us."

The great novelist Somerset Maugham in his notebook noted the following lines about India he visited during those days, "It wasn't the Taj Mahal. The Ghats of Benares, the temple at Madurai or the mountains of Travancore that had moved me; it was the peasant, the terribly emaciated, with nothing to cover his nakedness but a rag round his middle... That was the sight that had given me the most poignant emotion in India" (Quoted in Iyengar, 1960: 258). Rajani Palm Dutt too quoted an English historian M. L. Darling in his book *"India Today"* "The most arresting fact about India is that her soil is rich and her people poor". This is what gave Premchand too the fodder for his thoughts. When Mrs Premchand cried bitterly after reading the death of Hori in Godan, Premchand tried to pacify her. He told her that it was all imagination and not true. There was no Hori who died in penury. But the readers who read the last scene still cry and shed tears. In his doctoral thesis *"Premchand and Bhartiya Kisan"* (1982) Dr Ram Bakhsh proposes that Hori is not the only representative of Indian farmer. That may be a picture of a farmer of Premchand's India of that time but he is not the eternal representative of a typical Indian peasant. In Premashram, Balraj and Manohar are also farmers but they are revolutionary and rebels. Premchand portrays Hori as a calm, contented, restrained and composed person who is always superstitious and traditional. All these features are the characteristics of an average Indian peasant. If we keep in mind the farmer's agitation during that time, Premchand could have shown him in a different garb and light. But by experience Premchand understood and thought that a typical Indian farmer was basically an oppressed and wretched one who kept leaning on his fate, karma and dharma.

On the other hand there is life around the sugar mill. Its owner Khanna and social coquette Miss Malti are the cynosure of all eyes. There is an idealist Professor Mehta who is attracted to her and tries to persuade her to lead a normal life. Here's an example of a fight between a husband and wife. Khanna and his wife Govindi are debating what to do about a sick child; Khanna has been having a long standing flirtation with the same Miss Malti (an England-returned physician), and as a result has been neglecting his wife. Let us read how Premchand vividly depicts and creates a scene.

Bhisham was their youngest son. Sickly ever since birth, he seemed to have something or other wrong with him all the time. One day it would be a cough, the next a fever; sometimes he'd start having chest pains, other times it would be diarrhea. Ten months old now, he looked only five or six months. Khanna had become indifferent toward the boy, convinced he wouldn't live anyway. But Govindi for that very reason cared more about the baby than about any of the other children.

Khanna assumed an air of fatherly concern. 'It's not good to get babies in the habit of taking drugs, and you have a fetish for doling out medicines. You call the doctor at the slightest excuse. This is only the third day. Wait another day. The fever'll probably drop all by itself today.'

'It hasn't come down for three days,' Govindi persisted. 'All the home remedies have failed.'

'All right then, I'll make a call. Whom should I send for?' 'Call Dr. Naag'

'Very well, I'll get him, but remember that a big name doesn't mean the man's a good doctor. Despite the high fees he collects, I've never seen his treatment cure anyone. He's notorious for dispatching his patients to heaven.'

'Then call anyone you like. I only suggested Dr. Naag because he's been here several times.'

'Why don't I send for Miss Malti? Her fees are lower and a lady doctor knows more about children than any man could.'

Govindi flared up. 'I don't consider Miss Malti a doctor.' Khanna glared back at her. 'I suppose she was in England digging ditches. Besides, thousands of people owe their lives to her today. Doesn't that mean anything?'

'Maybe so, but I have no faith in her. She may have the remedy for men's ailing hearts, but she can't cure anything else.'

That did it. Khanna began to thunder, and Govindi let loose a torrent. Malti's name was like a declaration of war between them.

Khanna flung all the papers on the floor. 'Life with you has really gone sour,' he declared.

The following oft-quoted scene from the village life also gives the reader a kind of bewilderment and surprise that one can never forget the art of Premchand. This is not a piece of sheer art. It is a different kind of courage in which there are traditional values and there are social uprising of a different sphere. Other than using a word which is not considered acceptable now this piece is out and out revolutionary:

> Siliya's father Harkhu was an old man of sixty, dark and thin, wrinkled as a dried pepper and just as biting. 'There's no trouble, thakur. Today we'll either make a chamar out of Matadin or shed his blood along with our own. Siliya is a woman, and she has to go live with some man or other. We have no objection to that, but whoever takes her must become one of us. You can't make Brahmans out of us, but we can make chamars out of you. If you're willing to make us Brahmans, our whole community is agreeable. As long as that's not possible, then become chamars. Eat with us, drink with us and live with us. If you're going to take away our honour, then give us your caste."

Datadin raised his stick. 'Control your tongue, Harkhu. Your girl's over there. Take her anywhere you please. We haven't tied her down. She worked and she got paid. There's no shortage of labourers around here.'

Siliya's mother shook her finger at him. 'Bully for you, pandit! You're being terribly fair! I'd like to see you talk that way if your daughter had run off with a chamar. We're chamars, though, so of course we don't have any honour! We're not taking Siliya away alone. We're taking Matadin with her—the one who ruined her. You're so pious—you'll sleep with her, but you won't drink water from her hands. No one but this bitch would tolerate all that. I'd have poisoned such a man.'

'Didn't you hear what these people are saying?' Harkhu challenged the group with him. 'What are you standing there gaping for?'

At this, two of the chamars sprang forward and grabbed Matadin's hands while a third tore off his sacred thread. Before Datadin and Jhinguri Singh could wield their sticks, two chamars had stuffed a big piece of bone in Matadin's mouth. Matadin clenched his teeth but the abominable thing caught between his lips all the same. Overcome by nausea, he opened his mouth involuntarily—and the bone slipped inside...

The vomiting over, Matadin stretched out almost lifeless on the ground as though his back were broken, as though he only wanted a cupful of water in which to drown himself. The ritual propriety which had allowed him to flaunt his passion and his pride had been wiped out. That piece of bone had polluted not only his mouth but also his soul. His religion depended on absolute purity in eating and drinking; not that righteousness had been cut off at the root...

Translated by Gordon Charles Roadarmel (1968, 305-306)

I don't think you require further elucidation. I needn't tell you the pleasures of reading Premchand as a text. Reading *Godan* is reading the age of Premchand. In the above quoted lines Harkhu is sixty years of age. These sixty years are also Premchand's years. He was 56 when he completed the novel. The novel is the gist of those years' experience. The first half of the century will be before your eyes when you read the novel. The very idea of realism will change after its reading. The two worlds of the novel are real; they are face to face but never see eye to eye. From Bhartendu Harishchandra to Premchand whatever we receive in sixes and sevens, we get it together in this novel. When Dhaniya says, "You want suraj; you will not get suraj by just going to prison. You will get it by justice and Dharma." In the age of prosperity too, Indians disagree with the slogans such as "Shining India". Premchand too says, "*Bharat dhani ho raha hai. Hota hoga.*" The smile and shine on the face of the last man is what he wished to see.

Prabhakar Jha states that it is a novel, "expressing a Galilean perception of language, one that denies the absolutism of a single and unitary language, that is, that refuses to acknowledge its own language as the sole verbal and semantic centre of the ideological world." Therefore, he suggests that the main concern in the reading of Godan should be "the study of specific images of languages and the organization of these images into their dialogic interrelationships". On the other hand in his presidential address to the first conference of the Progressive Writers' Association Premchand said that literature is "the criticism of life" and the language used in it "is a means, not an end". In the speech, he also says that "the same event or situation does not leave the same impression on everyone. Every person has a different mentality and point of view." Another writer and critic Amardeep Singh, a professor of English at Lehigh University in Eastern Pennsylvania, sums up the detailed study of the novel " *Thoughts on Premchand's Godaan*"(2010) as follows, "*Godaan*, in short, is fundamentally a modern novel in both form and content. Its form clearly resembles multi-plot late Victorian novels by writers like Thomas Hardy, and in some ways its content is Hardy-esque as well – though thoroughly transplanted to the Indian/Hindi context without a trace of 'derivativeness'. The novel rings true both in its village scenes and in its urban/high-culture passages, and many of the debates and arguments its characters have, over issues such as caste-

and gender-relations remain relevant today. Despite Premchand's reputation as a political writer (which he himself reinforced in his public statements in support of the Progressive Writers), *Godaan* does not hit the reader over the head with patriotism."

Harish Trivedi is also right in this respect when he comments that while others believe that many of his works of fiction from the same final period are overcast with a resigned passivity which would have been unthinkable in the idealistic and broadly Gandhian Premchand of earlier years, Godan is balanced and perfect. On the other hand, Schulz sums up his findings about the novel as follows: Godan is a well structured and well-balanced novel which amply fulfils the literary requirements postulated by Western literary standards. The justaposition of the ways of life in poor village and the wealthy town serves to focus the reader's attention on the oppression of the poor by the rich. Even a very good man like Hori, who scrupulously observes and obeys the obvious laws and customs to which his dharma subjects him, is doomed in this struggle for survival. With his death, this is the real content of the novel Godan, the light of Dharma is extinguished, and apparantly for ever." Schulz understands of the novel in a Western Appraisal, if your Eastern mind disagrees. I am elated.

People praise Godan. Scholars and critics too appreciate it and find in it the culmination of his genius. We should remember that the 1930s was the time when a great many novelists were writing about peasants and their plight. In the West the causes were slightly different but in India exploitation, poverty and colonialism were the major factors. In the West authors like John Steinbeck and Ignazio Silone had published *The Grapes of Wrath* and *Fontemara*. In India, the Bengali writer, Manik Bandopadhyay had already written two major peasant novels by 1936. In the words of Devleena Ghosh, "All of these writers, Premchand included, did what historical documents cannot do-they recorded the experiences of a whole class and showed that human suffering need no longer elude the knowledge of those who did not experience it. Premchand's last work shows that knowledge of the exploitation on the scale of entire classes is accessible to us. It is also a painfully honest record of how a liberal humanist was compelled to discard some of his strongest views in the face of social reality."

Premchand is no Gandhian in Godan. Hori, is born, suffers and dies. Premchand is not the Premchand of the earlier days in the novel. He is mature and steady in his conduct and thoughts. His speech at Lucknow as the President of Progressive writers' association clearly indicated that he was for the realism of a different kind. It was not tilted towards idealism (aadarshonmukh). It was realism of the purest kind. He became interested in Life's truth (Jeevan ki Sachchaiyan). What was the truth about life? It was the existence of two worlds in one. The world of Hori and the world of Mehta were poles apart. The truth was that they lived and interacted but were different. The world of Dalits, marginalized and poor was one reality. The other reality was of the colonial master. The struggle for freedom was going on and the oppressor was unmindful of anything as his aim was explotation. This kind of realism with multilayered representations was present in the whole of India- British India and princely states. The realism of this kind was glaring at our heads in the entire world where the sun never set.

Just for a feel of English Translation of the novel two extracts are given below:

## Gordon C. Roadarmel

Hori Ram finished feeding his two bullocks and then turned to his wife Dhaniya. 'Send Gobar to hoe the sugar cane. I don't know when I'll be back. Just get me my stick.'

Dhaniya had been making fuel-cakes, so her hands were covered in dung. 'First eat something before you leave,' she said. 'What's the big hurry?'

A frown deepened the wrinkles on Hori's forehead. 'All you think about is food. But I have to worry that I may not even get to see the master if I reach there late. Once he starts his bathing and prayers I'll have to wait around for hours.'

'That's exactly why I'm suggesting you first have something to eat. And what harm would be done by not going at all today? You were just there two days ago.'

'Why do you go poking your nose into things you don't understand?'

Jai Ratan and P. Lal translation (1957)

After serving the two bullocks with feed and water Hori Ram said to his wife, Dhania, 'Send Gobar to hoe the sugar cane. I am going out and may return late. Hand me the staff.'

Dhania had been making cow-dung cakes and her hands were smeared with the dung. 'What's the hurry' she said, 'Have something before you go.'

Hori puckered up his wrinkled brow. 'Yout talk about refreshments when I am worried about the delay. If I am late I won't be able to meet the Master. If he sits down to his prayers I may have to wait for hours.'

'That does why I say have *something,'* Dhania said. 'Besides, what's the harm if you don't go today? You went to him only the day before yesterday.'

Why do you try to meddle with things which are beyond you?

**Mangalsutra**

Mangalsutra is Premchand's unfinished novel. He could write about 70 pages only and it was completed by his friend Jainendra Kumar after his death. The novel is the story of a writer "Mahatma" Pt. Dev Kumar, his wife Shaivya, his elder son Sant Kumar, a lawyer, and his wife Pushpa, his younger son Sadhu kumar, and a married daughter Pankaja. Had he completed it, it might have been Premchand's best. You can say that it is a veiled autobiography of Premchand. One wonders how "Gandhi in him had either gone asleep or the image of the Mahatma had been dislodged from the inner temple of his heart." Premchand now wanted injustice to be fought and put an end to it. The following extract from the novel has been repeatedly quoted by his biographers and critics to prove the point:

> It was impossible to bend Dev Kumar through threats. Before reason, however, he himself bowed his head. These days he pondered over the dilemma: "Why this chaos in the world??'

The theory of actions in this life and those in the previous one did not help resolve this question. If the entire universe is one, why should there be these differences? Why should one man who toils the whole life still starve, while another without the least effort lie on a bed of roses? Is it the universal spirit? Or, is it the complete absence of it? Reason says: "All are free here and they are also free to improve their prospects through their own strength and efforts." Doubt says: "Where is'the equality of opportunity? There is certainly equality in the market place: anyone can buy what he wishes to. But one needs money to buy. When some don't have money, this talk of equality of opportunity is meaningless!" This sort of searching of the soul had never taken place in Dev Kumar's life. The litterateur in him could not be satisfied with the existing social order. And there was no way to remove the imbalance. "Where is Justice?" he contemplated. "If a poor peasant steals a few sheaves of corn, he is arrested and punished. On the other hand, the rich who rob the people in broad daylight are honouredlby society and awarded titles. People armed with all sorts of weapons come down upon the workers and peasants. Enslave them and rob them in the name of taxes, levies, and so on and so forth. And they all draw huge salaries, have all the comforts and pleasures and indulge in licentiousness. Is this the world created by God? Is this justice?" And "there always have been, and will always be, pious people who claim that the world is based on religion and moral law. They sacrifice their own lives and quit the world. But why call them pious? They are cowards and greedy self-seekers. The pious is one who defends justice and gives his life for it. If, however, he willingly turns his face away, he is straying from the path of true religion. If the viciousness of the social inequality does not prick him, he is not only blind but is also a fool. He is not really pious. And here it is not necessary to be one. It is these pious men who, by propagating ideas of fate, God, and worship, have immortalized these traits of viciousness. Rather than live as we do and succumb to the existing social order; it would have been better if man had ended this. Man will have to become man. Surrounded as he is by beastly creatures, he shall have to arm himself. For, to allow oneself to be made a prey not piety but stupidity....

The main aim of this long quotation it to underline the fact that after a life long confusion and misunderstanding with regard to artificial and imaginary ideas about freedom, equality and justice, Premchand arrived at a juncture where he could very pointedly see and visualize the path of socialism and social justice. The first indication of his glorious intellectual turn can be vividly seen in *Godan* and the culmination and expansion of it can be deciphered from *Mangal Sutra*. It is the sutra which takes us to the Mangal or wellness of the entire humanity (Vishva Kalyan).

## Story-teller Premchand

To Premchand belongs the distinction of creating the genre of the serious short story—and the serious novel as well—in both Hindi and Urdu. Virtually single-handed he lifted fiction in these languages from a quagmire of aimless romantic chronicles to a high level of realistic narrative comparable to European fiction of the time; and in both languages, he has, in addition, remained an unsurpassed master."

-David Rubin: The World of Premchand (Oxford, 2001)

There is no doubt that in the beginning Premchand's stories appeared in Urdu and later in Hindi. Between 1907 and 1917, Premchand wrote mostly for "*Zamana*" magazine and only around 1917 he entered the portals of the Hindi language. To be precise, a book entitled *"Sapt Saroj"* was published by Hind Pustak Agency Calcutta and Mannan Dwivedi wrote its preface on June 8, 1917 as follows, "Premchand's name is on a very high pedestal in the world of Urdu literary world. Your books are decorating the Urdu panorama for a long time. The Urdu language press and magazines have been praisng the art of Premchand for a long time. It is heartening to note that mother tongue Hindi has also attracted him for some time now. Premchand entered the temple of his mother tongue to worship her with plenty to offer and mother too had embressed her devoted son. Your stories are really unique for Hindi readers. Hindi language magazines and papers are always eager to publish his articles. Many scholars think that Premchand's stories can be compared with Tagore Babu's fiction. It will be unfair and unnecessary to write about such a great and famous scholar and writer..."

Premchand has a huge corpus of short stories but no definitive edition of this corpus has yet been published. For some time the general impression was that Premchand's complete short stories have been put together in Hindi in the series known as *Mansarovar* consisting of 8 volumes, two volumes of which had come out in Premchand's lifetime from Saraswati Press owned by him. The remaining six volumes were published by his elder son, Shripat Rai. All the volumes of *Mansarovar* taken together contain 198 stories. However, it soon became apparent that the Mansarovar compilation is not an exhaustive one. Premchand's younger son Amrit Rai and a renowned scholar of Premchand Kamal Kishore Goenka later dug out a large number of stories and it was claimed that he must have written at least 300 stories. Premchand is considered the first Hindi author whose writings prominently featured realism. His stories describe the problems of the poor and the urban middle-class. His works depict a rationalistic outlook, which views religious values as something that allows the powerful hypocrites to exploit the weak. He used literature for the purpose of arousing public awareness about national and social issues and often wrote about topics related to corruption, child widowhood, prostitution, feudal system, poverty, colonialism and on the India's freedom movement. Sisir Kumar Das in the *"History of Indian Literature: 1911-1956"* puts it in detail that "a great novelist though he is, he is perhaps greater as a short story writer. The number of stories written by him is close to three hundred: over thirty five separate collections of his stories had appeared in his life time. Premchand did not have any particular model before him though he admitted that he admired the works of Tolstoy, Victor Hugo, Romain Rolland and Tagore, especially his short stories. Premchand's stories, like his novels, are intricately connected with his experience of the Indian village."

Dr Lakshmi Narayan Lal presents Premchand's growth as a story writer dividing his time into three phases namely: *First Phase*: 1917-

1920, *Second Phase:* 1920-1930, and *Third Phase:* 1930- 1936. In the first phase stories in *Sapt Saroj*, *Nav Nidhi* and *Prem Pachisi* are included. He had already written two long novels and he had before him a society marred with traditions and freedom struggle going nowhere. Almost all the stories of the first phase are told as if a traditional narrates where description is more than the depth of the characters. The stories have an element of chance embedded dexteriously. *Bade Ghar ki Beti, Paap ka agnikund, Panch Pameshwar* are some of the earlier stories. One needn't bother if a certain story was first written in Urdu or Hindi. The beauty is in the narration of events and presenting a glimpse of the social fabric. During the second phase, he got some expereice and was more refined in style and form than as he was before. In the forewords of *"Prem Prasoon"* and *" Prem Dwadshi"* Premchand said unequivocally, "Now a days the meaning of narration has become more wide and spacious. In it we include love stories, tales of adventure, amazing events, travelogues, science fiction, even friends-gossip and what not." He says that a story which doesn't shed light on some part of life is not a story; it must have the element of curiosity and should be able to enrich righteousness in the readers. In the first phase the sories were more idealistic and moralistic, now he turned towards idealistic realism (*Aadershonmukh yatharthvad*). The influence of Gandhi is also prevalent in many stories. *Satyagrah, Jail, Maiku* and *Mahatirth* are some of the stories of this phase. One should remember that Premchand is neither a Marxist nor a strict follower of Gandhism. Gandhi was a spiritualist and utopian who wanted to eradicate evils of society by following the traditional, ethical and moral path but Premchand was an idealist who wanted the change in thinking. In an essay collected in Vividh Prasang (1978) we can read Premchand's disappointment and dissatisfaction with Gandhi's way of doing things and indication that Gandhi's voice is not very dependable and heard. He calls for the "despritualization of national politics."

The third phase is more intense and natural where he is able to project his characters differently. He was able to write a few short stories in which the element of satire and humour was embedded along with delineation of social evils. Along with Gandhi one can see

Marx in a few stories of this time. This is the culmination of his art and craft. When we read his story "Pisanhari *Ka Kua*" we find the little girl with all her splendor and innocence. The description of *Laila* in the story of the same title Premchand depicts her beauty comparing her with the early morning dawn. *Kafan* is the masterpiece of this phase.

Premchand is a story teller par excellance. On his 136th birthday NDTV commented very aptly, "Premchand in his writings narrated stories of India, mostly before independence. The stories draw pictures of communal and class divide during those times, however his stories are very much relevant in present times as well (31-07-2016)." Short stories in *Prem Pramod* published by Chand Press, in *Prem Dwadashi* edited by Dularelal Bhargava, and in *Prem Pratima* published by the Bhargava Book Depot of Benaras etc are just a sign of his profundity. Premchand was preoccupied with themes relating to the non-cooperation movement; to the exposure of such evils as uneven marriages, dowry system and the social hatred on those women who give birth to daughters; to the innate qualities of the poor peasantry and Harijans and to their exploitation by the moneylenders and the so-called *sadhus;* and to the wickedness of the Brahmin priestly classes. Gulzar, the film-maker and a known personality said that when he first read Premchand's works *Haj –e-Akbar* and *Idgah* while still in school, he was speechless for a while, " As a child I used to see my mother baking tanduri rotis in a particular way. When I read Premchand I felt he had written about my mother. Later, after entering the college, I read Premchand's writing in English and got an insight into the zamindari system and the gap between the rich and the poor. While making films, I could feel that Premchand was extremely observant and even described animal movements and characters in great detail."(*The Hindu, 3-5-14)*

After Premchand's death at the age of 56, a number of unpublished stories were found and his son Amrit Rai presented them as *"Gupt Dhan"* (Secret Treasure). These stories are "clothed in Hindi". Similarly Kamal Kishore Goenka brought out a collection of his stories. You can never be sure if he wrote a particular story in Hindi first or in Urdu. Alok Rai, Premchand's grandson, says, *"Aisa Lagta hai ki kai* *baatein Hindi mein jyada swabhavik dhang se kahi ja sakti hain, aur kai Urdu mein. Is pratyakksh anubhav ki jad mein kya kya chupa hua hai-itihaasik, sanskratik, samajik-purvaghah, sahityik parampara-ye shodh ka vishaaya ho sakta hai." (*It seems tha there are several subjects that look more natural in Hindi, and there are other that look good in Urdu. In the root of this direct experience, their lies hidden strands of historical, cultural, social prejudices and it can be a matter of further research.)

Gordon C Roadarmel in the Introduction of *"A Death in Delhi: Modern Hindi short stories" (1972)* rightly states that many Indian readers feel more comfortable with Premchand's stories, written in first three decades of the century which expose weaknesses in the cultural, economical, religious and social system, but which retain a strong faith in many traditional virtues and patterns of life. In the words of a Western reader, translator and Premchand scholar David Rubin, "More than half a century after Indian independence, one cannot say that Premchand's world no longer exists. Here and there the surface of things has changed but, outside the big towns and cities, it would be premature to conclude that there has been a radical transformation of the conditions of every-day life in most of the rural districts." Rakhshanda Jalil very succinctly remarked, *"The world of Premchand, at first glance, is a seemingly black and white one peopled by villains and martyrs, a bleak world of unending poverty, unbreakable caste barriers and an unyielding social order."*

Once Premchand was asked to explain how he wrote his stories. In fact, the editor of "Naurange Khayal". An Urdu magazine of Lahore put this question to a great many story writers of the country and Premchand too replied in returen. He replied with a short essay in which he maintained that every story needed to develop toward a climax of some kind:

> I do not write a story just for relating an incident. I want to depict some philosophical and emotional truth in it. Until I find some such basis my pen does not move. On finding the basis I create my characters.... I cannot write a story until and unless it is fully developed from the beginning to the end in my mind. I develop the characters from the point of view that they should be in

accordance with the story. I do not consider it necessary to make an interesting incident the basis of my story. If in a story there is a psychological climax, then it may be related to any incident, I do not care....

Recently I wrote a story in Hindi which is named *"The Queen of Heart"*. In Mohammadan History I had read an incident about Taimur's life, in which his marriage to Hamida Begam was mentioned. The dramatic aspect of this incident at once struck me. How to produce a climax in history? This became my concern. In her childhood, Hamida Begum had learnt military science from her father and had also obtained experience in the battle field. Taimur had slaughtered thousands of Turks. How was a Turkish woman enamoured of such an antagonist; the climax would emerge by sloving this problem. Taimur was not handsome, therefore, the need arose that such moral and emotional qualities be produced in him as would attract a great woman like her. This way that story was completed.

The point about the climax was an important one, and he elaborated it. He denied that a story could be created "merely by using beautiful and smart words, and a brilliant style." Rather, a story must have "a climax, and that also a psychological one." And the whole story must "move in such an order that the climax should keep on drawing nearer." In the words of one of the well-known translators and Premchand scholar Frances W. Pritchett (Essays on Premchand-1986) "any reader of Premchand's stories knows that his practice follows his theory. Characters are developed "in accordance with the story," the action moves steadily toward a climax, and the climax itself is not only "psychological" but also designed to "depict some philosophical and emotional truth." Such climaxes occur at the end of virtually all Premchand's stories. In some the climax is apparent to the characters; it is a turning point in their lives; it causes marked changes in their attitudes. *"Bare bhai sahab"* (My Elder Brother), *"Mukti-marg"* (The Path to Salvation), and *"Poos ki rat"* (A January Night) are stories of this kind. In other stories, however, the characters do not change, but merely carry their typical characters further and further until it reaches some final extreme. This extreme is so striking, so aggressive, that its impact on the reader forms a real "psychological climax" to the story. Some of Premchand's most successful pieces are of this latter kind–stories like *"Kafan"* (The Shroud) and *"Dudh ka dam"* (The Price of Milk)."

Premchand once said that "An ideal short story, must throw light on some aspect of life; it must examine critically, and courageously, the conventions of society; it must deepen the inherent instinct in man for the good, the true and the beautiful; it must quicken his sense of curiosity and must be based on a psychological truth" It is true that the stories transport us into another world of a bygone era and evoke laughter, mirth, anger, hopelessness, amusement, tears, wonder, surprise, and a number of other feelings except horror and terror. But sometimes as Prof. Ravi Ranjan says in his *"Premchand ke katha sahitya ka samajshashtra"* that we are horrified to read the depiction of villages getting neglected in the colonial India. The exploitation by the British Raj is one of the themes of Premchand's stories.

Short stories (by Premchand): Aabi-Hayat, Abhushan, Aaga Peechha, Aap Beeti, Abhllasha, Actress, Adarsh Virodh, Aadhar, Adhikar Chinta, Agni Samadhi, Ah-e-Bekas, Ahuti, Akhiri Heela, Akhri Tohfa, Algyojha, Alha, Alim-e-Be-Amal, Amavas ki Raat, Amrit, Anaath Larki, 97, Andher, Ansuon ki Holi, Anubhav, Ashk-i-Nadaamat, Atmaram, Atmasangeet, Babaji ka Bhog, Bade Baboo, Badi Behan; Bade Bhai Saheb, Bade Ghar ki Beti, Bahishkar, Balak, Band Darwaza, Bang-i-Sahr, Banka Zamindar, Bank ka Divala, Bansari, Baraat, Basi Bhat men Khuda ka Sajha, Baudam, Baz Yaft, Be Gharaz Mohsin, Betj ka Dhan, Beton vali vidhva, Bhadeka Tattoo, Bhoot, Boodhi Kaki, Buhani, Chakma, Chamatkar, Chori, Daftary, Damul ka Qaidi, Dand, Daporshankh, Darogha, Decree ke Rupaye, Deeksha, Demonstration, Devi, Dil ki Rani, Dhikkar, Dhoka, Do Bahnen, Do Bailon ki Katha, Do Bhai, Do Qabren, Do Sakhiyan, Doodh ka Dam, Doosri Shadi, Duniya ka sab se Anmol Ratan, Durasha, Durga ka Mandir, Dussahas, Eaman ka Faisla, Ek Anch ki Kasar, Fateh, Fatiha, Ghaasvali, Ghairat ki Katar, Gham Nadari Buz Bukhar, Ghar Jamai, Gila, Grihadaha, Griha Niti, Gulli Danda, Gunah ka Ago Kund, Gupta Dhan, Guru Mantra, Hajj-e- ,Akbar, Har ki Jeet, Hinsa Paramo Dharma, noli ka Upahar, Holi ki

Chhutti, Ibrat, Idgah, Inteqam, Islah, Istifa, Ishq-e-Duniya aur Hubbe Vatan, Jadu, Jail, Jehad, Jhanki, Jeevan ka Shaap, Jeevansar, Jugnu ki Chamak, Juloos, Jurmana, Jyoti, Kafan, Kamana Taru, Kaptan Saheb, Karbala, Karmon ka Phal, Kashmiri Seb, Kaushal,Kavach, Kayar, Khak-i-Parvana, Khanjar-i-Vafa, Khauf-i-Rusvai, Khoon-i-Huriat, Khoon-i-Safed, Khuchad, Khudai Fojdar, Khudi, Khuvab-i-Pareesan, Kshama, Kusum, Kutsa, Laag Dant, Laanchhan, Laanchhan, Laila, Lal Feeta, Lekhak, Lokmatka Samman, Lottery, Maan, Maiku, Mange ki Ghadi, Mamata, Manavan, Mandir, Mandir aur Masjid, Manovritti, Mantra, Mantra, Manzil-i-Maqsood, Marham, Marz-i-Mubarak, Mashal-i-Hadayat, Mata ka Hridaya, Maut aur Zindagi, Meri Pahli Rachana, Milaap, Miss Padma, Mooth, Motayram Shastri, Motayaram ki Diary, Motor ki Chhinten, Mritak Bhoj, Mrityu J.ce Pichhe, Muamma, Muft ka Yash, Muktidhan, Mukti Marg, Naadaan Dost, Nai Pooja, Nairashya, Nairashya Leela, Namak ka Daroga, Narak ka Marg, Nasha, Nauk Jhaunk, Naya Vivah, Neki ki Saza, Neyur, Nigah-i-Naaz, Nimnatran, Nirvasan, Nyaya, Pachhtava, Paipooji, Panchayat (Pancha Parameshwar), Pareeksha, Parvat Yatra, Patni se Pati, Pisanhari ka Kuan, Poos ki Raat, Prarabdha, Prayashchitta, Prem Ka Udaya, Prem ki Holi, Premsutra, Prerana, Purva Sanskar, Putra Prem, Qaidi, Qanooni Kumar, Qatil, Qati1 ki Maan, Qazaki, Qaum ka Khadim, Qurbani, Rah-i-Khidmat(Seva Marg), Rahasya, Rajhat, Raja Hardaul, Rajput ki Beti, Rajyabhakta, Ramleela, Rani Sarandha, Rasik Sampadak, Riyasat ka Diwan, Roothi Rani, Roshni, Sabhyata ka Rahasya, Sacchai ka Uphar, Sadgati, Sair-i-Dervish, Samar Yatra, Sampadak Motayram Shastri, Sar-i-Pur Ghurur, Sati, Satyagraha, Saubhagya ke Koday,Saut, Saut, Sauteli Maan, Sava ser Gehoon, Selani Bandar, Shaamati-Aimal, Shanti, Sharaab ki Dukan, Shatranj ke Khiladi, Sheikh-i-Makhmoor, Shikar, Shikari Rajkumar, Shola-i-Husn, Shuddhi, Shudra, Sig-iLaili, Sila-i-Maatam, Sirf ek Awaz, Smriti ke Pujari, Stri aur Purush, Subhagi, Suhag ka Shay, Suhag ki Sari, Sujan Bhagat, Svatva Raksha, Swami, Swang, Swarga ki Devi, Taavaan, Tagada, Tathya, Tentar, Thakur ka Kuan, Tiriya Chantra, Trisul, Tyagi ka Prem, Uddhar, Unmad, Vafa ki Devi, Yair ka Ant, Vajrapat, Veshya, Vichitra Hoti, Vidhwans, Vidrohi, Vikramaditya ka Taigha, Vinod, Vishwas, Yeh bhi Nasha voh bhi Nasha, Yehi Mera Vatan Hai, Zanjiri-Havas etc.

Prem Batisi, Prem Chalisi, Prem Chaturthi, Prem Dwadashi, Prem Pachisi, Prem Prahhakar, Prem Pramod, Prem Prasoon, Sapta Saroj,Nav Nidhi,Maan Sarovar -8 volumes are different short story collections by Premchand in which his stories are presented. Kamal Kishore Goenka and Amrit Rai also presented a few collections after getting a number of stories translated from Urdu or those that were found in due course of time. Now the number of Premchand's published stories are around 300. Once Premchand's work came under public domain there are umpteen number of publishers publishing his stories in the manner they find appropriate and marketable.

## Duniya ka sab se Anmol Ratan (1907)

*Duniya ka sab se Anmol Ratan* (the most valuable jewel in the world) is Premchand's first original short story which was written in Urdu in 1907. The language of the story is Urdu and the Persian words often make the story very difficult to follow. The story begins in the Urdu tradition but ends in the Hindu tradition. Even the names of the main characters are Dilfareb and Dilfigar – you have to ask the meaning of these words. The theme of the story is based on popular Romances which were fondly read by common folk and the underlined current of patriotism and ultimate sacrifice for the sake of the country make it worth reading even today. The precious drop of Rajput blood is the most valuable jewel which is shed in battle with a Muslim army!

Let me give you an excerpt from the story which begins as follows:

> "Disheartened and dejected, Dilfigar (the injured heart) sat under a thorny tree, shedding tears of pangs of love. He was a true devotee of the Goddess of Beauty, Queen Dilfareb (bewitcher), and not one of the classes which displayed perfumes and scents and gaudy dresses to win over the beloved or who acted as beloveds, parading as lovers. He was rather among the simple-hearted and artless lovers who undergo the tribulations of wandering through jungles and hills in search of the beloved. Queen Dilfareb, he remembered, had asked him to bring to her

court the most valuable thing in the world, if he wanted her to accept him as her lover."

Determined to win over Dilfareb, Dilfigar sets out to secure the "most valuable thing in the world." He brings the tear drop shed by a murderer, about to be hanged, on seeing a young child. "Is this drop the most valuable thing in the world?" Dilfareb says, "No." He then brings a part of the ashes of a beautiful woman sacrificing her life on the funeral pyre of her husband. The sweetheart rejects this too.

Then Dilfigar goes out and meets a young man who claims to be "the son of my mother, and the beloved of India" about to die of wounds inflicted in a battle. On learning that the lover is from a country other than his own, the mortally wounded says to him: "If you be a foreigner, come and sit on this little patch of land, stained with my blood. This is all that is mine. None but death can deprive me of this. I am sorry you have met me at a time when we are unable to play the host. The country of my forefathers has passed out of our hands. We are now stateless. We have, however, told the enemy and the aggressor that a Rajput sacrifices his life gladly for the motherland. The corpses lying about here are of those who have been killed in battle. And although I am stateless, I consider myself to be blessed to be dying in the enemy's camp." When the Persian lover applies balm to the wound, the young Rajput says: "Why have you put this balm? Let my blood flow. Don't stop it. Have I been born to live like a slave in my own country? I think it is better to die than to live the life of a slave. And there can be no better death than one in the defence of the motherland."

Tbe lover takes this drop of blood to Dilfareb, who now accepts his proposal because she is also in agreement with him "the drop of blood shed in defence of the motherland is the most valuable thing in this world."

And the story ends "All of a sudden then, the embellished curtain was rung down. He saw a bevy of pretty girls, among them Dilfareb whom even Zulekha would envy. Full of charm and grace, she sat on a gorgeous throne. Dilfigar was stunned to see her beauty; she appeared to be like a painting on the wall. Rose Dilfareb from her throne advanced towards Dilfigar and held him in her arms. The damsel's surfounding Dilfareb danced with joy and they sang. The courtiers offered presents to Dilfigar and installed him as the royal consort-the Moon and Sun put on the throne, with all honours."

*Duniya ka sabse Anmol Ratan, Sheikh-i-Makhmoor, Yehi Mera Vatall Hai, Sila-i-Maatam and Ishq-e-Duniya aur Hubbe Vatan,* were published in a collection entitled *Soz-i-Vatan* in early 1908. It was a collection of short-stories in which the theme was patriotism. The *Saraswati* magazine of Allahabad, which did not take notice of Premchand's *Prema* and *Kishna* novels too mentioned this book of short stories in its column of book reviews for December 1908. The book was banned because the British Governemnt found it biased and seditious. The CID investigation also found that the person writing under the name Navabrai was none other than a Government servant named Dhanpatrai. That is why he had to take another nom-de-plume. Navabrai was dead and the name Premchand, as suggested by his friend Nigam, was born. The pen-name "Premchand," appeared for the first time on his story *Bade Ghar ki Beti*, published in Zamana of December 1910. Francesca Orsini says that with a few, sure strokes the narrator presents the socio-economic contexts and the psycho-social characteristics of each character. The girl's father, a once rich zamindar, has dissipated all his wealth in lawyers and outward show. Anandi, one of his seven daughters, talented and well loved, is consequently forced into marry into a much humbler family, but she adjust gracefully to her new circumstances. Her husband is a typical middle class product of modern education, a clerk who commutes and mediates between town and village and who, despite his B. A., is not anglicized but rather takes part in Hindi literary-religious activities and has rather conservative views on women. His brother, by contrast, is a simple uneducated youth who spends all his time wrestling. In a pattern that will be repeated in most of his stories, Premchand takes a common, everyday occurance or a familiar social practice and shows its critical consequences while in the same time, taking in turn the points of view of all involved. Anandi's change of heart makes her bade ghar ki beti. For Premchand the mission of fiction was to bring change in the readers by presenting familiar social practices and suggesting ways to eradicate conservative practices prevalent in our society. He thought that literature could change society and the purpose of writing is to bring change.

Let me make it clear that Premchand did try to change the way and style of his stories befitting to the readers of the Hindi Heartland. It is evident from the prefaces of *"Sapt Saroj"*, *'Prem Prasoon'*, "Prem Dwadshi" . *"Mansarovar"* he wrote. On the one hand you have stories of earlier years such as *Asrar-eMa'abid* whose title was later translated by its Hindi editor as *Devasthana Rahasya* or, literally, *The Secrets of the Sanctum Sanctorum* (1903-4) *in* which the language is heavily loaded with the choicest words from Arabic and Persian:

> *Is do angusht ki zaban men vo qoowat-e-goyai au zor-e-bayan kuja ki us qudarat-ekamila ka ek shimma bhi mariz-e-bayan men la sake jisake mahaz adna ishare par yah gulzar sarapabahar wajoodpizir hua. Is deeda-e-kor men wah teziy-e-bisarat kuja ki us sana'at-eezadi ka mushahira kar sake jisaki jat se yah gunagoon khilaqut zahoor men ai.*

On the other hand, there is a story of a village goldsmith "Mahadev"in which the Hindi spiritual word *"Atma"* is in the title itself and the story is full of expressions such as *"Pran pakheru ud gaye"* Mahadeva is best known in his village for chanting at all hours of the day and night two lines from his favourite bhajan: *'Satta Gurudatta Shivadatta Data/Rama ke charan men chitta laga.'*and his parrot is described by Premchand as follows:

> The parrot would now come and settle on the top of the cage, and now sit at the door of the cage and look at its bowls for food and water, and then fly off. If the Old Man was *moha* incarnate, the parrot was incarnate *maya.* This went on till it was evening. The struggle between *maya* and *moha* was lost in the darkness.

Once asked about the way he weaves his stories and can use the language so effortlessly Premchand gave his hearty laugh and replied "'Well, I said to myself—let me write a language that will show them ...'. After a pause he added, 'After all, I am the son of a kayastha, am I not!' (Rai 1982, 347)

In *'Babaji Ka Bhog'* (A Meal for a Holy Man 1920), Ramdhan is an ordinary farmer. Though he belongs to the 'ahir' caste which is traditionally associated with cow-herding, he has no milchanimals, and has only plough-oxen. After paying his rent, debts and taxes, he has practically nothing left: 'The barn had been emptied of the crop. The moneylender had taken half and the landlord's agents had grabbed the other half, the straw had been sold to get the ox-trader off their neck. A small sack was all that fell to their share. By threshing it over and over again, they had managed to get a maund of grain out of it. Somehow or the other; they had reached the end of spring. But what about the rest of the year'! God only knew what the oxen would eat then or indeed the people of the house.'

In *'Samar Yatra'* (The Battle Journey, 1930) an old woman says: "Tell me honestly, all of you people here, have you had a full stomach anytime these past six months? ..."

*Sava Ser Gehun* (1924) is a story in which the plight of a peasant is portrayed in such as a natural way that we get s clear picture of the condition of a farmer whose land is divided and taken away by crafty system. The protagonist of the story, Shankar, has only five-sixths of an acre of land and one bullock after the division of property between him and his brother. This is not enough to ensure a livelihood so Shankar who was a "kurmi kisan"became a sort of labourer. Premchand puts in in this way: 'In the end cultivation became a means for maintaining status, livelihood depended on wage labour'. Shankar was poor, minded his own business, neither borrowed nor lent anything...He did not worry about being cheated, nor did he know the art of trickery. If food was available, he ate it, if not, he chewed grain; if even grain was not to be found, he drank water, prayed to God and went to sleep.'" He borrows some wheat from the village priest to feed a holy man and finds, after seven years, that his debt has increased two hundredfold because of interest. He has to become a bonded labourer and work without wages on the priest's land to pay off part of the debt. His son inherits both the debt and the slavery when Shankar dies in penury.

## Kafan (1936)

As it is already said that Premchand also wrote *Kafan* ("The Shroud"), in which a poor man collects money for the funeral rites of his dead wife, but spends it on food and drink. Though Premchand's last published story was *Cricket Match*, which appeared in *Zamana* in 1938, Kafan is his last story which was penned in 1936. Here is "a story of total dehumanization of man caused by poverty and privations. No other Indian writer has been able to capture the complex mood where the traces of remaining humanity get buried under a bout of frenzied hysteria. When Ghisu weeps for his wife, the father consoles him like the village priests ' be glad she's slipped out of this maze of illusion...' and they stand up, begin to sing then and all the drunkards join them. Then they started to dance, they jumped and sprang, fell back, twisted, geticulated, they mimed their feelings, and finally they collapsed, dead drunk right there."(Das 1995:270)

In the words of Frances W. Pritchett, one of the first English translators of the story "I think *kafan* is the best South Asian short story, in any language, that I've ever read. The harshness and bleakness of the story, the utter awfulness of the two characters, balanced against the (sporadic, limited, but genuine) sympathy we're forced to feel for them, and even a sort of morbidly comic effect–how far beyond the achievements of Premchand's previous stories! And above all there's the extraordinary final scene at the wine-house, in which the whole human condition seems to be held up for reflection in the light of pie-in-the-sky longings, bread-on-the-ground cynicism, touches of (sincere?) compassion, absurdity, and the wild mood swings of intoxication."

Dr T. C. Ghai who translated 18 short stories of Premchand till date commented on this story as follows, "Coming from Premchand, often a half-hearted realist and an idealist-reformist, it is an amazing story. To fully comprehend what Premchand is doing here, we should forget both realism and idealism. The straightforward and seemingly realistic narrative is very deceptive and disguises a very complex texture of meaning, which perhaps could have been achieved only through a subversion of the realistic mode. Many things in the story look improbable, unconvincing, distorted and unnatural from a purely realistic point of view. But the net result is very rewarding. Premchand is able to pack so many things in a small space using this subversive technique."

Dr Totaram Gautam collected 14 English translations of this story and found each one of these unsatisfactory and lacking in grace, poise and fiancé of the original and Prof. Harish Trivedi says that "in English translation he appears to be not even a shadow of what he is in original." The two translations of the story namely of Madan Gopal (Premchand's biographer and translator) and Princhett's (An American Professor of South Asian literature), convey the philosophical and emotional truth and psychological climax aptly according to Premchand's wish that he wanted his stories to contain *aadarshnonmukh yathard* or idealistic reality. In the words of a reviewer Sejal Mahendru(2014), " The grueling poverty, systematic oppression and heart rending pathos of the original story are retained in both the cases, showing that cultural distance does not have an impact upon the unified meaning of the work if it is taken out of the context of its production. This authenticates Bakhtin's view that the essential features of a great work of art transcend its own space, time and culture."

*An extract from the first notable translation of the story by Frances W. Pritchett follows:*

Ghisu stood up, and as if swimming in waves of joy he said, "Yes, son, she'll go to Heaven! She never tormented anyone, she never oppressed anyone; even while dying, and she fulfilled the greatest desire of our lives. If she doesn't go to Heaven, then will those fat rich people go–who loot the poor with both hands, and go to the Ganges to wash away their sin, and offer holy water in temples?"

This mood of piety too changed; variability is the special quality of intoxication. It was the turn of despair and grief. Madhav said, "But the poor thing suffered a great deal in her life. Even her death was so painful!" Covering his eyes with his hands, he began to weep, [and sobbed loudly].

Ghisu consoled him: "Why do you weep, son? Be happy that she's been liberated from this net of illusion. She's escaped from the snare; she was very fortunate that she was able to break the bonds of worldly illusion so quickly."

And both, standing there, began to sing, "Temptress! Why do your eyes flash, temptress?"

The whole wine-house was absorbed in the spectacle, and these two drinkers, deep in intoxication, kept on singing. Then they both began to dance–they leaped and jumped, fell down, flounced about, gesticulated, [strutted around]; and finally, overcome by drunkenness, they collapsed.

*"The Winding Sheet" translated by Jeffrey Krouse with Dr. Hanif Fauque (2003)*

Gheesu stood and, brimming with delight, said, "Yes, my son, she will go to heaven. She never hurt a soul. When she died, she fulfilled our greatest wish. If she doesn't go to heaven, do you think these rich snobs will? These filthy rich pigs who rob the poor with PDF created with pdfFactory trial version www.pdffactory.com both hands and then just bathe in the Ganges and pour out water for the gods in the temple to wash away their sins?" With this the mood of optimism suddenly changed, as is common when drinking, and was followed by a round of despair. "But father!" wept Mahdo. "The poor woman suffered so much in her life! She even died in pain and anguish!" Covering his face with his hands, he broke into sobs. "Why are you crying, son?" said Gheesu. "Be happy that she was set free from the delusions of this world. She left all these troubles behind. She must have been a real saint to die so young!" With that the two of them stood and began to sing: O you deceitful seductress! Why do you beguile us with your charms? Everyone in the bar was captivated by the spectacle as the two men went on singing in a drunken stupor. They began first to dance, acting out every detail of the song by their gestures, then to jump and cavort; Gheesu stood and, brimming with delight, said, "Yes, my son, she will go to heaven. She never hurt a soul. When she died, she fulfilled our greatest wish. If she doesn't go to heaven, do you think these rich snobs will? These filthy rich pigs who rob the poor with both hands and then just bathe in the Ganges and pour out water for the gods in the temple to wash away their sins?" With this the mood of optimism suddenly changed, as is common when drinking, and was followed by a round of despair. "But father!" wept Mahdo. "The poor woman suffered so much in her life! She even died in pain and anguish!" Covering his face with his hands, he broke into sobs. "Why are you crying, son?" said Gheesu. "Be happy that she was set free from the delusions of this world. She left all these troubles behind. She must have been a real saint to die so young!" With that the two of them stood and began to sing: O you deceitful seductress! Why do you beguile us with your charms? Everyone in the bar was captivated by the spectacle as the two men went on singing in a drunken stupor. They began first to dance, acting out every detail of the song by their gestures, then to jump and cavort, then dead drunk on the floor.

In "*Itihas aur Alochana*" (1957; History and Literary Criticism) by Namvar Singh there is an essay on Premchand "*Vyapakata aur Gaharai*" (Breadth and Depth, or The Extensive and the Intensive) and he says "It is often the case that if a writer is clear as a running brook he is called shallow and if he is turgid, profound. *Kafan* and several other stories by Premchand reveal that he has breadth and depth both in abundance."

For Premchand the point about the climax was an important one. He was not inagreement with the thought that a story could be created "merely by using beautiful and smart words, and a brilliant style." Rather, a story must have "a climax, and that also a psychological one." And the whole story must "move in such an order that the climax should keep on drawing nearer." Frances W. Pritchett presents the example of the story "The Chess player" in "The Chess Players: From Premchand to Satyaajit Ray" as follows:

> By comparison to Ray's film, however, Premchand's story is finally almost invigorating. Premchand removes himself so far from Lucknowi culture, and judges it so harshly and insistently, that the reader never really enters imaginatively into its death throes. Lucknow is falling apart, and the British pick up the pieces; there is no hint in the Hindi story that the British have acted in a

particularly shabby or unexpected way. (Here again, the Urdu story is more detailed and accuses the British of premeditated treachery. Premchand has a firm grip on moral truth. Lucknow has succumbed to *vilasita*, it is dying, it is dead—and serves it right, too. The best use we can make of Lucknow is to learn from its fate, and never be guilty of the same shameful political apathy ourselves. Yet after all this has been said, it is Premchand, rather than Ray, who is ready to offer a sort of epitaph for Lucknow: his chess players "were *vilasi*, but they were not cowards." There was something there after all to admire. Premchand judges, he condemns, but he can also praise. Ray does neither. Premchand takes great pains to prepare us a "psychological climax," while Ray takes equal pains to deny us one. Climax gives way to anticlimax, with fifty years of the twentieth century in between.

Premchand published Shatranj ke Khilari (The Chess Players) in the magazine Madhuri in September-October, 1924. Since then it has seen several translations/transcreations and one cinematic adaptation. The first was Premchand's own, re-titled in Urdu as Shatranj Ki Bazii (A Game of Chess) and published sometime before 1928 in his anthology of short stories Khavab-o-Khayal Ki Kahaniyan kî (Stories of Dreams and Visions). Several cross-cultural translations have been brought out in English, before and since, most of them bearing the title The Chess Players. David Rubin's translation is one of them.

Here is an extract from the concluding part of the story "The Chess Players" translated by David Rubin:

> The two friends drew the swords from their belts. It was s chivalric age when everybody went around carrying swords, daggers, poniards and the like. Both of them were sensualists but not cowards. They were politically debased, so why should they die for king or kingdom? But they did not lack personal courage. They challenged one another formally, the swords flashed; there was a sound of clanging. Both fell wounded, and both writhed and expired on the spot. They had not shed a single tear for their king but gave up their lives to protect a chess queen.

Darkness was coming on. The Chess game had been set up. The two kings each on his throne sat there as though lamenting the death of these two heroes.

Silence appeared over all. The broken archways of the ruins, the crumbling walls and dusty minarets looked down on the corpses and mourned.

There are not less than 300 stories and a separate book is required to deal with all of them. I fail to do justice with him and have to satisfy myself with this much.

## Playwright Premchand

Premchand is a novelist and story teller. He is not a dramatist in the sense as William Shakespeare is. But undoubtedly his narration and dialogues have dramatic effect. It seems, in his childhood he was very fond of Ramlila and wrote an skit to make fun of sexual habits of an uncle. He wrote a skit : *Honhar Birwan ke chikne chikne pat* when he was barely fourteen years of age. Let me give you a glimpse of a skit played in the novel "Godaan". It is a hilarious comedy with short and pungent dialogues. It is a farcical drama staged by the villagers. A poor farmer knocks the door of a wealthy thakur. He is crest fallen and weak. He implores and prays for some financial help. The thakur after much dilly-dallying agrees to lend him rupees ten. The farmer is asked to put his thumb impression on a promissory note prepared by the thakur. The poor farmer signs on the dotted lines. Thakur then gives him a five rupee note. The farmer is taken aback. He signed for 10 but got only 5.

"But they are only five, master," he says.

"They are not five; they are ten. Go home and count them again."

"No master, they are really five."

"One rupee as your nazrana,"

"Yes, master."

"One rupee for writing the note."

"Yes, master."

"One rupee for the government paper."

"Yes, master."

"One rupee as the dasturi?"

"Yes, master."

"One rupee as interest."

"Yes, master."

"And five rupees in cash. All these do add up to ten or not?"

"Then, master, please keep these five, too, with you for me."

"What a fool you are!"

"No, master. One rupee as nazar to the senior thakurani."

"one rupee for her pan-beeda."

"One rupee as nazar to the junior thakurani and another for her pan~beeda."

"The balance, one rupee, for your last rites."

Dramas are of two types, one for reading and the other for staging. Premchand's dramas are meant to be read and not for being staged. Roughly speaking they are closets of a kind. Some of his renowned plays include **Karbala, Tajurba, Prem Ki Vedi, Roohani Shadi,** and **Sangram**. National Council for Promotion of Urdu Language (Kulliyat- e- Premchand - Volume 15) published his plays under the editorship of Madan Gopal in 2010. Some of his plays are either translations or based on writings in European languages. Most of the writing of Premchand was in Hindi/Urdu and he usually translated them vice versa.

## Sangram

Sangram is one of the plays written by Premchand. There is a comparative study of village and city life in it. The problems posed here are similar to what he delineates in Premashram. In a sentence the theme of the play can be as follows, "Until the time we get swaraj, our conditions won't improve." The all powerful Zamindars and helpless peasants are at daggers drawn. Unless the zamindars follow the path of dharma the condition of farmers can not improve. Not only they but the whole system- the police, Zamindars' agents, bureaucracy, all are there to exploit the farmers. The British government officials are also hand in gloves with the oppressors. This is a drama in which the dramatist also portrays those Indians who are the agents of the British government and try to win the favour of their masters by informing them about those who are in league with those who wish to bring the downfall of the British empire. There are petty officials who lead a life of luxary and there are others who are oppressed and suppressed and lead a miserable life.

The drama takes the reader to understand that the highest kind of sin is lust for woman. It leads to nowhere and those who commit this sin are left in the lurch. The lusty behavior for a woman leads Sabal Singh to a mirage. It is a desert with no desert-crossing. All his sense of propriety goes hayware and he is destined to doom. He has to repent for his deeds and go for a pilgrimage as penance. The theme of the play is very similar to that of another novel Premashram and we find that Sabal Singh is like Mayashankar of Premashram but Premchand wanted to try his hand in this field also. That is why one of the reviewers wrote in Saraswati magazine, "even though we cannot refute the author's view, we are convinced that, if he had wished, Premchand could have written it as a novel."

Sabal Singh, the village Zamindar, is kind and gentle up to the time when he looks at the wife of a farmer and wants to seduce her. Haldhar's wife Rameshwari is kept by him after he gets the poor farmer arrested. The charges are flimsy. The ground is concocted but the power of the zamindar is supreme. All are helpless before him. Not only Sabal Singh but his brother Kanchan Singh also is in the league to get Rameshwari. In this way there are three men for a lady.

There is another prominent character in the play. Sadhu Baba Chetan Das is a slave in the hands of lust. He is Sadhu in name only. Nothing saint like will you find in his character. He preaches what he never practices. He preaches that "it is the duty of a Kshatriya to wage a battle for land, wealth and woman, all of which are for the man who can take them through force and might. And in this battle, all thoughts of piety, dharma, enlightenment, prestige and status are tantamount to cowardice." In a word, we can call him a "fraud".

After reading the play like all other readers you will also be surprised and ask why after all Premchand wrote this play. I never heard someone tried to present it on the stage. Yes, Premchand must have thought that the story-line was such that a drama would be better than a novel. As far as the characterization of a number of characters is concerned a few characters stand out and shine. There is no doubt that the drama is entertaining and educative. According to Premchand, the plot of the story was such as would lend itself to treatment only through a drama. But according to Saraswati's reviewer, however, "even though we cannot refute the author's view, we are convinced that, if he had wished, Premchand could have written it as a novel."

## Karbala

Karbala is a drama written by a Hindu. Karbala is not history but a historical drama. It is not a play to be enacted on the stage. The aim of the drama, and of the principal character's portrayal, is to make the Hindus pay a tribute to Hazrat Hussain. When Khwaja Hassan Nizami, a Muslim, wrote a biography of Lord Krishna, it was considered that a Muslim had paid his tribute to Lord Krishna; therefore Hindu critics lauded his attempt. On the other hand when Premchand attempted to write a drama on the life of a Muslim it was neither lauded by many Muslims nor liked by Hindus of his time. *"In musalman harijanan par kotin hindun variye"* (Let us sacrifice scores of Hindus on these Muslims) said Bhartendu after reading Raskhan. But no Muslim said anything of such type for any Hindu. That is why all talk about Hindu Muslim unity remained mere talk and India had to be divided. "*Karbala*" was sold in Hindi but there was no one to publish it in Urdu because it was thought that it might hurt the feelings of Shiyas. Nobody thought that the purpose of the play was to cement the bond between the two communities. However, it took two years before the Urdu version of the drama could be completely serialised in Zamana, i.e. from July 1926 to April 1928. Before publication in Urdu, Nigam wrote to Premchand that he should not write anything which would hurt the feelings of Shias, Premchand replied: "You can rest assured that I have been extremely careful to ensure that no disrespect of any sort is shown to them.

Every single word has been weighed carefully, so that the religious susceptibilities of Muslims are not injured. The purpose of the drama is political-to cement the bonds of Hindu-Muslim unity." He further replied, "I read the life of Hazrat Hussain. His zest for martyrdom moved me and I felt like paying a tribute. The result was this drama. If Muslims do not concede to Hindus even the right to pay tribute to Muslim caliphs and imams, I am not keen either."

## Prem Ki Vedi

Prem Ki Vedi is more like a one act play. Premchand takes up the problems arising out of inter religious marriage. He wants to discuss the obstructive role of religion in marriage. That is why he takes up a number of characters who are Hindus and Christians. Miss Jenny, Mrs Garden, Mr William is on the one hand and Mr Yograj and his wife Uma on the other. After Uma's death, Yograj loves a Christian girl who is very liberal and broadminded. The girl, in fact, is his late wife's friend and Yograj somehow looks in her the reflection of his wife. She gets attracted to Yograj when she goes to console him. But she doesn't want him to convert into Christianity for the sake of marriage. Yograj wants to marry her at any cost. He doesn't bother about religion and society but both of them can not meet unless one of them converts. Ultimately they couldn't live happily ever after in the wedlock of marriage and Yograj dies due to his unfulfilled desire of marrying her. Premchand is an out and out idealist in this play and all the characters are just his mouthpiece. The theme of the play can be expressed in a sentence as follows: The ways of wealth, knowledge and materialism can lead to strife, but the way of God is love and that is what one should accept.

## Chapter - 4

# The Engaged Intellectual Premchand

Prof. Francesca Orsini (Professor of Hindi and South Asian Literature at South Asia Section, School of Languages, Cultures and Linguistics), an author and researcher describes Premchand as *the engaged intellectual* taking an active part in all the debates of the day and sharing hardly anything with Hindi intellectuals of his time neither their deep allegiance to the glorious Aryan past nor their consequent alienation from the history of Indo-Muslim rule. Ruth Vanita, another prominent Premchand scholar (The *Co-wife and Other Stories*) puts Premchand in an animated way, "there are many other Premchands, some of them less in tune with modern progressive tastes- the Gandhian Premchand, the Hindu Premchand, the Romantic Premchand, the Conservative moralist Premchand. Reading the three hundred or so stories collected in *mansarovar* is an instructive experience, not only for the number of stories of indifferent quality that one encounters but also for the unexpectedly wide range of plots, themes and genres and for the recognition when one recreates the immortal ones, like "The Shroud" (Kafan), "Voice of God" (Panch Parmeshwar) and "The Winter's Tale" (Poos ki raat)." In the same articulated way Harish Trivedi wrote an oft-quoted paper – *Hindi Premchand, Urdu Premchand.* There is a Dalit Premchand also and his Dalitism is beyond any doubt. It is not *sahanubhuti* but *swanubhuti*.

Premchand took an active part in all the debates and discussions and commented on burning issues of his time. In this chapter an attempt has been made to present multifaceted, versatile and the engaged intellectual Premchand in different avatars such as Dalit Premchand, Educationist Premchand, Journalist Premchand, Translator Premchand, Translated Premchand, Feminist Premchand, Islamophile Premchand, English Premchand and Hindi -Urdu Premchand...

## Dalit Premchand

In 1936, Premchand announced at the conference of All India Progressive Writer's Assocaition:

> It is the duty of a writer to protect and argue in favour of those who are oppressed, sufferers, deprived, whether they are individuals or a group.
>
> ('jo dalit hain, pirit hain, vanchit hain, chahe vah vyakti ho ya samuh, uski himayat aur vakalat karna sahityakar ka farz hai.')

Sympathy with the underdog is perhaps Premchand's most characteristic feature and victimization of the powerless is the recurring theme of his stories and novels. But many Dalit writers and critics often complain that Premchand is too rhetorical and insensitive to Dalit issues and blame him for lampooning of Dalit characters. They cite the example of his story ' *Kafan*' and say that the Dalit characters are shown in poor light and they are projected as being stereotypes or representatives of the entire community. "The caste is deliberately imposed on character. It is being tried to portray that being from cobbler community, it explains that they are lethargic, slothful, work-shy, and notorious. In his words, it was the community of cobblers *(chamar)* that was notorious in whole village." (Mazumdar: 2012: 219). V. B. Rawat in "*Premchand and his Dalit writings*" claims that in *"kafan"* Premchand made all chamars look like they were kammchors. Similarly Akira Takahashi, Osaka University of Foreign Studies, poses a rider, "none of the researches and biographical works on Premchand and his literature has told us that he had an adult friend from the so-called "untouchable" castes through whom he tried to know their pitiful plights firsthand. Judging from the cursory and arbitrary descriptions seen in his works, we cannot escape the conclusion that he knew about their realities only superficially and conceptually." But when we read some of his stories such as "*Quzaki*" and "Gulli *Danda*" we find that he had some friendship in his childhood with the Dalits. Ruth Vanita counter-argues that it is not so because the woman described in this story is extremely hardworking and efficient and she is also a chamar. Giving a talk on *'Sociology of Literature: Insights from Hindi Novels'* at the *Bihar Virasat Vikash Samiti* in Patna, Subhas Sharma pointed out that Premchand, though born and brought up in an upper caste family, depicted a blind illiterate and poor Dalit Surdas as the central character in his novel *'Rangbhumi'* (TOI, 23-12-13). Premchand expresses the pains and helplessness of common men in their language and the aim is not to provoke them or incite them to attempt *hara-kiri* as they were being subjected to social and political untouchabilty of their times. His characters are from the poorest of the poor who are replete with insatiable desire to better their lives. Yes, the thoughts of a Marx and a Gandhi are in the background but they are ahead of them. The spirit with which Surdas directs his little kin Midhua is worth reading again and again:

> Where will we live now, Dada?
> We will construct another hut.
> And if someone again puts it on fire?
> We shall build it again.
> If someone does it a thousand times?
> We shall continue constructing for a thousand times.

This is the message the novel "Rangabhumi" given to the young and not the message which is believed to be given by some section of our society. How can a word or a form of address incite others to insult? It is insulting on our part to condemn Premchand because he used a certain expression of his time and was unaware of the rage of a few persons after 80 years of the publication of his novel. The kind of commotion which was created on Premchand's birthday in 2004 when nearly 25 copies of this hefty novel were burnt in Delhi just to show that a novelist creates a world of his own based on his experiences and imagination. There are a number of characters in Premchand who belong to the so called upper caste and are mean and wicked. Don't you remember the story "Sava *Ser Gehun*" in which the character Vipr is the villain? Premchand's comment in the end is worth repeating "This world is full of such viprs and farmers." That is why when Premchand is read with preconceived notions, the reading remains incomplete and partial. I too studied Rangabhumi in my childhood and never got into the kind of thinking. The character of Surdas will move you every time you read the novel and I have no hesitation to say that he is more powerful than Shakespeare's King Lear. The only thing required from the reader is "ripeness" and "maturity".

It should also be added here that Premchand in most of his stories shows Dalits as hardworking and noble, oppressed but God fearing. Look at the stories such as *Thakur ka kua* and *Poos ki raat* and you will agree with me. For instance, In *Poos ki raat* the protagonist Halku is a hard working farmer who is unable to make both ends meet, exactly like what Ghisu and Madhav resist to become in "*Kafan*". Halku is not lazy. He is not a miser. He doesn't buy a blanket just to keep the money to pay his debts. He is efficient and expert, responsible and responsive but unable to withstand hunger and winter. The reader can very well understand his plight and the reason of his inaction, similarly as he understands the indolence and inaction of the father and son duo in "Kafan". ("If Ghisu worked one day, he would take three off. Madhav was such a loafer that whenever he worked for half an hour he'd stop and smoke his pipe for an hour"). One is responsible but not responsive; the other is irresponsible and inresponsive. You don't condemn any of them but the element of pity is different for each of them.

It is interesting to note according to a newspaper article published in *The Hindu* (13-9-13) by Kuldeep Kumar that "When he was alive, Premchand was the target of fierce and abusive attacks from Brahmins and other upper castes because of his sympathetic portrayal of the oppressed lower castes and untouchables. He was dubbed as "anti-Brahmin" by his upper caste detractors who accused him of spreading hatred against them. It's an irony of fate that the same Premchand is being dubbed as "anti-Dalit" these days by many Dalit writers and critics."

Shrinath Singh, an upper caste, wrote a number of polemical articles in *Saraswati* against Premchand during his life time. Mr Singh quoted a number of passages from his short story *Sadgati* (1931) and said that if in fifty years from then, Premchand's books were to be taken as representative of this age, readers of his books would then think that Hindus of this age, and in particular the Brahmins, "led a life full of hatred ... that the Brahmins of India were the most tyrannical, selfish, hypocritical and deserved to be hated." A Brahmin member of the Hindi Sahitya Sammelan of Allahabad, asked Ram Vriksha Benipuri, "why he, a Brahmin, was getting mixed up with the supporters of a Kayastha (Premchand)!" When we watch the film adaptation of the story Sadgati directed by Satyajit Ray we are really overwhelmed with a mixed of emotions. Hatred and anger for others but pity and sympathy for Dukhi played by Om Puri.

In Sadgati (Deliverance, 1931) Premchand gives us a detailed description of how an untouchable tanner, Dukhi, makes gifts to a Brahmin. 'We'll put the offerings on a leaf. But don't you touch it. Take Jhuri, the Gond's daugher to the village shop. Make a full offering. A seer of flour, half a seer of rice, a fourth of lentils, and eighth of ghee and four annas at the edge of the leaf ... You don't touch anything, or everything will be ruined.'

The untouchable is not allowed even on to the verandah of the Brahmin's house. The Brahmin's wife says to her husband "... you forget caste rules. A washerman, a tanner or a bird shooter can't come into the house with his head held high. Is this a Hindu's house or a hotel?'

The Brahmin and his wife express the majority opinion of the village:'These people eat anything, clean or unclean, without worrying about it ... They're all polluted.'

When Dukhi dies while splitting wood for the Brahmin, most of the villagers are only concerned that his corpse is polluting the way to the village well. No tanner will remove his body for fear of the police so the Brahmin has to do it himself.'

... How could a Brahmin lift up a tanner's corpse! It was forbidden in the scriptures and no one could deny it ... So the Brahmin got out a rope. He made a noose at the end, managed to get it over the dead man's feet and drew it tight...He grabbed the rope and dragged the corpse out of the village. Having returned home, he immediately bathed, read prayers to Durga and sprinkled Ganges water round the house...

Madan Gopal wrote that Premchand didn't bother about the propaganda and gave befitting reply to these fierce polemicists. He continued writing against the so called upper caste Hindus, mainly the associates of Varnashram Swarajya Sangh. Through his articles in *Jagaran*, "he lifted the curtain from the hideous way the Hindu dead bodies are treated before and during cremation; he exposed the deceit of the sadhus and mahatmas, the hypocrisy of the priests and mahants and the debauchery in the temples, the fraud of the yagnas and havans to cheat the honest and the simplehearted folk." What would be the response of Sumnakshar and his ilk who wanted Premchand banned in 2004?

Kamal Kishore Goenka in an article *"Premchand ka Dalit-Vimarsh"* published in *Bahuvachan (* July – September 2014) calls him *"a literary messiah of Dalit upliftment"* and says that long before Gandhiji raised this issue Premchand wrote stories such as " *Dono Tarf se*" in 1908 underlining Dalit cause. Even his mini story *"Rashtr ka Sevak"* is an out and out Dalit literature. Out of Premchand's 300 stories not less than 40 belong to Dalit Consciousness. One can see his short comments in *Jagaran* and detailed articles in *Zamana* and *Hans* and find that he is very critical of the so called upper caste Hindus and is always with the Dalits and the Wretched of the Earth.

Here is a list of 40 stories provided by Kamal Kishore Goenka (2014: 18) in which the theme is Dalit centred:

1. Dono Taraf Se (March, 1911) 2. Sirf Aik Aavaj (August-September 1913)3. Banka Jamidar (October, 1913) 4. Anath Larki (June, 1914) 5. Khoon Safed (July 1914) 6. Apni Karni (September – October 1914), 7. Maha Teerth (September 1917), 8. Pashu se Manushya (January 1920) 9. Ruhe Hayat (January, 1921) 10. Vidhvansh (25 July 1921)11. Muuth (January, 1922), 12. Lokmat ka Samman (October 1922)

13. Sailani Bandar (February 1914)14. Sobhagya ke Kode (June 1924) 15. Sava ser Gehun (November 1924) 16. Sabhyata ka Rahasya (February 1925) 17. Shudra (December 1925)18. Mantra (February 1926)19. Kajaki (April 1926) 20. Lanchan (August 1926) 21. Mandir (May 1927) 22. Matara (March, 1928) 23. Khudi (1928), 24. Prem Ka Uday (August 1929) 25. Ghasvali (December 1929), 26. Samar Yatra (April 1930), 27. Maiku (June 1930) 28. Devi (1930), 29. Rashtra ka sevak (1930), 30. Sadgati (1930), 31. Khel (April 1931), 32. Tawan (September 1931)33. Thakur ka Kuvan (24 August 1932) 34. Roshni (November 1932) 35. Gulli Danda (February 1933)36. Balak (April 1933) 37. Dudh ka Dam (July, 1934) 38. Devi (April 1935)39. Kafan (December 1935) 40. Jurmana (1936)

*Rastra Ka Sevak (The Servant of the Nation)*

The servant of the nation said: There is only one way for the freedom of the nation and that is the conduct of brotherhood with the downtrodden and the treatment of equality with the oppressed and lower caste.

The whole world praised him: What a broad vision! What an emotional heart!

His beautiful daughter Indira too heard him and started thinking deeply.

The servant of the nation embraced the lower caste young man in public.

The world said: He is a farista, a messiah, the protector of the nation.

Indira saw it and her face began to shine.

The servant of the nation took the lower caste youngman to the temple, had *darshan* of the deity and declared: Our god is in poverty, in the Wretched of the Earth.

The world praised: What a pious heart! What a noble soul!

Indira looked at him and smiled.

She went to the servant of the nation and pleaded: Respected father, I want to marry Mohan.

> The servant of the nation looked at her daughter with love and affection and asked: Who is Mohan?
>
> Indira replied with utmost enthusiasm: Mohan is the same young man you hold in your arms, took to the temple and one who is truthful, brave and gentle.
>
> The servant of the nation looked at her with burning eyes and turned his face away.
>
> (Reprinted in *Gupt Dhan* Page 80, translated by Gopal Sharma)

According to Mamta Kalia (2009) When Premchand was writing about the have-nots of society, there was no specific bracket of Dalit thought in literature. Modern day analysis has resulted in making this a whole area of social concern. "*Producing Dalit Texts in English*" is full of pitfalls and dangers in the words of Julia Perczel as expressed through her thesis submitted in 2014 to the Central European University, Budapest (Hungary). Barbara Harlow in "Resistance *Literature" (*1987) codifies the shared aesthetic and ideological foundations of resistance literatures and emphasizes that resistance literature calls attention to itself and to literature in general as a political and poloticized activity. Laura R. Brueck devotes an entire chapter of her recent book, "*Writing Resistance: The Rhetorical Imagination of Hindi Dalit Literature* (2014), to analyze the complicated reception of Premchand by Dalit writer-activists- that is, by those who have come in to consciousness ( *Chetna*) about the pervasive oppressiveness of the caste system. Brueck opens her books with a descritption of the burning of Premchand's novel, Rangbhumi(1925), at a public park in the center of India's capital, New Delhi. On July 2004, BDSA publicly burned multiple copies of Rangbhoomi, claiming that the novel is offensive to Dalits and dangerous to the 'soft minds' of young students who may become biased against Dalits as the protagonist of the novel Surdas is repeatedly called "Surdas Chamar" (and the result of these movements was that one fine morning NCERT removed this controversial( ?) word from their course book.) This is also to be noted that Om Prakash Valmiki and other Dalit writers continuously used this word because as Sharan Kumar Limbale wrote in his book,

"Towards an Aesthetics of Dalit Literature", "The reality of Dalit literature is distinct and so is the language of this reality. It is the uncouth-impolite language of Dalits. This language does not recognize cultivated gestures and grammar. Standard language has a class. Dalit writers have rejected the class of this standard language. Dalit writers have rejected the validation of standard language by the cultured classes because it is arrogant." "The Dalit community rejects the social organisation of the high caste society. In the same way it also rejects the ideology connected with this social organisation, the tradition connected with this ideology and the literature that is born out of this tradition. The dalit is absent, invisible, excommunicated, and repressed in the creative imagination of the writers of such literature." This statement adds insult to an injury. It has been written by Purushottam Satyapremi in, *"Dalit Sanskriti ki Avadharana ka Pranadhaar Dalit Sahitya" (1998*) and can't be ignored. You can read Christopher R. King's 2010 translation, *Rangbhumi: The Arena of Life*, to understand the wide context of such critiques. In fact, the event was staged to raise awareness about the ways mainstream society unthinkingly colludes with an upper-caste mindset and ultimately condones caste-based discrimination. In her discussion, Brueck uses the example to pose more general questions about the vexed relationship of politics to aesthetics in literary criticism and comments "a towering icon of Modern Hindi literary mainstream, Premchand has also come to inhabit special and more contested terrain in the Hindi Dalit literary sphere in subsequent years."The Dalit aesthetic principle of *Dalit Chetna* has been variously applied to exclude Premchand's writings from inclusion in the field of Dalit literature. As Premchand was not a Dalit by birth or caste, he was said to be unaware of real Dalit experience and he is just sympathetic to the Dalit cause. Sharan Kumar Limbale (2004) clarifies that Dalit Literature is writing about Dalit by Dalit writers with a Dalit Consciousness. K. Srinivasulu asserts that Dalitness denotes "a community of oppressed castes with specific experience of being treated as untouchables and being humiliated through the conscious denial of self-respect and honour by the caste Hindus" . Kanval Bharti says that Premchand's writing cannot be considered Dalit literature, which is based on Dalit consciousness (Chetna) and a struggle for social transformation.

In his words, "I am not saying that Premchand was against Dalits or that I am against Premchand. Only that when doing an evaluation of Premchand as part of Dalit literature, it should be according to Dalit consiciousness and thus Dalit writers' remarks on Premchand are based on and show respect for the authority of Dalit consciousness."

That is why Namvar Singh says, "Look at the time when he was writing, at that time Dalits were not struggling. He couldn't foresee this fight for Dalit cause. So he writes out of sympathy (Sahanubhuti*).*"Vir Bharat Talwar and Ramnika Gupta also tried to underline the fact that Premchand's Dalit characters show struggle and radicalism of high order. For example, in Godan there are a group of people who thrust a cow's bone into the mouth of Matadin Pandit who was accused of molsting a Dalit girl named Siliya. The episode is a stark example of caste- transgression, and a confrontation over it provokes one of the more disturbing scenes in Premchand's novel:

> Siliya's father Harkhu was an old man of sixty, dark and thin, wrinkled as a dried pepper and just as biting. 'There's no trouble, thakur. Today we'll either make a chamar out of Matadin or shed his blood along with our own. Siliya is a woman, and she has to go live with some man or other. We have no objection to that, but whoever takes her must become one of us. You can't make Brahmins out of us, but we can make chamars out of you. If you're willing to make us Brahmins, our whole community is agreeable. As long as that's not possible, then become chamars. Eat with us, drink with us and live with us. If you're going to take away our honour, then give us your caste.'
>
> Datadin raised his stick. 'Control your tongue, Harkhu. Your girl's over there. Take her anywhere you please. We haven't tied her down. She worked and she got paid. There's no shortage of labourers around here.'
>
> Siliya's mother shook her finger at him. 'Bully for you, pandit! You're being terribly fair! I'd like to see you talk that way if your daughter had run off with a chamar. We're chamars, though, so of course we don't have any honour! We're not taking Siliya away alone. We're taking Matadin with her–the one who ruined her.

> You're so pious–you'll sleep with her, but you won't drink water from her hands. No one but this bitch would tolerate all that. I'd have poisoned such a man.'
>
> 'Didn't you hear what these people are saying?' Harkhu challenged the group with him. 'What are you standing there gaping for?
>
> At this, two of the chamars sprang forward and grabbed Matadin's hands while a third tore off his sacred thread. Before Datadin and Jhinguri Singh could wield their sticks, two chamars had stuffed a big piece of bone in Matadin's mouth. Matadin clenched his teeth but the abominable thing caught between his lips all the same. Overcome by nausea, he opened his mouth involuntarily–and the bone slipped inside.
>
> The vomiting over, Matadin stretched out almost lifeless on the ground as though his back were broken, as though he only wanted a cupful of water in which to drown himself. The ritual propriety which had allowed him to flaunt his passion and his pride had been wiped out. That piece of bone had polluted not only his mouth but also his soul. His religion depended on absolute purity in eating and drinking; not that righteousness had been cut off at the root. (305-306)

You will appreciate that Premchand allows a kind of change of heart when Matadin not only accepts Siliya's aborted child and cremates it but also says in a philosophicizing manner, "He who does his duty is a true Brahmin and he who doesn't is a chamar."

In a paper on *"Premchand's Eternal Contribution to Dalit Literature*" (2014) Shruti Jain and Anuj Kushwaha maintain that he never glued a message onto a piece of fiction rather he documented Dalit's history, poverty, helplessness, the way difference was enforced on them and its psychological outcome in their own words and language. We think that by not letting the reader know the usual message at the end of the novel, the reader gets more than just receiving the simple message (that one should not mistreat the lower caste people, that Dalit should be considered the part of social – egalitarian society and should be given equal rights and so on).

In the words of Talwar (2000) "Whatever influence of Gandhiji on Premchand, in Godan the aggressive act of putting the bone into Matadin's mouth shows the influence not of Gandhi but of Ambedkar. If Ambedkar's ideology is a central tenant of Dalit literary aesthetics, Premchand is very much a Dalit Writer." There is no doubt that Premchand was born before casteism in Hindi literature was born and flourished and the autobiographies of Dalits were noticed by us. Their English translations underlined that it was not *Sahanubhuti* ((sympathy) which was the hallmark but *Svanubhuti* ( self experience) which was found to be more important in Dalit Chetna.

Again, if you take Namvar Singh's words as the new understanding, it was said by him at Kathakram Samman Samaroh - 2009 that Premchand's stories are not the stories of rural life as svanubhuti but a depiction of it by an outsider as the life of village folk was not as miserable as depicted by Premchand. Take a remarkable story to counter all such arguments. There is a Ghaswali in the story 'Ghaswali'. Her name is Mulia. She is a poor Dalit woman who is sexually harassed by the upper caste landowner Chain Singh. He is in the habit of seducing women and thinks that it is his birth right to do so as the so called lower caste women are for use and misuse. He never imagines that these insignificant women can ever say 'no' to him. He is eager to win Mulia but she refuses his advances. She not only says no to him but also asks him to see reason: *'agar mera aadmi tumhari aurat se is tarah baten karta, to tumhe kaisa lagta? ... mujhse daya mangte ho, isliya na ki main chamarin hoon, neech jati hoon aur neech jati ki aurat zara-si ghurki-dhamki ya zara-se lalach se tumhari muthi mein aa jayegi. Kitna sasta sauda hai! Thakur ho na, aisa sasta sauda kyon chorne lage?'* (If my man would have talked to your wife the same way, how would you have felt... You ask me for kindness, because I am a chamarin, from a low caste, and a low caste woman is easy to win either by threats or by small temptation. What a cheap bargain it is! You are a Thakur. Why would you give up such an inexpensive deal?)

Mulia is a Dalit character created by Premchand to stress the need to protest and rebel against the so called traditional mind-set. He shows that Chain Singh ultimately changes himself.

Just one more example should suffice to make the reader understand that it is not necessary to be a Dalit reader to understand and feel like a Dalit. The experiences of Mulia, Ghisu, and Madhav, Surdas or other such characters are not your experience. It is not my experience too. I am a professor of English in a foreign country, though I was born in the same district in which Om Prakash Valmiki was born. When I read Chinua Achebe, things do not fall apart. I understand. Similarly the rhythm and resonance of a Dalit's life may differ with my experience as I am outside of it or I am "other" another. But once I enter in the realm of fancy even for a moment and the story gives me access to the world of another experience, I am a changed man. In the words of Henri Lefevre, "the rhythm of the everyday differs from the one which these individuals inhabit; it is incomprehensible to those who are outside it; the reader has momentary access through the story. His moment of empathy is the product of an aesthetic intervention. The story allows the reader to be insider enough to experience this rhythm, and outsider enough to comprehend it."

It will not be out of place to add here in the context of the current Dalit discourse on Premchand in which experts(?) label Premchand as *"Samanto Ka Munshi"( an agent of feudalism)*and a *Kayasth* conditioned by birth as anti-Dalit. They overplay his essays such as "*Mahajani Sabhyata*" wherein he propounded, according to his biographer Madan Gopal (1964: 448) the thesis that the old social orders based on feudalism and imperialism, which imposed disadvantages and disabilities on the common people, had a brighter side too. The individual in those orders retained his qualities of head and heart. Even the tyrant king and the extortionate zamindar were capable of showing kindness and mercy. This essay is Premchand's last testament. He wanted the zamindar as well as the moneylender, all who sucked the blood of the poor, to be eliminated.

B. R. Ambedkar, who chaired the committee that drafted India's democratic constitution, concluded his presentation with a powerful pointer: "On the 26th January 1950 (the founding of the Indian Republic with its new constitution), we are going to enter into a life of contradictions. In politics we will have equality and in social and economic life we will have inequality." Therefore, the reader and the translator have to be careful and capable of reading and presenting Premchand and his text avoiding words that might hurt the feelings of the present day over-sensitive reader because the inequality paradigm is hard to equal. It is also to be noted that more often than not readers of Premchand in the universities in India and abroad go to him for sociological purposes also to find out what he says about the society of his time, not for aesthetic pleasure and to read him as literature only.

Paul Giffard-Foret [(Postcolonial Text, Vol 11, No 1 (2016)] a researcher from Université Sorbonne Nouvelle-Paris says that the policing of Dalitness by a section of Dalit intellectuals is to be measured against the degree of narratorial authenticity. It remains a highly contested terrain that has crystallized around the literary figure of Munshi Premchand. For instance, while showing indebtedness to Premchand's legacy as an engagé writer, Ajay Navaria's re-worked version of Premchand's story *"Dooth ka Daam"* (The *Price of Milk* - 1934) depicts a different scene. In *"Hello, Premchand!"* Dalit characters consigned to death or a hopeless existence are resurrected, educated, and politicized. Mangal of "Hello, Premchand!" is determined and able to continue his studies, following his mother's last wish that her son ought never to "have to carry piss and shit". This is an inspirational and extension of Premchand's legacy and must be studied. The story is a fine example of showing marked difference between pre-class rural communalism and modern metropolitan individualism felt bitterly by Dalits like Mangal. The Derridean "supplementarity" is at work here.

Therefore Premchand is a representative of Dalits, an advocate who readily agreed to present their case before the masses and was their well-wisher. Sarah Beth Hunt in her study "Hindi Dalit literature and the politics of representation" (2014) says, "the notion of representation, in fact, lies at the heart of the discursive public sphere and becomes a way of justifying the limits of participation, since not every individual can speak for themselves, but rather, their interests must be represented by someone who speaks on their collective behalf." What Premchand did was simply this.

## Feminist Premchand

Premchand is an enlightened male feminist to the core. But with a rider; he is a feminist of his time. For instance, the Gujarati novelist Goverdhan Ram Tripathi in his novel *Saraswatichandra* (1887-1900) was not able to get his widowed heroine finally remarried, though he himself was a champion of women's lib. It is repeatedly stressed that the novelists of the time were really interested in documenting women's plight and were trying to ameliorate their suffering. Similarly Premchand was keen to reform and review their condition but under strict Indian ethical codes of behaviour. That is why at the surface level he looks like a bundle of opposites when it comes to his treatment of women. In his personal life he married a widow but only after abandoning his first wife. (It is said that he used to send some amount of money to her for sustenance but we are not dead sure about it.) Premchand's first wife, supposedly possessed by evil spirits, and he himself participated in the rituals by the witch doctor to drive the spirits away. He also supported the *Sharda Bill* which aimed to raise the minimum age for marriage and to give the widow the right to her deceased husband's property. That is why there are scholars who treat him as a revolutionary and way ahead of his time. There are others who call him conservative and traditional, *a lakir ka fakir*. In fact the truth lies in between these two extremes. It is not only interesting and amusing to note that most of the students who wish to go for research want to work on Premchand. This is the first choice of those who are new to the field. Female students invariably select him as their favourite author. That is why there are books such as *Premchand ka Nari Chintan, Premchand ke Nari Patra, Premchand ka Nari Vimarsh, Striyon Ki Samasyaon ke Prati Premchand ka Dristikon* etc. In English too one can find the work of Geetanjali Pandey, *'How Equal? Women in Premchand's Writings'* (1986), in which she concludes that Premchand upholds for women a clearly conservative ideal. This fact is also underlined by Javrimal Parekh in an article *'Premchand Aur Nari Samasya'* (1980) and Dr. Bharat Singh in "Premchand *ke Nari Vishyak Vichar"*. Even a Sri Lankan scholar Ranjini Obeyesekere (1986) says that the question of women's rights surfaces his work and it is a powerful motif. Nirmala Jain in "*Women in Premchand are writing: Feminist or Chauvanist?" (1986)* concludes that Premchand does not offer any revolutionary programme for the upliftment of women. He wants to restore to them their traditional responsibility which has been lost due to various historical and socio-economic factors, rather than advocate a path of total war or revolution. His portrayal of women, however, is important from another point of view. For they provide the keynote to a distinctive life style. From this point of view it would be rewarding to focus on two of his significant characters: Suman (Sevasadan) and Dhaniya (Godaan). The former brings to the surface the life style of the urban middle class and the latter the saga of the Indian rural life. Charu Gupta in her paper *"Portrayal of Women in Premchand's Stories: A Critique"* (1991) broadly sees four images of women, emerging in Premchand's stories: the ideal woman, the counter-model of woman, the suffering woman and one who protests. These images are not distinct or completely seperate from each other. There are a lot of interconnections between them and they often run into each other.

In a letter to Dr. Indernath Madan, Premchand once wrote that his ideal of a woman is a combination of sacrifice, care and purity at one place. The ideal woman for him is one who has sacrifice without a hope for reward; care without showing any dissatisfaction and purity like Caesar's wife which does not bring any regret. *(meri nari ka adarsh hai ek hi sthan par tyag, sewa aur pavitrata. Tyag bina phal ki asha ke ho aur pavitrata sijar ki patni ki bhanti aisi ho, jiske liye pachtane ki avashyakta na ho.)* It is this ideal what you see reflected in Premchand's work.

It is not necessary to read Premchand as reactionary or conservative. It is also not appropriate to read him as an epitome of virtue and goodness as far as gender equality is concerned. He is a man of his time who wanted to better *the* lives of the women. What Gandhi was doing in the political space Premchand did in the literary arena. His experiments in writing were to place and replace women in a typical Indian family system where man was still the supreme commander but woman was also there and claiming her rightful place in her own way. For instance in the story *'Beton Wali Vidhava'*(1932) the main character Phoolmati says to Uma ( her daughter in law) in a rebellious tone, "Is this the law of Manu and you want to follow the same law? .... I planted the tree and I only cannot stand in its shadow; if this is the law, then I wish it burned."(The burning of Manu Smriti by some people in independent India and

Ambedkar's own sense of growing social pessimism which led him, eventually, to embrace the egalitarianism of Buddhism, in a powerfully evocative public ceremony of religious conversion indicates what this character says.)

Such stories are the reflection of Premchand's anger and aghast for the social and religious bondage of women. Shivrani Devi noted in her book *"Premchand Ghar Mein"* that he used to ask her to stop using Purdah (veil). "You are not the wife of a newly-wed. Why should you observe purdah then? I have been seeing it for the last several years, and am fed up. Why should you observe it-just because of the stepmother?"

But it doesn't mean he wants women to abandon their culture and controlled behaviour. Nobility of character is what he wants in women. In a story entitled *"Shanti"* ( 1920) Premchand speaks through the male character, "I want to again see you as a woman who is shy, walks with her head down, offers prayers, reads Ramayan, does household work, spins charkha, is scared of god and is completely devoted to her husband."

Most of his stories show a kind of veiled bias against Western culture and there is a conscious attempt to restore and preserve Indian culture. For instance, "Miss *Padma*" (1936) is a story in which the westernized woman is depicted with derision and not with devotion.

The story is a sort of indication about the present day live-in-relationship and should be read by today's metro-youngsters. Chetan Bhagat should turn it into a novel which can be a sequel of *Half-girl friend.*

Premchand's treatment of women characters is idealistic but it seems that as a writer he is duty bound to protect and argue for them. He is with them as they are also oppressed like Dalits. In

*"Vaishya"* a prostitute named Madhuri exclaims, "No woman sells her body willingly... if I am corrupt, then those people who come here are no less." Women are in fact dynamic social force in Premchand as they develop and transform themselves in conflit and turmoil. For instance, in *Gaban* the character of Jalpa develops significantly when she comes out of the house and struggles to get her husband Ramanath out of the turmoil he is forced to be in. Sofi in Rangabhumi is another example. Rohini in Kayakalp and Nirmala in Nirmala all are in a kind of conflict and struggle to find a respectable place in the society where man is the supreme commander.

When we talk of women's rights we find that Premchand is very traditional. In Godan Professor Mehta tells Malati that marriage is a social contract and neither man nor woman has a right to break it. "You are free before the contract but once you are married it is not possible to break the bond." Similarly he is hell bent on purity of character. He doesn't want to present an independent butterfly. "The question of women's rights surfaces the work. It is a powerful motif but the creation, balance, and patterning of Premchand's major female characters seem governed by the need to explore it. The Indian concept of ideal, womanhood, the traditional expectations of the roles of wives and mothers, the feasibility, the viability, and validity of those expectations in the changing social context of modern India are issues implicately and explicitly introduced in the novel"opines Ranjini Obeyesekere in *"Women's Rights and Roles in Premchand's Godan (1986)".*

Though Premchand seems to be avoiding details of the beauty and sexual desires of women and is guided by his time (as Chetan Bhagat, namely in *One Indian Girl,* is perhaps at ease with the depiction of sexual act too!), he indicates as is sex is just a point in one's life. In *Sevasadan, Suman's* suppressed desires goad her to go towards prostitution. In *Premasharam*, Gayatri is carried away by sexual fulfillment and has to commit suicide in the end. In *Kayakalp,* Devpriya is an epitome of carnal desires. Somehow Premchand is not for such projection and whatever we read now is also due to the time we come across with the text called Premchand.

In the novels "*Nirmala*"and "*Sevasadan*" the protagonists suffer. Nirmala suffers and Suman suffers. There greatest sin is being a woman. Like Thomas Hardy's heroines their suffering is continual and happiness is just but an occasional episode in their lives too. But there are stories in which women are different. They suffer but they react. They are not fragile but highly explosive. For instance, there is Kusum. She begs and implores to be accepted by her husband. Premchand comes forward as the narrator and says "*'striyon ko dharma aur tyag ka path parha-parhakar hamne unke atmasamman aur atmavishvas dono ka hi ant kar diya. Agar purush stri ka mohtaj nahin, to stri bhi purush ki mohtaj kyon ho?'* (By continuously preaching women about religion and sacrifice, we have ended both their self-respect and self-confidence. If the man is not dependent on the woman, then why should the woman depend on the man?)

Slowly but surely, there is a sea chage in Kusum and she retorts vehemently: *"vartman stithi mein patni banna gulami na sahi, purush se kamtar darja swikar karna hai. Prem to arthik samta ka naam hai. Is asamanta mein prem ka astitv ho sakta hai, mujhe to isme sandeh hai."*(In the prevalent condition to be a wife may not be abject slavery, but it does mean accepting a lower status to that of a man. Love stands for economic equality. I have doubts whether in the present disparity, love can sustain.)

To conclude, one can say that Premchand's women are really the better half of the Indian society. His stories in Chand magazine (established by Ramrakh Singh Sahgal in Allahabad in 1922) are really women-centric and his women are vocal and argumentative. His contemporary women writers like Mahadevi Verma and Subhadra Kumari Chauhan presented women suffering meekly without a word of protest and the narrators speak for them. But Premchand makes the women speak and protest. Nikhil Govind in "Between Love and Freedom: The revolutionary in the Hindi Novel" says Premchand had struggled hard to make the case through the 1920s for marriages based on the choice of the participants and not on family, village and caste considerations. And yet in the novels written from the 1930s the desire of the protagonists exceeds the simple proprieties of companionship and choice and extends rapidly into forbidden, the extra-marital, the quasi-incestuous.

## Political Premchand

Premchand dedicated his life and work for the service of the mother land. In a letter to Anand Rao Joshi written on 26-11-1930 he elaborates, "My whole career has been devoted to politics. I have been dabbling in politics for the last thirty years, although not directly. All my works have a political bearing". Premchand was born in the same decade in which the Indian National Congress was born. It was natural that he too got inspired by the movements for India's Independence. Premchand started taking interest in political affairs while at Kanpur during the late 1900s, and this is reflected in his early works, which have patriotic overtones. His political thoughts were initially influenced by the moderate Indian National Congress leader Gopal Krishna Gokhale, but later, he moved towards the more extremist Bal Gangadhar Tilak. He considered the Minto-Morley Reforms and the Montagu- Chelmsford Reforms as inadequate, and supported greater political freedom. Several of his early works, such as *A Little Trick* and *A Moral Victory* are based on the Indians who cooperated with the British Government. He did not specifically mention the British in some of his stories, because of strong government censorship, but disguised his opposition in settings from the medieval era and the foreign history. He was also influenced by the teachings of Swami Vivekananda. In the 1920s, he was influenced by Mahatma Gandhi's non-co-operation movement and the accompanying struggle for social reform. During this period, his works dealt with the social issues such as poverty, zamindari exploitation (*Premashram*, 1922), dowry system (*Nirmala*, 1925), educational reform and political oppression (*Karmabhumi*, 1931). Premchand's focus on the economic condition of the peasantry and the working class, and his opposition to the rapid industralization can be seen in works like Rangabhumi (1924). In the words of K. P. Singh in "Premchand's ideology" (1976) his is the most powerful and authentic account of the national movement and people's lives: their aspirations, struggles, victories and defeats, injustice, exploitation, courage, cowardice, and in particular the community life of rural India, peasant common sense, non-conformist and sacrifice, these all have been etched with a sense of realism.

Premchand once said "I am doing my bit for India as he (Gandhi) is striving to promote the welfare of peasants and workers, and he has launched a movement for that; I am writing to provide enthusiasm to this cause. He wants unity between Hindus and Muslims; I wish to merge Hindi and Urdu to create Hindustani." His stories dealing with almost every aspect of social and national life constitute a social document. Robert O'Swan very briefly put it as follows "Sentence by sentence and story by story Premchand created a fictional Indian Nationalist movement so comprehensive that the reader finally feels he has seen almost as much happen in almost as many situations to almost as many individuals as happened in all of Uttar Pradesh from 1920 to 1932." What Gandhi did through politics, Premchand tried to do through his writing. Once he expressed his feeling in a letter to one of the friends Banarsidas Chaturvedi," *I have only one ambition and that is that my country should become free. Before I die, I would like to write some good books but their aim too should be the Independence of the country."*

In an introductory book on Premchand in the series called "Makers of Indian Literature" ( 1968) Prakash Chand Gupta says the work of Premchand is dominated by patriotic overtones. In the background of his work we hear constant echos of the voices of Ram Mohan Roy, Vivekananda, Dayananda, Gandhi, Tagore, Nehru, Bhagat Singh, Chander Shekhar Ajad, and European fighters of freedom and human emancipation, like Mezzini, Garibaldi, Karl Marx, and Lenin. (Premchand is reported to have "dressed' some twenty stories by Count Tolstoy in Indian garb and got them published under the title *Prem Prabhakar.)*

When you read his stories such as *Juloos and Idgah,* you will notice how he presented Hindu- Muslim unity and women in perspective. Premchand had a burning passion for Hindu-Muslim unity, and was very critical of the fanatically inclined, be they the Muslim *mullahs* or Brahmin priests. In the words of Madan Gopal, "He used to say that Hindus should realize that their weakness would weaken the country. "So long as the Hindus are weak, and the

Muslims know that the Hindus are weak, Hindu Muslim unity is meaningless." With the idea of making the Islamic history and culture better understood by the Hindus, he writes a drama, *Karbala in which* references to the presence of Hindu soldiery in the army of Hussain is worth noting. The story *Nyaya* is based on the Prophet's life. *Mandir aur Masjid* is the story of a Muslim zamindar, Choudhury Itarat Ali, and his extremely loyal Rajput *chaprasi,* Bhajan Singh. Itarat Ali is an epitome of Hindu-Muslim unity. He is what an ideal Hindu or an ideal Muslim ought to be. The novel *"Kayakalp"* is also, in part, a study of Hindu- Muslim unity. *"Rangbhumi"*also has flashes of this problem. "One of the characters speaks what Premchand wants and desires to comment, "There are some people in both the communities whose prestige and prosperity is dependent on the continuance of tension between the two communities. I sincerely believe that whether you are a Hindu or a Muslim, you should be a truthful and a good man. No one community can have the monopoly of all the good qualities. Not all the Muslims are gods, nor all the Hindus *kafirs.* Anyone who hates the members of the other community is as far removed from God as possible."

In the words of Shantanu Mukherji"Best tribute to Premchand will be to widely disseminate his literature harping for a pluralistic society with tolerance and peace as the hallmarks of an exemplary national unity. Such dissemination includes story telling of Premchand's works to the students and youngsters lest they are not drawn towards the parochial forces with limited vision, who are constantly threatening to split the society on communal and caste lines."

*Patni se Pati (Samar Yatra)* is a story I would like you to read for understanding the impact of Gandhi and his Congress among the masses. A blind beggar is singing and begging for alms: *Vatan ki dekhiye takdir kab badalti hai?* (Let us see when does the fate of the nation change?) Mrs Seth was different from her husband. He hated anything swadeshi and she loved everything swedeshi. When she heard the blind boy singing and begging, she opened her box to give her a pice but the box contained only rupee and no change. She found a pice which was out of circulation. She gave it to the begger. The next day she went to a congress gathering where she found that the same blind beggar donated that coin to the Congress party. The president of the meeting was overjoyed to find a blind begger giving a coin and he announced that the coin was more than a thousand rupee given by a rich man. Mrs Seth was so overwhelmed with emotion that she took the same coin she gave for 200 rupee. This was the impact on common men and women but Congress was not able to encash it into a full fledged revolution and movement then. Premchand's writing is full of such events. He shows that the people are with the movement and their struggle. He had full faith in Gandhi but was apprehensive about Congress.

To sum up it can be said that the issues which were very dear to him were the poverty ridden life of the poor villagers, peaceful and non-violent struggle for freedom from the British yolk, a natural and permanent change of heart of the cruel and heartless exploiter, idealistic people giving away their extra land for the welfare of landless labouers and farmers, Hindu Muslim unity and the closeness between Hindi and Urdu.

## Educationist Premchand

"Teaching is only a means of livelihood," wrote Premchand in March 1920. "There is little fame in it." Premchand was a novelist and story teller but for his livelihood he was a school teacher. As a matter of fact, about a third of Hindi and Urdu writers in this period were teachers. How he struggled to get himself educated and how he could secure jobs as teacher make a very interesting reading. It is also worth noting that he slowly but surely developed his theory of education the traces of which can be collected from his stories, novels, speeches and essays.

In his address to the fourth convocation of Dakshin Bharat Prachar Sabha, Madras (29-4-1934) Premchand said that our educational institutions were factories of slavery as they made our youth slaves of needs, exhibitionism and inactivity. He also found that the supremacy of the English language in every walk of life was like the shackles on the feet of a prisoner and it affected the head and heart of the nation.

In one of his essays on Primay Education (1909) Premchand compares the condition of schools in India with that of the schools in the United States. He once read an article written by Nihal Singh (1908) that a high school with a fine building and a library and a separate laboratory existed in every village with a population of two thousand in the US. (Do you still have such a luxary in India?) Premchand wrote that even a college in India could not boast of these facilities. A village school in U. P., according to this article, consisted of a class of boys sitting on a worn-out jute rugget spread over unswept ground under a tree amidst dirt, the twenty to twenty-five children half-dozing. Opposite them sat a teacher on a broken chair, with a dilapidated table before him. The children were "learning everything by heart," and none would appear to have an untorn shirt. Their dhotis went down to their knees, their eyes downcast. "Yes, that is the condition of the school in Aryavarta which once boasted of Taxila and similar other universities. How far have we travelled?" We seemed to be so far behind in the race of development, according to· Premchand, that "we may not perhaps have even the heart to reach the goal." "The principal requirement for any reform of our primary educational system," he wrote, "is that of competent teachers. Government has entrusted the job to teachers who do not get more than four or five rupees a month. How can one who is not free from material worries be inclined towards devoting attention to his work? Worse still is the condition of teachers in the "aided schools where teachers get only three rupees and fifteen annas (after the deduction of the money order fee of one anna). The teachers' wages are half of those of the water-carrier in towns or even that of a manual labourer. The teacher, therefore, either turns towards cultivation or extorts higher fees on the sly, resulting in a reduction of the number of students. The teacher is also overworked and cannot give adequate attention to all the students. When the parents find that their wards are not getting proper education, they withdraw them from the school." Added Premchand: "Teachers trained in Normal schools (trained teachers) too find themselves out of place; for they had been taught to teach one class only, whereas in the village school they teach four." Premchand suggested fifteen rupees as the minimum wage, the minimum degree for the teacher being a certificate in Urdu and Hindi upto the Middle standard. This, he agreed, called for larger expenditure, but "national education is an item where nothing is wanted. Surely, the Government can, on this truly useful work, spend Rs. 50 lakhs as against the present 19 lakhs, if it wishes. When the expenditure on wars is mounting every day, and when money is wasted on amenities of highly paid officers, the argument of paucity of funds is untenable." The author also suggested that the system of appointing village school teachers as postmasters needed a review. "Rather than waste money on the two or three schools for training six teachers each in every district, through a teacher with a normal school degree, it would be far better if we restrict the work to one school in each district with a teacher who has a certificate from the Allahabad Training College, Such a teacher, English-knowing and familiar with modem teaching methods, could train the teachers-to-be far more adequately. Unfortunately, wrote Premchand, Government thought of spending more money on the inspection of schools, irrespective of the fact whether there was education or not. In fact, the expenses on inspection far exceeded those on education itself. "When will the Government understand that inspection can never be a substitute for education?"

The curriculum too called for a review. "The readers now being prescribed are useless .... Their language deserves to be touched up.... The primers should be done away with ... geography is enough.... Drawing is meaningless, and should be replaced by a little primer in regard to health.... The place of rules of languages should be taken by teaching of the principles of agriculture.... And of considerable importance is the subject of letter writing." The author also draws a picture of the premises of upper primary schools which "remind one of a cattle shed or an orphanage," their walls crumbling, their floors kuccha, their roofs falling and their doors worn out. "At least half of the money meant to be spent on construction goes to the middlemen. School buildings in many of the villages are premises placed at the disposal of the teacher by the zamindar who wishes to earn salvation through such free use of his house. With this, however, goes the client." Here's the concluding paragraph: "Such being the condition of our educational system, it is a shame that our public workers too are ignorant of the pressing problems. How many of the journalists or lawyers who are accustomed to passing resolutions, have toured a district to ascertain how many schools have buildings? The Director's reports do not say what percentage of teachers could pride themselves on their school buildings. And in the light of the ability and education of the members of District Boards, to expect of them to agitate on these problems is hoping for the impossible."

It seems Premchand wanted change in the Primary Education System and thought that it was possible only with the assistance and patronage of the government and the desire of the common folk. He himself also wanted to do something. He got opportunities too. He served not only as a teacher but also as headmaster. He got a chance to work as a Sub Deputy Inspector of Schools too!

The novel Karmabhoomi begins with the views of the main character on the education system in India. Premchand comments, "The great compulsion with which fees are collected in schools and colleges surpasses the hardships experienced in collection of revenues. The same heartless bureaucracy which dominates government offices also dominates the working of our educational institutions...Money reigns supreme in our educational institutions as in courts- with greater rigidity and with greater hardship. If you are late you are fined; if you are unable to buy books, you are fined; if you commit a mistake you are fined. Is it an educational institution or an institution to impose and collect fines? That, then, is the object of Western education which is being praised to the skies. Is it any wonder, then, that these institutions turn out pupils who sell their lives for money, who would strangle the poor and who would sell their soul for a mess of pottage."

The real degree we need is that of humility, service and simplicity. If we do not have this degree i.e. if our conscience is not awakened, the paper degree is worthless.

Amarkant, the protagonist of the novel Karmbhoomi hates the system of education and says: these teachers are in no way behind an ordinary trader or government servant. They are also corrupted by the same lust for money and power and the same weaknesses.

Our educational system and institutions are only appendages of the government. Being themselves stepped in darkness how can they spread light?

The main theme in *Premashram* is said to be zamindari system but in fact the sub-theme is also introduced right at the beginning of the novel in the discussion between the illiterate peasants of Lakhanpur. "What is the use of education?" "In what way is the educated man superior to those who are uneducated? Has he become more human, more just?"

The questions are repeated as a refrain throughout the novel. When Prabha Shankar is perturbed by Gyan Shankar's behavior he comes to the conclusion "Education should normally have the effect of making a man more satisfied and contented, restraining his egoism and making him more generous rather than bringing him under the control of the demon of selfishness, meanness and unscrupulousness".

Kadir Mian is another important character who tells Prem Shankar about the meaning of true education: "During my long life I have seen hundreds of educated men but, except for you, I did not meet a single one who did not cut our throats. The whole world speaks highly of education. It seems to us that education makes a man a greater crook. It teaches people to squeeze the neck of the poor. God gave you true education. That is why other educated people have become hostile to you"

From the very beginning, Premchand was against English Education. He was not against English but the way English educated people were treated in the society. In his first significant novel *Sevasadan* when Sabal Singh goes in search of an employment, he realizes that he is not "educated"enough in the prevalent sense of the term. He says to himself, "My character may not be very high but is better than many; my thoughts may not be very grand but I am not mean. But all the doors are closed for me. I can become either a peon or a constable. This is my ultimate reach. It is a great injustice to us. Our wisdom, character, intellect, sensibility are of no use if we have no knowledge of English. We are the wretched one and we not only tolerate this insult but also are very proud of it."

## Islamophile Premchand

Premchand was for Hindu Muslim unity. He wrote an article entitled *"Malkana Rajput Mussalmanon ki Shuddhi,"* which was published in Zamana of May 1923. Premchand took up cudgels on behalf of the Muslims who deprecated the shuddhi movement launched by the Bharatiya Hindu Shuddhi Sabha, formed by several sections of the Hindu society, including the Sanatanists, the Arya Samajists, the Jains and the Sikhs. While Premchand agreed that the shuddhi movement had been originally started by the Muslims, the launching of the shuddhi movement by all sections of Hindu opinion to him signified a grave danger to the Muslims.

Premchand regretted the failure of the Hindus to view Khilafat movement from the comprehensive perspective of Mahatma Gandhi and said "The truth is that the Hindus have never understood the importance of Khilafat but always looked at it sceptically." He opined, "The Hindus have never been known for their political generosity, but the kind of narrow-mindedness they have displayed at this occasion, one is forced to conclude that this community is at the peak of political bankruptcy. Could the entire Hindu community collectively go in a frenzy motivated by a few so-called nationalists driven by hysteria?" Premchand was also a great admirer of the two brothers, Mohammed Ali and Shaukat Ali. "I consider the transformation in the ideas of the Ali brothers," he wrote to Nigam, "to be genuine. Only such conversion, shuddhi, can be lasting." The reference was to the presidential address to the annual session of the Indian National Congress at Kakinada. In an article entitled "*Qahat-ur-Rijjal*" (or A famine of wise men), in Zamana of February 1924, Premchand wrote, "The attitude of the Hindus shows that the nation has gone bankrupt. If the Hindus had even one Kitchlew, or Mohammed Ali, or Shaukat Ali, the movement of the Hindu Sangathan or shuddhi would not have led to such heat and would have resulted in the reduction of incidents that had taken place under their impact. It is, indeed, sad that even though the Congress as an organisation has not had anything to do with these movements, its individual members have left no stone unturned for the shuddhi movement. Not one of the top leaders of the Congress has openly raised his voice against these movements... even leaders like Motilal Nehru, Jawahar Lal Nehru, Bhagwandas and Sri Prakasa who, one hoped, had the moral conviction to come out with their views openly expressed themselves one day against the movement and contradicted their statements the next day."

Premchand was aware of the pranks of the so called "*religious loafers*" and admonished them against their ill-deeds. He used his art of story telling to indicate the role played by Muslims in nation building. He satirized those who stood in the path of Hindu-Muslim unity. He was equally against those priests and mullahs who instigated their communities against each other. Moteyram is one such Brahmin priest who recurs again and again in his stories since we first met him in Jalva-i-Isar (1912). On the other hand we have a balanced character in the story *Mandir and Masjid*. He is a Muslim zamindar named Choudhury Itarat Ali who holds in equal respect both Hinduism and its temples and Islam and its mosques. He defends Bhajan Singh, his servant, from the wrath of the Muslim fanatics.

There are some stories by Premchand to showcase the life of the Prophet such as *Nyaya* in which there is a memorable episode from the life of the Prophet and his son in law. The impartiality of justice is the theme of the story where the Prophet says "Justice must not err." *Rajabhakta, Pareeksha, Vajrapat, Kshama, Laila, Fatiha, Vinod, Mandir aur Masjid and Shatraj ke Khiladi* etc are just a few examples of his stories dealing with lives of the Muslims, their values, message and way of life. Just look at an innocent childlike story "Idgah" in which Premchand portrays the concept of brotherhood enshrined in Islam:

> Wealth and position don't matter here. All are equal in Islam. Sach a beautiful management, such beautiful arrangements! Lakhs of heads bow together in reverence, and rise together... and it goes on. Such a wonderful sight! The collective acts, their expansion, eternity filled the heart with respect, pride and happiness, as if the thread of brotherhood strung all these souls together.

Gopal Krishna Maniktala, a short story writer underlines Premchand's contribution in familiarizing common men with the teachings of Islam particularly presenting a well-meaning positive image of Islam and the Prophet (PBUH). Mr Maniktala collected Munshi Premchand's articles which appeared as clarifications and rebuttals against articles published in books such as *Islam ka vish viraksh* (poisonous tree) and *Andha Aitmad Aur Khufia Jihad*. Maniktala's five books *Prem Chand Aur Tasneef-i-Prem Chand — Kuch Nae Goshe (1985), Prem Chand, Kuch Nae Mabahis (1988), Prem Chand, Hayat-i-Nau (1993), Prem Chand Ka Secular Kirdar Aur Deegar Mazameen (2001) and Hoori Ka Dosra Janam (1999)* are not only important books for any student of Urdu fiction but also for those who wish to dig deep into his thought process. Munshi Premchand was bred in an atmosphere which was truly Indo-Islamic. He was grounded in Persian and he could be deemed culturally part of a composite culture. One of the Premchand's stories which is being talked about these days in *Nabi Ka Naati Nirvah* which was published in Monthly *Madhuri*. This study defends the Prophet on an issue which has been overplayed with a great deal of sarcasm by anti-Islam fanatics and proves that a good number of articles in defence of Islam are going to cause a stir in contemporary India. It is true that Munshi Premchand was a true Kayasth in letter and in spirit as evidenced by his drama Karbala which is, perhaps, the most moving tribute to the martyrs of Karbala. Premchand has manifested India's homage to Imam Hussain by showing that a large Indian army was standing nearby the Camp of Hussain imploring him to allow them fight alongside his camp but the offer was not accepted on the plea that this would cause more bloodshed. (Dawn 21 May 2003)

Munshi Premchand's devotion to the Prophet (PBUH) and Islam is not a secret. Premchand asserts in the preface of his Hindi version of *Karbala* that in order to be realistic, he could not put too many Sanskritized words in the mouth of Muslims' he has tried to keep the language of the play a ' shared' communal language that Hindus and Muslims both speak. In making the point Premchand suggests that religious identity in India is related with language. Premchand by first publishing Karbala in Hindi rather than in Urdu, according to Syed Akbar Hyder, an assistant professor at Asian Studies University of Texas, validates the Hindi Urdu polarization at one level but at another level he reengages this space by articulating in Hindi an Islamic allegory, already held in reverence by many Hindus. Through the Hindi Karbala, Premchand postulates the plausibility of an affectionate nexus between Hindi and Islam, Islamic history and the history of Hindusism, thereby attempting to enervate Urdu's hold on Islam, Islam's hold on Urdu, Hinduism's hold on Hindi and Hindi's hold on Hinduism, In the play's preface, Premchand describes the battle of Karbala as the Islanic counterpart of the epic struggles of the Mahabharata and the Ramayana. By invoking such an analogy at the very outset, Karbala is domesticated and stripped of its foreignness, so as to make it more comprehensible and appealing to Hindus. Premchand wrote Karbala to cement the bonds of Hindu Muslim unity and to mount a successful campaign against communalism. (Reliving Karbala, 2006)

When Nigam wrote to Premchand that he should not write anything which would hurt the feelings of Shias, Premchand replied: "You can rest assured that I have been extremely careful to ensure that no disrespect of any sort is shown to them. Every single word has been weighed carefully, so that the religious susceptibilities of Muslims are not injured. The purpose of the drama is political-to cement the bonds of Hindu-Muslim unity." He wrote to Jainendra Kumar when Acharya Chatursen Shashtri wrote a pungent article "Islam *Ka Vish Vriksha*" that "we shall have to counter this communal propagamda effectively."On the other hand, Geetanjali Pandey in her paper *"North Indian Intelligentia and Hindu Muslim Question*" (1984) studies Premchand's writings and shows that though he is a consistent supporter of communal unity his reactions to specific situations on issues at times deviated from this stance. A body of inherited assumptions, deeply rooted in his mind, militated against the secular nationalist values to which he was attached and produced ambivalence in his responses to the Hindu-Muslim question.

It will not be out of place to place on record the tribute paid to Premchand by an ardent admirer and a man of letters Khwaja Hasan Nizami, "There is not a single short story, novel or article in Urdu by Premchand that I have not read. I am always on the look out for something written by him, there have been various currents and cross currents in the life of our nation. The eyes of one community have been bloodshot against the other. Communalism prevented the outlook of most among us. In fact, how many of us were there who didn't succumb to the all pervading poisonous atmosphere? Premchand in sharp contrast stood firm and steadfast. His head was clear. So was his heart."

In an article published in "Hans"( Nov 1931) and republished by Savyasachi in Uttargatha and reported by Kuldeep Kumar in The Hindu dated July 31, 2017 we find the following mention of Premchand and the information he provided about the protection of cows by Hindus and the eating of beef by Muslims and poor Indians.

> Beef is primarily eaten by those who are so poor that they cannot afford mutton or chicken. Also most of the so-called "untouchable" Hindus too eat beef. In the Arab lands, cow is not found. Therefore, there is no question of Islam prescribing eating of beef. If the two communities come closer and start respecting each other's sensitivities, Muslims will themselves give up eating beef as those Muslims who live in close proximity of the Hindus in villages do not eat beef.

The cow protection movement has been a religious and political movement aiming to protect the cows whose slaughter has been broadly opposed by Hindus, Buddhists, Jains and Sikhs. The opposition to slaughter of animals including cows has extensive and ancient roots in Indian history, Premchand too was aware of this but he said. "We have the right to consider holy any animal we like but to hope that followers of another religion will consider it equally sacred is nothing but to incite violence. In the matter of cow-killing, the Hindus have adopted unjust ways since the beginning. We have the right to consider holy any animal we like but to hope that followers of another religion will consider it equally sacred is nothing but to incite violence. Cows are eaten all across the world. Would you pronounce a death warrant against the whole world for it?" (As told by Dr Apoorvanand *Delhi University 31-07-2017)*

## Urdu Premchand- Hindi Premchand

There are two Premchands, nay three Premchands: Hindi Premchand, Urdu Premchand, and English Premchand. Urdu

Premchand wrote in Urdu and also translated his work himself in Hindi. Snehal Shingavi in *"Premchand and Language: On Translation, Cultural Nationalism, and Irony"* (a paper presented at the International Seminar on Premchand in Translation, held at Jamia Millia, New Delhi, 28–30 November 2012) says that understanding Premchand as a novelist under the sign of translation is helpful in allowing us to cut through some of the hagiographic modes of thinking about him and understand the real contradictions that he faced. Long before Harish Trivedi in an article *"The Urdu Premchand: The Hindi Premchand"* (1984) opined that Premchand played an important role in shifting the center of gravity of North Indian literary publishing from Urdu to Hindi and its consequences for the communal politics of language, with the result that the Hindi Premchand and the Urdu Premchand have now almost completely different critical legacies. Similarly Premchand's grandson Alok Rai in his study *"Hindi Nationalism"* looked at the history of Hindi language as a narrative of "intimate destabilisation and dispossession". He stressed that Khari Boli "Hindi" was deemed suitable for the rising Hindu - savarna middle class and even Braj Bhasha with its heavy traditional overtone failed to complement their identity politics (pp 102-3). Premchand once said "my way of living and my culture are, in fact, a blend of the Hindu and the Muslim. The impact of Muslim culture on me is actually deeper than that of the Hindu. I learnt Persian and Urdu from a *maulvi* long before I started reading and writing Hindi."Jafar Raza in his doctoral thesis *"Premchand: Kahani ka Rahnuma"* (1970) says that Premchand is an Urdu writer and in Hindi he is merely a writer in translation. He is the forerunner of Hindi Premchand who wrote in Hindi and scarcely translated into Urdu.

When Premchand found that in Urdu it was very difficult to survive and it was not financially viable to write only in Urdu and earn his livelihood, he started shifting towards Hindi. Muslims used to make fun of those who wrote in Urdu. They called such a Hindu writer *"Bu-e-kachori.* He really struggled to master the Hindi language. Mrs Premchand wrote in *"Premchand: Ghar Mein": ve kisi kahani ka anuvad Hindi mein karte, aur kisi ka Urdu mein..."* Hari Bhau Upadhyaya wrote in his memoirs: I recollect when Premchand started writing in Hindi; he very often copied the style of Urdu. When

I used to work for *"Saraswati"* magazine, I came across the manuscript of one of his stories in which he wrote- *Yah aapka bada aadhkya hai.* By this he meant- *ye aapki badi zyadti hai.* When I read this I couldn't control my laughter." (Hans, *Premchand Ank, May 1937, page 802*)

No doubt that Premchand belongs to both Hindi and Urdu. Now that the people reading him in Hindi and Urdu both are hardly found so we are amazed to know that he started writing in Urdu and bulk of his writing is still in Urdu. In fact he translated some of his early stories into Hindi from Urdu. If you want to understand his creative process and the way he treats language as an expression of thought you should sometimes look at both the versions of his stories. For instance the very Urdu title of one of his novels "Bazaar- *e- Husn*" becomes *"Sevasadan*" in Hindi. You can see that the title in Urdu captures the image of romance and beauty but in Hindi *"Sevasadan*" it is dull and filled with grief and remorse as if it is the story of an orphanage. However, Vasudha Dalmia finds the Hindi title appropriate as the story is the redemption of the heroine rather than focussing on the courtesan's quarters itself. The Urdu version of his novel *"Godan*" appeared three years after the Hindi version and it is someone else's translation. Thus Hindi and Urdu were like two eyes with which he looked at and expressed. T. Graham Bailey in his *History of Urdu Literature* (1928) says that Premchand found the fulfilment of his true sensibility and genius in the last phase of his career when he started writing in Hindi.

Compare the Urdu of the concluding paragraph with the Hindi one of the story "The Chess Players":

**Urdu**

Andhera ho gaya tha. Bahzi bichi hui thi. Donon badshah apne apne takht par raunaq afroj the. Un par hasrat chayi hui thi. Goya maqtulin ki maut ka matam kar rahe hain. Charon taraf sanneai ka alam tha. Khndhar ki bosida divaren aur khasta hal kangure aur sar-ba- sujud minar lashon ko dekhte the aur insane zindgi ki besibati par afsos karte the jis men sang-0- khisht ka sibat bhi nahin.

It was dark. The chess game was laid out. Both kings sat magnificently on their respective thrones, stricken with sorrow, as if mourning the deaths of those who had been killed. There was silence all around. They would look at the decaying walls of the dilapidated mosque, the damaged turrets and the minarets which had crumbled to the ground; looked upon their bodies and bemoaned the impermanence of human existence which lacked the stability of even a brick or stone.

## Hindi

Andhera ho chala tha. Bazi bichi hu I thi. Donon badhah apne apne singhasanon par baithe hue mano in dono viron ki mrityu par ro rahe the! Charon taraf sannata chaya hua tha. Khandhar ki auai hua mehraben giri hui divaren aur dhuli dhusarit minaren in lashon ko dekhti aur sir dhunti thin.

Darkness was coming on. The chess game had been set up. The twokings each on his throne sat there as though lamenting the death of these two heroes. Silence spread over all. The broken archways of the ruins, the crumbling walls and dusty minarets looked down upon the corpses and mourned.

## Translator Premchand

You will be surprised to know that Premchand translated a few writers of English, Urdu and Russian into Hindi and Urdu and probably learnt and polished his style in this way. His translation of Ratan Lal Dhar Sarshar, for example, is from Urdu. But his translations of Tolstoy, Gorky, Shaw, Galsworthy, Maupassant, Anatole France and Dickens and several others are through English. Charles Dickens (The Story of Richard Doubledick), Oscar Wilde (Canterville), John Galsworthy (Strife, Justice), Hendrik van Loon (The story of Mankind), Maurice Maeterlinck (Sightless), and others translated by him are through English. Towards the end of 1916 when he read "Les Miserables" he was so deeply impressed that he asked his friend Daya Narayan Nigam: "Has it been translated into Urdu? ... If not, I would like to do the translation. It would take about a year."

Apart from English literarture, Premchand held French literature in high esteem. In the Hindi translation of Anatole France's novel

*Thais* (1890) as *Ahankar* (1925) Premchand said "In Europe, the delightful literature of France is the best of all" (qtd. in Trivedi 1997, 407). Premchand translated Maurice Maeterlinck's (1862–1936) symbolist-absurdist play *Les Aveugles* (1890) or *The Sightless as Shab-e Tar* (Dark Night) through English in 1919. It was published four months after the Jallianwala Bagh massacre. In a way the publication was a veiled protest against British oppression and censorship. In the 1962 Hindi version (Andheri *Raat*) of this translation the Arabic/ Persian script was replaced with Devanagari and many difficult words were also changed by Premchand's son Amrit Rai. Appropriating Sujit Mukherjee's concept of "new writing"as new aesthetics, Madhu Singh (2012, 176) concludes that "being equally proficient in English and Urdu, Premchand adhered to the lexical, semantic and stylistic equivalences without compromising on the spontaneity and grace of the target language... Shab-e Tar may be seen as an effective engagement with world literature and specifically with the renewing of the aesthetics and politics of Maeterlinck's play."

Christine Everaert in her study "Tracing the boundaries between Hindi and Urdu" (2010) argues that the different endings in Premchand's translations were deliberate and caused by the author's and/or translator's (presumably Premchand himself) consideration of the differing reading tastes of Urdu and Hindi audiences. Urdu fiction is often more poetic and nuanced, whereas Hindi fiction tends to be more didactic, especially in the case of Premchand's early oeuvre. She gives an example of the Urdu story "Apna Apna Khyal" translated into Hindi as "Manovratti". The denouement of the Hindi version (i.e., the revelation that the young woman sleeping on a park bench is innocent and not a prostitute, as some passersby speculate), is missing in the Urdu version or may have been added to the Hindi version depending on which version was composed first. The argument seems to me very similar as in the case of Bazar-e- husn translated into Sevasadan.

It is worth noting that *Premchand translated George Eliot's Silas Marner as Sukhdas. The little book (of 59 pages in large type) retained only the "bare bones" of the story and adapted it to Indian conditions. It carries an introduction by Premchand about George Eliot and her works, as also a preface wherein the writer said that the original novel was a unique portrayal of the working of the human heart. Premchand wrote, "The author had so well portrayed the subtlety of thoughts that according to experts of English novel, it is considered one of the best novels in that language." Sukhdas is a different kind of "translation" of the novel. It had been disrobed of its British clothing and dressed in Indian attire. All the dresses, ideas, places, conventions, were steeped in the "nationalist" colours. Premchand is reported to have also "dressed" some twenty stories by Count Tolstoy in Indian garb and got them published under the title Prem Prabhakar.*

*He translated Jawahar Lal Nehru too.* Acharya Narendra Dev wrote a letter to Premchand urging him to translate into Hindi Jawaharlal Nehru's *'Letters from a Father to a Daughter'*. Premchand honoured the request. *He was so enamoured by the work of Alexander Kuprin's depiction of prostitution in Yama/The Pit (1910; English tr. 1930) that he recommended it to many friends and wanted it to be translated into Hindi. He was on the deathbed and yet was ready to go to pay a public tribute to Gorky! In fact he could not even read out his own address-someone else had to read it on his behalf. (This was the last address he ever delivered.)*

As Premchand used to translate most of his work from Urdu to Hindi and there is a distinct flavour in the two Premchands: The Hindi Premchand and The Urdu Premchand, it is worth noting that Premchand has his distinct ideas about translation, and his own work as a translator is perhaps based on it. Though there are only a few attempts to underline Premchand's theory of translation, it will be asking for more to expect that his translators should follow his example in this regard.

It will not be out of context to say that Premchand not only valued translations but also valued the translators who toiled to enrich literature. Rudra Narayan Aggarwal, a translator of repute who translated Tolstoy's War and Peace and W. M. Thackeray's Vanity Fair and died of TB in a Lucknow hospital was taken care of by Premchand. Premchand wrote to Jainendra Kumar: "There would be very few people as hard working as Rudra Narain Aggarwal ... He is down with TB in a hospital in Lucknow .... There is none to help him, none to sympathise with him. And he is dying. Such is the condition of litterateurs in India."

I must include an extract from Premchand's preface to Rangbhumi's Urdu edition which tells the readers something more. Premchand not only translated his work himself but also took help of others too when he was preoccupied with several other projects. In the preface to the first edition of Volume II of Chaugan-i-Hasti, published by Darul Ashayat of Lahore in 1927, Premchand wrote:

> Rangabhoomi's first edition in Urdu is being published some three years after the Hindi edition. While preparing the manuscript of the Hindi edition, so many changes were made in the original Urdu manuscript that it was not fit to be sent to the press. There were also several chapters that were added to the Hindi edition. These had to be incorporated into the manuscript for the Urdu edition. Consequently, the entire manuscript in Urdu had to be brought into line with the Hindi edition. I am extremely grateful to my esteemed friend Munshi Iqbal Verma Sahr Hitgami who undertook this onerous task upon himself....

Premchand mentioned in a letter to his friend Nigam that he was ready to give Sahr an amount of four aanas per page but he wanted eight aanas per page or Rs. 465. It is said that he was paid Rs. 200 for his services.

Similarly when he found that it was worthwhile and profitable to get published in Hindi, he decided to translate or get the Urdu essays and biographical sketches translated which were published in zamana. He had in his mind to take the help of another translator Jag Mohan Dikshit for this work. The translator's invisibility in this sense in Premchand's case has not been underlined so far. Madan Gopal, his biographer mentions the following regarding the translation work done by the students who wanted to curry favour with him.

> We find Premchand sending the same short story simultaneously to the Urdu and to the Hindi journals. The translations at times were done indifferently by his favourite pupils who considered an assignment of this nature to be a matter of pride and also a

qualification for getting to know the secret of writing short stories, and were touched up by Premchand. (p. 113)

Munshi Manzurul Huq Kalim used to make fair copies of most of Premchand's short stories written at Gorakhpur from August 1916 to May 1918. The bulk of Premchand's writing is made possible by several invisible hands about whom we have never heard.

## Translated Premchand

We are very proud of our past and claim that the stories such as in *Panchtantra, Hitopdesh,Kathasaritsagar* and even the tales in the *Mahabharata* and *Jataka tales* are the first ever stories. The Sanskrit language is considered a treasure of tales both moral and spiritual. In modern times when the world was turning towards short stories, Indian tales reached them via Arabic translations. In the nineteenth century, many writers got inspiration from Sanskrit, Persian and Arabic literature to write stories of such kind once again. That is why *Baital Pachisi, Singhasn Batisi, Rani Ketaki ki Kahani, Nasitopakhyan, Gulbakavali, Tota maina* and several other stories were composed in Urdu and later were translated into Hindi. Urdu translations of *Alif-Laila or Gulistan and Bostan* were tales of adventure and romance but were far from real life. These efforts were to bring about the western short story style but Urdu and Hindi writers failed to do it while the narrators in the Bangali language were successful. Hindi short story developed first in translation mode. Premchand too tried his hand and translated a number of stories including those of Tagore and Tolstoy into Urdu. It is said that Premchand collected twenty stories written by Count Tolstoy, the Russion mastermind, and translated them in such a way that they looked Indian in more ways than one and got them published under the title *Prem Prabhakar*. He translated a few Hindi /Urdu stories of himself into Hindi too. For instance *Roothi Rani*, a Hindi story, was translated by him and was published in Zamana (1907) with a note *"Adapted and translated from the original in Hindi."*

"You may consider me to be the editor of your Hindi department. I shall translate important, useful and interesting items for your journals and newspapers, also some notes and critical assessments.

I shall also send you brief worthwhile thumbnail sketches of Hindi poets" wrote Premchand to Zamana's publisher once.

"A text lives only if it lives on, and it *lives on* only if it is *at* once translatable *and* untranslatable. ... Totally translatable, it disappears as a text, as writing, as a body of language. Totally untranslatable, even within what is believed to be one language, it dies immediately. (Derrida: *"Living On/Borderlines"*) Translation is necessary for the perpetuation and life of the text. For the survival of Premchand it is necessary that he should be translated as much as possible. In the Introductory preface to the book *"Post Colonial Translation: Theory and Practice" (1999)* Susan Bassnett and Harish Trivedi conclude "When the very first translation from Sanskrit into English was published in 1785 (the only one to precede Jones' *Sacontala*), of the *Bhagavad-Gita* by Charles Wilkins, the then Governor-General Warren Hastings remarked that 'works such as this one will survive when the British dominion in India shall have long ceased to exist' (quoted in Brockington 1989: 97). He could not have foreseen the post-colonial turn in world history, through which the *Bhagavad-Gita* now augurs to circulate and survive rather better in English translation than in the original language – perhaps even within India in the decades to come." Derrida, taking a hint from Walter Benjamin, also talks about survival through translation. Translation is not only survival, it is reincarnation of the text and every single attempt in this direction should be welcome.

Unlike other contemporary renowned authors such as Rabindranath Tagore, Premchand was not much read outside India during his life-time. Siegfried Schulz, a German Scholar of Premchand, believes that the reason for this was absence of good translations of his work. Also, unlike Tagore and Iqbal, Premchand never travelled outside India, studied abroad or mingled with the renowned foreign literary figures. In a letter written to Kesho Ram Sabarwal dated 18-5-1928 Premchand expressed his acute desire to be translated, "I have felt not a little flattered by the many kind things you have said of me. What can be more gratifying to an author than appreciation from men of light and culture? I shall deem it a privilege to be introduced to the Japanese public although I am afraid my presentation of life will hardly be appreciated by them. What has a poor Hindi writer to give to advanced Japan? If you think, however, that my works can appeal to Japanese reading public, you have the whole at your disposal. You may translate anything which suits you..."Sabarwal too replied in detail and the following lines are worth quoting, "People in Japan have very high opinon of your writings. It is a pity that they have not enough of it to read in their own language and it is my earnest desire to remove their handicap if I can."

After independence he became one of the authors worth translating in more senses than one. *M. Asaduddin, Professor of English at Jamia Millia Islamia University Delhi and the editor of a notable book, "Premchand in World Languages: Translation, reception and cinematic representations" (2016) very adroitly exclaims that "Premchand's revival and receiption in contemporary times are largely propelled by the translations of his work in English, because the bulk of Premchand translation now is happening in English."* Presently those who want to get name and fame must be available in translation. Now the usual sceptical Western retort is: But show us – in English translation! (Trivedi and Mukherjee (eds. 1996: 239). Publishers world wide tend to rely on the selection of authors who have been successful in the English-language market instead of making their own risky and more costly choices. They pick up Premchand only when he is available in English first.

Three early estimates of Premchand exist in English, *Munshi Premchand: A litereay Biography* by Madan Gopal (Bombay, 1964); *Premchand: His Life and Work* by Hans Raj Rahbar (Delhi, 1957); *Premchand* by Indar Nath Madan (Lahore, 1946). *Munshi Premchand of Lamhi village* (1969) written by Robert Oscar Swan (Brandeis University), and Premchand*: His life and work* (1979) by VS Naravane are some other notable books. There are many other interesting books on Premchand. For instance, 'A *Premchand reader' (1967)* by N. H. Zide and others had been published by University of Chicago and was primarily oriented towards students in the USA. Premchand's novels namely "Godan" is available in English translation by Jai Ratan and P. Lal (Bombay, 1957). Another English translation has been completed by Gordon Roadarmel of the Department of South Eastern

Languages, University of California, Berkeley. In fact, Gaudaan or Godan or The gift of the cow has been translated by not less than six scholars including the incomplete translation by Agyeya. In his essay, *"On Transcreating Premchand,"* P. Lal talks about his position as a translator of Premchand and discusses *twenty-four Stories by Premchand,* a book which he translates with Nandini Nopany. He refers and criticizes Roadarmel's translation of Godaan too and says that his translation aims at "Indian reader who has working knowledge of English" but it is a fact that Roadermel's translation got wider acceptance in the West. Kathryn Hansen doesn't like P. Lal's translation and his way of appreciating himself and she points out that the translation of these stories in *Twenty Four Stories by Premchand* often digresses from "literalness into a morass of misconstructed idioms, improper usage, and grandiose images that are simply not in the original text" In his review of Roadarmel's translation of Godan, Robert O. Swan writes that many translations of Hindi text, Godaan, were tried in the past and most of them failed, but this translation is of "highest order" because the language of the translation is "as clear and as stylistically suitable as can be expected of English" in the Indian setting (218). He defends the title "The Gift of a Cow" for Godaan as it has a "better chance of being understood in New York," though it may not carry the "connotation freight" of the original title of the book. Vasudha Dalmia is right when she says that Godaan is a "vibrant" novel which "poses a challenge to the best of translators". Inge C. Orr (1977) says that Premchand when translated apprears naïve, over idealized, in short unconvincing".

*Godan, Nirmala, Sevasadan, Rangbhoomi, Karmmabhumi* and *Ghaban* are the six novels of Premchand that have been translated so far. There must be other translations too but I am not aware of any. Three selections of Premchand's short stories are also available in English: *Short Stories of Premchand*, translated by Gurdial Mullick (Bombay, 1946); *A Handful of Wheat and Other Stories* (New Delhi, 1955); *The Secret of Culture and Other Stories*, translated by Madan Gopal (Bombay, 1960). In his book *"The Best of Premchand"* (1997) Madan Gopal presents 50 stories in translation. Many other stories of Premchand translated into English appear from time to time in various Indian and foreign newspapers and magazines. One such collection of short stories translated into English is published in *Thought, Mahfil and Indian Literature.* The Oxford India Premchand, published in 2004, offers the reader about a thousand pages of Premchand in English translation. This omnibus edition of his works gathers together two distinguished novels (Nirmala and Gaban) and two short-story collections (The World of Premchand and Widows, Wives and Other Heroines). It also includes an introduction by Premchand scholar Francesca Orsini. Nandini Nopany and P. Lal (1981) also translated 24 stories of Premchand. David Rubin, one of the best translators of Premchand, translated Premchand's stories in three volumes—The World of Premchand (1969), Deliverance and Other Stories (1988) and Widows, Wives and Other Heroines: Twelve Stories (1998) and he translated Nirmala (Alok Rai also translated Nirmala). Carla Petievich has aptly said "It is always a pleasure to read David Rubin's translation because he "[re]confirms his position as Premchand's foremost translator in North America, if not of the entire Anglophone world"

David Rubin in his book *"The World of Premchand"* (1969) published in the most comprehensive way in the UNESCO Asian Fiction series, says that Premchand continues to interest us today because of the originality and clarity of his vision and his ability to dramatize universal human problems. His validity as a critic of society stems in part from the fact that he himself had his roots in that society and never set himself above it; in confirmation of his integrity, his criticism remains inseparable from his love and is never tinged with spite." Inge C. Orr (1977) says that the reason that few of Premchand's works have been "translated into other languages" is that they, when translated, "appear naïve, over-idealized, in short, unconvincing". Commenting on present day writings in comparison with Premchand's work, David Rubin opined "The present day writing tends more towards a psychological literature, more refined (and alas, more chic) in nuance and language, and consequently less vigorous... language cleansed of Premchand's inexhaustible fund of humble metaphors and proverbs, similarly the subject matter tends to be the restricted world of psyche of the writer himself, turned inward, away from the epic horizons of Premchand's multifarious world. Premchand makes many of the present generation of writers look very small." *"The Co-wife and other stories"* (Penguin edition 2008) is also a noteworthy translation of Premchand by Ruth Vanita. It brings together 20 of his classic tales to provide a glimpse of the author`s range and diversity. She aptly said, "what distinguishes Premchand's writings is that, in them we feel the tempo of the times in which he lived. Usuallly he catches our attention by a few striking phrases and straight away plunges into action...While victimization of the powerless was doubtless Premchand's main theme, placing him in the company of the great truth tellers like Charles Dickens, Thomas Hardy, Leo Tolstoy and Fyodor Dostoevsky. ." In the words of Harish Trivedi, *"Translating Premchand is a tricky task perhaps because he is not a realist writer. He treates large urgent themes with a moral dimension, and goes for idealistic endings in which characters must repent, reform and reconstitute their lives and themselves before they can live happily ever after. The cliché is to form a mere trick of the plot. It is the eesence of his radical humanism." Trivedi finds even the King's translation of Ghaban inept and full of mistakes. The translator is not able to translate even the title of the novel correctly. The translator says that Premchand wrongly gave this title because according to his reading no embazlelment has taken place here. It is also very bad in taste that the name of the translator is given on the cover page and Premchand's name is conspicuous with his absence."*

The above understanding indicates the complexity of translating Premchand. In the age of translation when Premchand can be read in translation, the job of a translator is also to present the text in a manner suitable to the target readership. Premchand wrote at a time when Indians reading English fiction and fiction in English were few. Now there are millions who read Chetan Bhagat and Raja Rao both. When Gurdial Malik translated him in 1946, his readers were limited, now we find cyber-space filled with blogs where Premchand is discussed and read. M. Asaduddin in his edited volume *"Premchand in World Languages: Translation, reception and cinematic representations" (2016)* underlines the complexity of translating Premchand as "the reception and reputation of a writer in the receiving culture depend on the quality of translation and the version the translator has chosen from, one needs to be sensitive to the complexity to arrive at a judgement." In one of the chapter's of this book Snehal Singhavi concludes that " Premchand as a writer only makes sense under the sign of translation, as a writer whose intellectual concerns are only made manifest by putting his translations( and translations of his works) at the centre of our attention." On the other hand, Harish Trivedi opines that Premchand appears to be not even a shadow what he is in the original.

Still there are limited number of translations from Premchand's voluminous oeuvre, given his high status in the canon of Hindi prose writing, compared to the number of translations of later Hindi writers (Nirmal Varma, Yashpal, Mohan Rakesh, and Uday Prakash, to name only the most prominent ones) is surprising. Does his work not appeal to the modern publisher/critic/reader? Have they lost their cultural and social meaning? It is also a fact that each of his translators translates him is if he/she is the first translator and has no knowledge of the translations if any. The recent republication of the Godan translation and its critical acclaim and a revival of interest in readership suggest otherwise, but generally mainstream publishers are more interested in contemporary writing of a less overtly social-realist and occasionally idealist nature. Though Premchand is perhaps one of the more sought after writers after Tagore, he is ordinarily read in English for sociological study of his time. As U. R. Ananthmurthy says in the article *"What does translation mean in India?"(2008)* raising relevant questions related to the translation scenario in a multilingual country like India. "I must try to change our academic notion of the word "translation" and make it more homely, if I want to make more sense... I read Saul Bellow as literature but Premchand is read in the universities of the United States of America for sociological purposes. That is their problem, not ours. But that may well become our problem too, if we should also globlise and become prisoners of the homogenized modern world system." Ananthmurthy understands of translation and Premchand is based on his personal expereice as a writer, professor and thinker. Indranath Chaudhuri too wrote in an article published in The Navbharat Times ( 10 October 1993) and opined that "in Western Universities when

Indian literature is studied it is with socio-anthropological interest, without regard to universal values or the importance of understanding the continuity of the Indian literary tradition and what is specifically Indian in the aesthetics of a given work."When researchers like Devleena Ghose turn to Premchand to find in his writing reliable sociological evidence, it should be understood that Premchand is being seen as a chronicler of his time, "Premchand's writing is not only an important document of the nationalist movement, but also of peasant conditions at this time. His fiction is true to the historical record and complements the social history of this period, thus bearing out David Craig's contention that the more effective a piece of fiction in its own medium, the more reliable it is as sociological evidence."

Amrit Rai, Premchand's son, in the introduction to the two volume anthology of Premchand's stories found and collected after his death and published with the title "*Gupt Dhan*" (Secret Treasure) wrote about the kind of change he made while transcribing Premchand's stories from Urdu to Hindi, "I thought it unfair to Hindi readers to publish these stories in their original form. So I clothed them in Hindi, in the style of Munshiji, as far as it was possible for me. How far I have succeeded in this effort to not only preserve the soul of the story but the language and style as well will be judged by you. As for me, I feel satisfaction in the thought that I have pulled all my resources in the endeavours." Snehal Shingavi in her study *"Premchand and the politics of language : on translation, cultural nationalism and irony"* states that Premchand as a writer only makes sense under the sign of translation, as a writer whose intellectual concerns are only made manifest by putting his translations ( and translations of his work) at the centre of our attention.

Gayatri Chakrovorty Spivak in her celebrated essay *"The Politics of Translation"* (2000) says that the translator must surrender to the text. Her plea that a translator should adopt a procedure of "love" and "surrender" towards the original is a traditional Indian viewpoint of all translators and I am sure that Indian readers also go to Premchand in translation with the same amount of love and surrender as a translator goes. I would like to use here two Hindi words " *Shradhdha*" and " *Bhakti*" and conclude that reading

Premchand is an event filled with devotion and love for him and for India where the past is never a foreign country, it is always present. What is still left to translate should be translated to reveal and represent him to the readers in English.

## Journalist Premchand

*As a journalist writing on topical matters from the beginning of his writing career around 1910 and right up the last decade of his life when he was himself the editor of significant journals – Hans ( monthly 1930- ) and Jagaran ( weekly 1932-) and Madhuri (1927-1931). Nigam admitted to Madan Gopal, Premchand's biographer, that Premchand himself was writing Zamana's popular monthly column entitled "Raftar-i-Zamana" (the March of Time) on current developments in national and international fields-with or without the initials of "Navabrai." Between1900 and 1910, Premchand wrote on national and international issues and topics under Navabrai's name in Avaz-i-khalq (Banaras), Zamana (Kanpur), and Adib (Allahabad). In the words of Harish Trivedi, Premchand offered 'virtually a running commentary on the evolving national scene in his notes and columns as well as in longer analytical essays.' In Vividh Prasang (1962) Premchand's son Amrit Rai collected such writing and just a look on the titles will reveal their diversity and depth. "The National Stage: The Struggle for Independence", "Hindu- Muslims", "Untouchability", "Workers and Peasants", "Religion and Society", "The World of Women", "National Language" are some of titles. Between 1900 and 1910 Premchand wrote on many current topic under Navabrai's name in Aavaz-i-khalq (Banaras), Zamana (Kanpur), and Adib (Allahabad). He wrote biographical sketches of Oliver Cromwell, Raja Man Singh, Gopal Krishna Gokhale, Swami Vivekananda, Garibaldi, Queen Victoria and Thomas Gainsborough. He wrote critical pieces on Sharar and Sarshar, Krishan Kunwar, and Akbar's poetry. His varied interest and wide reading compelled him to write on such subjects as constitutional rule in Turkey, the swadeshi movement, how to popularise swadeshi, the industrial training centre at Baroda (Kala Bhavan), the Urdu language and the novel, and primary education in U. P. etc. In a journal Chand, established by*

*Ramrakh Singh Sahgal in Allahabad in 1922,Premchand regularly reported on news and features concerning women and supported them.*

Through the character of Omkar Nath, The editor of "Bijli" in the novel to average editor of his time. He is not an editor to present the facts and truth but is busy in getting favours from the government and the rich. When he finds some report against Rai Sahib he tries to get some monetary consideration in lieu of hushing up the matter. He knows that it is not appropriate to do so and is also against moral principles, yet he is not at all afraid of pouncing on such a rich man who is busy in exploiting the rich. Premchand comments very aptly, "It is a pity that people are not bothered about what is published in the newspapers. There is no dreath of money for temples and schools but there is no one to donate something for the sake of propagation of newspapers and magazines. Though we can attain the aim of education for all through newspapers by spending little amount of money, we restrict our spending on school education. If some amount of money or grant is given to the journalists as it is provided to the schools and colleges, these poor persons will not waste their time and energy in collecting advertisements."

*Premchand knew that Journalism required sacrifice and hard work and he himself was not in a position to take up journalism as a career. He wrote to his friend Nigam, "One cannot yet make journalism a career. There is so much to worry and so much to bother about in this field. There is none to pay more than fifty to sixty rupees." "Mrityu ke Picche" is a story of an editor named Babu Ishwar Chandra. He is inspired by the ideals of service to the nation and becomes the editor of a paper to serve the people. This story tells us Premchand's ideals about journalism as a profession. The protagonist of the story resembles Daya Narain Nigam too, the editor of Zamana, who used to face similar difficulties and hardships in keeping the journal going.*

Premchand was of the view that whosoever is in the field of public service should be free from material longings. His idea of a great man was different. For him a great man is one who does great things and not the one who has great wealth. "I can not imagine a great man rolling in wealth. The moment I see a rich man, all his words of art and wisdom are lost upon me. Any great man not dissociated with Mammon, therefore does not attract me. I am glad Nature and fortune have helped me and my lot is cast with the poor. It gives me spiritual relief." For him an ideal journalist should be a man of frugal means.

During the formative years of Hans, even from the very beginning Premchand wanted to use journalism and the journal for the sake of the country. Since it was a kind of dharma to oppose the foreign rule and help the leader Gandhi in the best possible ways, Premchand treated his vocation as a tiny contribution for the mammoth cause. Therefore he wrote in the first editorial of Hans "It is said that when Shri Rama was building the bridge across the straits (of Mannar), little birds and animals helped him by bringing a little of the earth to build the bridge. The battle in which the country is now engaged is far grimmer. India has sounded the bugle for the non-violent battle. Leaving the peace of the pond, Hans, with a little lump of earth in its tiny beak, has started to help cross the straits (help in the struggle for freedom)." According to his biographer Madan Gopal Hans was the third son and Jagaran was the foster child for him. The first issue of Hans had his signature story Juloos. Hans used to have varied topics but all were in a way related to the freedom struggle. For example editorials and essays on topics such as "The role of literature in the struggle for Independence," "Dominion status and swaraj," "The duty of the youth," "Get ready for the struggle for independence," "Machine-gun and peace," "Need for propaganda in villages," "The big stick," "Simon Report," "Boycott of the Round Table Conference " were in abundance.

Premchand's association with another magazine Madhuri(1927-1931) is also important, though he was just an associate editor. Madhuri gave him ample opportunities to speak out and give a befitting reply to those who used to write and speak against him. During 1927, the same Saraswati magazine which once welcomed him in the Hindi arena started writing against him. It seemed every one wanted to prove that Premchand was a one novel wonder and his novel Premashram was not as good as Sevasadan was. Hemchandra Joshi and Ila Chnadra Joshi both wrote articles against him. Avadh Upadhyaya wrote a number of articles attacking him. Priestly Brahmin class of Allahabad was against him and a sketch on Motyeram Shastri published in Madhuri of January 1928 took him to court. Saligram Shastri, a vaidya of Lucknow, charged Premchand and Krishna Bihari Mishra, editors of Madhuri, under Section 500/109 of the Indian Penal Code. But the magistrate dismissed the case, and advised the complainant to "quietly leave the court through the backdoor."

While discussing about writers and their profession Premchand told his wife as follows:

> The government and the public, both think that writer is their slave. After all even the author has his own existence. If he writes according to others, what will remain of him? The author has his own sanctity. Government puts him in jail; the public threatens to kill him, the author should get scared and stop writing.... a writer produces, he does so out of his own emotional conviction (kuredan)... there are disputes in the whole world...You cannot run away from them. You should confront them (Premchand Ghar Mein, p. 149)

Premchand's views are loud and clear. He wanted to write for his own pleasure and not for the appeasement of any group of people. He wanted to think independently and write independently.

## Filmy Premchand

*It is said that good stories only can give us good entertaining and socially worthwhile cinema. Premchand tried his hand in story writing for the films and in fact went to live in Bombay for a while. He acted in a small role of a rustic in film "Mazdoor" based on his story and he was the dialogue writer for the film. The film was not a blockbuster. He had to come back home. The other story which Premchand wrote was Navajeevan. It was round the theme of Rajput chivalry-a theme which had been the favourite of Premchand during the earliest phase of his literary career. Mahalakshmi Cinetone's film version of Sevasadan is also to be mentioned which was produced by Nanubhai Vakil. Its Tamil version, in which M. Subbalakshmi appeared for the first time in films, is reported to have been an excellent film.*

In independent India prominent directors including the famed one like Satyajit Ray took up his stories and presented films worth remembering. In 1977 Satyajit Ray gave us " The Chess Players" based on the story " Shatranj ke Khiladi" in which Amjad Khan, Sanjeev Kumar and Saeed Jaffery acted and Amitabh Bachchan was the narrator. In the same year another Bangali director Mrinal Sen directed a Telugu language film "Oka Oori Katha" based on Premchand's story "Kafan" and the film was an award winning one like The Chess Players. Hrishikesh Mukherjee gave us a film based on his novel "Gaban" in which Sunil Dutt, Sadhna, Minu Mumtaj were the lead actors. Before it came another remarkable film based on "Godan" (1963). It was a film in which Hori was Raj Kumar and the music director was Pt. Ravi Shankar. Who can forget Rafi's song "Pipra Ke Patva..."? In 1982 Satyajit Raj again brought a film "Sadgati" based on a story by the same name in which Om Puri played the role of the protagonist Dukhia.

*Gulzar immortalized Premchand's work on Doordarshan.* A poet-lyricist-writer-scenarist, he has to his credit over 50 screenplays, five anthologies of poetry, two collections of short stories, 16 books for children and countless memorable lyrics. The 26-epsiode serial, *"Tehreer Munshi Premchand Ki"* (The Writings of Munshi Premchand), had been commissioned by Doordarshan. It includes multiple episodes of the celebrated Hindi-Urdu litterateur's best-known novels, Godaan (The Gift of a Cow) and Nirmala. The stories taken up by him are *Eidgah,Sava Ser Gehun, Boodhi Kaaki, Namak Ka Daroga, Hajj-e –Akbar, Kafan, Poos Ki Raat, Thakur Ka Kuan and Namak ka Daroga.* Gulzar adapted Premchand's books into small-screen because he says that he finds the author close to his heart."I have met Premchand in three stages of my life. I met him first in school when I read *'Hajj-E-Akbar'* and *'Idgah'*. I could very well relate to the story of *'Idgah'* because I had seen my mother making *chapattis* in tandoor and her hands used to get blisters. Second time I met him in my college when the interpretation of these stories become big. I started relating with the socio-political scenario of the society and last I met him when I turned director. I understood how beautifully, he used to bring out the small nuances of our day-to-day life."

## English Premchand

Premchand was the voice of the Indian village and wrote in chaste Hindi and Urdu, though he often wrote his notes in English. He was well read and well-versed in English. He was a permanent certified English teacher (Certified by J. W. Bacon on 14-9-06 Government Central college, Allahabad). According to Kamal Kishore Goenka (1988: 361) one of the characteristic features of Premchand's creativity was that he used to write the outline of his stories, novels and essays in English first and then he used to write in Hindi or Urdu as the case might be. This was the way he got the seed from English and the contribution of English language in his thought process can't be overlooked. He himself acknowledged a number of times that English was the language of the elite and he was a writer of the land where English couldn't be a language for his creative expression. He was against the slavery of the English language. It is interesting to recall that the Hindi Sahitya Parishad's correspondence with which Gandhiji and Premchand both were associated was carried out in English. When a member of the Parishad expressed his displeasure to Premchand, the latter wrote back: "The Parishad is a child of the Congress and when Congress carries on its correspondence in English, why do you think that the Parishad should be free from slavery to the English language?The Parishad's secretary is a non-Hindi person but a devotee of Hindi. If you press your point too far, he too will abandon it". (Madan Gopal 1964: 425) Once an admirer asked him, "Why do you reply all your letters in English?" He gave a hearty laugh, bambook laughter, "I am a B. A. in English, Man!"

In Premchand's *Bazaar-e-Husn* (Courtesans' Quarter, in Hindi *Sevasadan*), two characters engage themselves over the issue of "mental slavery" to the West. A little later, a third character intervenes and exclaims: "As long as the educated among us remain under the spell of English, no national language can come into being. And if intelligent people like you are devoted to English, a national language will never be born ... people have found a lofty language like English and have sold them over to it. I don't understand why people think it honorable to speak and write in English. I too have studied English. I spent two years abroad and learned to speak and write from the best English teachers, but I hate it. It feels like I am wearing nothing." What he called slavery is a way of life now.

While he devoted his prescribed time to teaching and supervising the work of the school there was seldom a day when he came to the school without a copy of one English novel or another. If there was a period when he did not have to take a class, he would read the novel and then think about it. He was so lost in weaving out the plots of his novels or his short stories that anyone who went to him found him in the condition of an "opium eater" or a daydreamer. When he wanted to write a play he asked a copy of *Twelfth Night* by William Shakspeare. In Kanpur when he used to spend his evenings at Zamaana's editor Nigam's house along with Durga Sahai "Saroor", Naubat Rai "Nazr", Pyarelal "Shakir" and several others he used to invariably discuss the novels of Walter Scott and Charles Dickens. The friend circle used to persuade him to write as the European trend was.

Premchand's creative impulse was extraordinary and there is a definite and unique place of English in his thought process and style of presentation. He was a graduate scholar in English literature and Persian. "Premchand was studying for an MA in English Literature but unavoidable reasons prevented him from completing the course. He had secured a second-class B. A. degree in English Literature, Persian and History from the Allahabad University. During his intermediate days, Premchand studied English Literature as a subject," says Kamal Kishore Goenka who taught at Delhi University and completed his PhD on Premchand in 1972. The unavoidable reasons made "a bright prospect for the future and his ambitions-of taking an M. A. degree and of becoming a lawyer-became utopian. It was like wanting to "climb the Everest with one's feet bound with chains wrought, not in iron but, in the heaviest-known metal"says Madan Gopal.

Premchand was about 40 years of age and was already feeling old and sick but the keen desire of becoming a professor of English was there in him. Premchand himself said to one of his friends about this when his friend Imtiaz Ali Taj was contemplating going to the UK for further studies. He said, "It is very unfair to your own self, as also to the nation, not to avail of this chance. When these years of youthful ambition are past, you, like me, would regret it. Had I passed my M. A. in my early years, my plight wouldn't have been as helpless as it now is. I devoted my early years to the writing of short stories, and my wordly needs are now forcing me to take a degree."

Hindi was the language he learnt later. In fact he had to write in Hindi because he was banned and censured by the British government when his writing in Urdu was found to be inflammatory according to them. He couln't stop writing. He just stopped using his name and got the pen name Premchand instead. His writing in Urdu didn't give him enough money and day by day it was becoming to get him published in Urdu. Though he used to write in Urdu and Hindi , he noted down the spark of the ideas in English to turn it into a story or novel at a later stage. The English outline was the seed or idea with which he used to write in Urdu or in Hindi as he deemed fit and someties he himself translated it into another language. There are a number of articles, interviews, and letters etc which are in English. It is already stated that he was a trained ELT expert and knew the value of English. In fact his letters and personal correspondence are in English. In this section a glimpse of Premchand in English is given to understand that he could have written in English as well. K. M. Munshi once suggested to Madan Gopal, Premchand's biographer that without the summaries of the short stories and novels, a reader in English would not be able to get an idea of the development of Premchand as a writer. We find that Madan Gopal wrote brief summaries of a number of stories which make Premchand's biography a little bit old fashioned but when we read Premchand's notes we understand that it is necessary for both the writer and the reader not to overlook these notes. Dr Devraj's valuable paper *" Katha Ke Tatv"* (1957) says that these Engish outlines by Premchand are a valuable document to understand the process and product which the novelist and story writer presented before us a finished product. In his words, "I have read somewhere that in America there are a number of libraries where the rough drafts, pieces of paper, comments written on the margins of a manuscripts or a book are kept with a great care, so that we can understand the writer better and not only understand him as an author but as a person who struggled a lot to refine his art and expression. Through these notes we can see the way the author really making a story happening. Now is the time when we should also start such an endeavour in India, so that we also get an accurate picture of the writer and use this material to understand him and also to evaluate him properly." In this article Dr Devraj quoted the statement of Premchand's son Amrit Rai that he had seen a 25-30 page English outline of Premchand's last unfinished novel *"Mangal Sutra"* but now he couldn't get hold of it. This is a very unfortunate condition that we don't understand the value of these papers and notes and do not know the art of preserving manuscripts and other documents. How amazing it is that the seed in English and the tree in Hindi/Urdu has similarities and differences both. It means Premchand used to get the spark or the idea of a story or a novel and used to very quickly note it down in English. Then the whole edifice of the novel or the story used to be structured on it. You will note the difference when you find that the *gaudan* in the novel by the same title "Gaudaan" is performed by the wife but in the outline it is planned in another way. According to Hindu customs, the *gaudan* is performed by the son and it is done by the son in the outline. This kind of end might have been ordinary but the extraordinariness had been filled in by the novelist when this gaudan was performed by the wife. This act fills the novel with tragedy and remorse,we feel that in the life of the protagonist happiness was just an occasional episode with a general drama of pain through out.

You will find that Premchand used to plan beforehand because he was too busy and had to look after writing, publication, publication of magazines and several other works. He was continuously writing in Hindi and Urdu. His correspondence with so many people was also time -consuming. Banarsi Das Chaturvedi, the editor of Vishal Bharat, the sister publication in Hindi, who had met Premchand once in 1924 or so, had carried on correspondence with him mostly in English! It was also the habit of Premchant that as and when he got the idea of a story, novel, essay, play, and even translation, he used to note it down in English. Two outlines of his yet to be started novels in English are available which might have been penned in 1930s. We are unfortunate that Premchand could never write the novels based on these outlines and he died in 1936 at the age of 56. To illustrate the point, let me give you these outlines as found out by the researchers.

## 1. An outline of "Rangbhoomi" by Premchand

I. Prabhu Sewak turns a staunch nationalist. Extremely bold and desperate, revolutionary tendencies...

II. Vinay and Sofia living quietly in a cottege in hilly village. Vinay is chivalrous and full of love. He is devoted to Sofia. As he has again to be united, she doesn't consent, once or twice when he approaches her. She snubs him. She says she will not have him unless given by Rani and Kuar. Then they read in the read in newspapers the changing attitude of Kaur sahib. The moment is at stake. Nobody is to take care. Sofia then comes out with the intention of preserving the moment and if possible to win over the Rani.

III. She comes directly to Rani. A scene, Rani obdurate, turns his face. She pleading. At last Rani brought accord. Vinay is beyond himself with joy to receive her letter of welcome, written by the Rani.

IV. Mr John Sewak has succeeded in acquiring the land. The struggle.

IV. Tahir Ally comes out of his jail and is broken hearted to see the plight of his family. ( He goes to Mahir Ali -) Mahir does not come even to see him. He falls ill and dies of grief.

VI. Ghisu, Mithua and Vidayadhar all turn bad characters. They one night try to violate Radhika. She raises an alarm. Surdas at once arrive on the spot and takes hold of two of them. Mithun makes his escape. Surdas's true evidence. Bajrangi glad to hear the judgement, but Jagirdar is enraged and vows revenge. Bhairo saves him. Then struggle is in the end over, Indraduta now takes the field.

VII. Prabhu Sewak and John Sewak united. The scheme is abolished. The mill is runnng. P. Das goes away again to Europe. While J. Sewak is grinding his wheel with desperate and pitiable patience.

VIII. Nayak Ram dreams a drama that Vinay has jumped and he jumps after him. He broke his knee apart. Takes much time to restore. Then he comes to his home, sees everything in ruins.

IX. The struggle begins. In the meantime marriage between Sofia and Vinay is also settled. Dates are fixed. Vinay now seeks excuses to keep away from the struggle for fear of imprisonment and death. Sofia is glad to have him by her side. She tells him to remain with Surdas. She does not quite like Vinay's cowardice. All volunteers are ready to join in the struggle but vinay's cold- heartedness. On the last day... there... in a stir, some violence is feared. Police and military came in the town and spot. The next day she herself goes the scene. Vinay accompanies her. They watch the scene. People are flocking, brick bats are thrown. Vinay tries to conduct Sofia safely home. Firing is ordered. She goes Surdas falling on the ground. He is overcome by emotion and runs towards her. Vinay is ashamed. He comes forward to pacify the mob but is hooted. In this agony, at his unpopularity, at his weakness, at his moral frustration he is overcome by a sudden grief and remorse. He stabs himself to death.

Police and military succeeded in driving away the mob.

X. Sofia leads Surdas to hospital and attends upon him. Daily thousands come to have a look of Surdas. Bajrangi and others come. Rani also comes and showers him with flowers. Ten days pass. Surdas is happy and smiling. He never complains. Then Sofia all of a sudden comes to know of Vinay's self-sacrifice. She is much unnerved. She respects at her whole life. When Surdas passes away the whole town accompanied. Raja and one are the only defaulters. Sofia returns to Rani and is warmly received. Rani drops a tear (but never loses heart). And weary of life, hating the life- losing her son, losing her daughter, Rani becomes mad. Her brain is turned. She leaves home and is never heard of Sofia...

(*Premchand ka aprapya sahitya* 361-363)

## 2. Kayakalp: an outline

Kayakalp is the first novel of Premchand. This is the novel written in Hindi and is not a translation. In the manuscript one can find the following outline in English.

Bibhuda Singh is yagyanarain-crafty, parsimonious, selfish, but serviceful, tactful.

Vishal Singh is Bechan Lal- simple, honest, wanting in moral courage.

Kalyan Singh is Chandrika Prasad- sneaking in the presence of superiors, cannot manage household, suspicious.

The new Rani's father is Nana- flatterer, selfish, dishonest, unscrupulous, drunkard, hopes to bild his fortune with his daughter.

Chkradhar's father-flatterer, kind, generous, mild, simple-hearted.

The pundit (Vibhuda Prasad) and his wife both turn Hindu Sangathankars

Bibhuda is a Persian- readman. Knows very little Sanskrit. His dialogue must be an educated mussalman.

Chakradhar always seeks God in man.

## Ideas

Trials and troubles mould the human character, they make heighest heroes of men. Power and authority is the curse of humanity. Even the highest fall a victim to power and lose their charcter. Chakradhar rose morally while struggling for existence. His fall began when he came in power.

Rani is rejuvenated. She forgets her previous birth, who she was, how she got rejuvenation. Raj Kumar begins to decline from the same day. Rani afraid to approach him. Struggle. In the end Rani loses her balance. Passion overcomes her. She approaches Raj Kumar. A love scene. The next day Raj Kumar, seized by a fatal sickness dies. Rani again sinks into self gratification. She builts her Rangshala. She agais birth in leads a life of flippancy.

Raj Kumar takes his birth in Kuar Vishal Singh's house from Ahalya. When the boy grows into a lad, he starts a tour through India. He reaches Telari, sees the Rani, memories begin to revive. Rani making approaches.

Chakradhar comes out from Jail a nobler and purer. All the extreme hostility of human nature dawns upon him and his sense of duty is awakened. There as it was never before.

The story should be put in Lucknow. Necessary changes should be made.

The Raja has three wives. He inherits the gaddi. He falls in mad love with Ahilya. Ahilya knows him (she knows how dull and pitiable his life is) She is also fond of riches. She marries him for money. But the Raja is sincere and overpowering tendencies gains her heart. The mutual love arises. The Raja is so immersed in love that all considerations are vanished from his heart, wealth even his son. He no longer pines for a son.

She is faithful to the Raja. Whatever she does, Raja approves. The Rani to come to live with her, although at first they hated her and thought she was coming to exploit the Raja.

Chakradhar remains poor.

Manorma is an ideal housewife and love. She makes Chakradhar happy in whatever she gets, always happy and cheerful. Chakradhar's character is very high. He devotes himself to service and uplift of his brothern. Rani pays money for Chakradhar.

Ahilya dies in the end. The Raja forsakes his Raj and draws a deed of which he makes Chakradhar a secretary.

Ahilya secretly in love with Chakradhar, but never utters a single sentence. Chkradhar too is ardent lover of Rani but never gives vent to his feelings.

In the end it turns out that Manorama was the daughter of Thakur Hari Sewak from Loungi. They had cast her away and entrusted her to the care of a man and had been paying monthly for it.

$23^{rd}$ chapter – Chakradhar proposes marriage to his partner.

Arrival at Agra. Jashodha Nandan's house is broken into and he is murdered. Ahilya spirited away. Chakradhar gets the news and hurries to Agra. He interview Khwaja Saheb. For a week-no trace. Then Khwaja Saheb takes upon himself to search her out. At last he finds her in safe custody.

24th chapter – Chakerdhar gets the news and proceeds to Agra. Kwaja Sahib hands ahalya over to him. Ahalya ready to kill herself, but Chakerdhar marries her then and there.

25th Chapter-Their married life want and poverty. She is a good housewife and manages to live in comfort in whatever she gets. A son is born to her.

26th Chapter – Manorma agony, she invites her and she is recognised by the Raja.

27th Chapter – Ahalya and Chakerdhar's parting with her.

28th Chapter – Manorma sister to Ahalya. Ahalya pines and is about death. Raja is murdered.

29th Chapter – Chakradhar now comes and lives with Ahalya. Gradually his interest is awakened in the state affairs. Manorma is jealous. Chakradhar begins to cut her expenditure.

Manorma grudges this.

30thChapter – Manorma is furious. She conspires to murder. Chakradhar at the hour repents and commits suicide.

31th Chapter- The whole state is opposed to Chakradhar only to his fairness and freedom from bias. Hindu- Mohd quarrels grow- Gusguru Sewak heads a Hindu riots, Chakradhar leaves the state in disgust and works silently for the cause of unity with unflagging zeal and stubborn hope.

32th Chapter- Rani Deva Priya is widowed and remains widow 20 years. Then she is approached by a young prince. She is brought back to Jagadish Nagar.

(Page 363-366)

Madan Gopal (1964: 230-31) mentions that "within the pages of the manuscript of Kayakalpa are also found suggestive details of the principal characters of the novel. These details, it is interesting to note, are in English! We quote from the manuscript.

"IDEAS: Trials and troubles mould the human character; they make heroes of men; power and authority is the curse of humanity;

even the highest fall a victim to power and lose their character. Chakradhar rose moraily while struggling for existence; his fall began when he came to power." On another page are some interesting suggestions indicating that he used to draw his characters from actual life. Along with the imaginary names of the principal characters, he would also mention real names as aide memoirs. The following sentences (in English) are significant: "Vibudha is Yash Narain Upadhyaya -crafty, parsimonious, selfish, but serviceful, tactful; Vishal Singh is Bechanlal-simple, honest; Kalyan Singh is Chandrika .... Chakradhar is J. Prasad-very shy." Here are some more suggestive traits (in English) of the characters of Kayakalpa. "The new Rani's father is Nana-perfectly selfish, dishonest, unscrupulous, drunkard, hopes to build,' nis fortune with his daughter.;' "Chakradhar's father-flatterer, kind, generous, mild, simplehearted." "The Pandit (Vibudha Prasad) and his wife both turn Hindu sanga t hankar s. " "Vibudha is a Persian-read man. Knows very little Sanskrit. His dialogue must be of an educated Mussalman." "Chakradhar always seeks God in man." "Rani is rejuvenated. She forgets her previous birth, who she was, how she got rejuvenation. Rajkumar begins to decline from the same day. Rani afraid to approach him. Struggle. In the end Rani loses her balance. Passion overcomes her. She approaches Rajkumar. A love scene. The next day Raj kumar, seized by a fatal sickness, dies. Rani again sinks into self-gratification. She builds her Rangashala. She again leads a life of flippancy. " "Rajkumar takes his birth in Kunwar Vishal Singh's house from Ahalya. When the boy grows into a lad, he starts a tour throughout India. He reaches Telari, sees the Rani, memories begin to revive. Rani making approaches."

### 3. The outline of "Karmbhumi"

1. Amarkant awakened. The whole outlook is transformed,his past life is reviewed-His up at once.

2. While working Amar finds Sakina and Munni both there and a scene of humiliation and shame comes upon him. He falls at their feet and begs forgiveness.

I. The municipal resolution passed.

II. Governer's visit of inquiry-His decision.

III. Amarkant awakened. The whole outlook transformed. While working scene-orders of release arrive just them. Jubilation.

IV. All proceed to Hardwar. Naina and Rein and all the others come from Benares to welcome.

Sukhda forms her ministry. Amar cooperates whole heartedly. No ill will. They work together, talk together, form plans together, but their privateselves are apart withone another. Mani devotes herself to the personal comforts of Amar.

The two bills are brought before the council. Both are defeated by jobbery and underhand dealings. Some most reliable friends succumbs to temptations. The ministry is short lived and dissolved and the interested parties find Amar their most uncompromising enemy and plot to assassinate him. Amar remains undaunted. The murderous attack comes. Mani saves Amar. They are then disappointed with democracy and begin to work set up a missionary institution of selfless workers with no wheels to find. This is the hope of the future.

Samar Nath gives away his all in cherritable objects. His fortune is the nucleous of the funds required for new movements. (Page 366-367)

## 4. The outline of "Godan"

We find the following outline of "Godan" in the hand-written manuscript and it is sad that the first two points are missing there. So one can just imagine those lines.

**3.** Hori purchases the cow. The whole village comes to have a look, Shobha is indifferent but Hira grows jealous. He poisons the cow. Hori sees it, but cannot report him to police.

**4.** The whole village goes to the Zamindar to celebrate his Desehra festival. Hori sells his store of barley. He could not hide his face. He wants to increase his tenatry. Zamidar must be impressed. The party goes to Zamindar, there is a drama, a show, a Dhartiyagya. The Zamindar is humane and generous. He tells his story. He is also a member of Distt. Board. There are officers to feast and please, endowments to pay. The tenants come satisfied. Jhunia also comes to the show. Gobar proposes. He is not married and marriage means money. Jhunia surrnders herself.

**5.** Jhunia gets a daughter, Panchayat, Gobar goes away to Calcutta. Panchayat excorts heavy punishment. For redemption Hori has to start on pilgrimage. His heridatry property is mortaged. He is unable to pay the interest. Gobar does not return. Then Sona is to be married. There is no money, no property. He is a day labour now. The girls also go to work with him. The whole mentality is changed.

**6.** The property is to be redeemed. The girl is married. The property comes into possession. Then a quarrel with Hori's brothers for Mahua. Hori is beaten. He fights a suit against brothers. The brothers are jailed. Hori enjoys the scene. But in the end takes care of his family.

**7.** Bhola's son separate. Jhunia is dead. His only child. Bhola begins to rear the child. He has surrerendered his share to his sons and becomes sadhu. The Zamindar takes care of the daughter.

**8.** Zamindar's eldest son is a vakil and a member of council, and also a municipal servant and a nationalist leader. He should be exposed for his hypocrisy, the younger son is a poet and an author with some impulse. He marries Jhunia's daughter. His family outcasts him. He is a social worker and is honoured by the tenants.

**9.** Hori's younger daughter is sold off. The crops have not failed but they brought only enough for rent. There were cattle to feed. What could he do? He was weak. Jhinki was labouring hard to pull on. Then the old man sells off the girl, without the knowledge of his wife. He manufacures a tale to hide his shame.

**10.** Gobar returns a sober man. Tell something of his sojourn abroad. Jhunia has been forgotten,but when he has made good deal by doubtful means, his spiritual awakening takes place. He hurries home. His father is on the death-bed, but he would not receive him back. Gobar is reunited to Jhunia.

**11.** Bhola has brought a widow his wife much younger. He comes to live with Hori. A hut is built for him. He has taken to thieving as he can get no work. Jangi is attracted to this woman and secretly they meet. Then one day the woman gives him up and goes to Jangi. Bhola lives with Jangi shamelessly for years. At last one day the wife scolds him for her and beats him with a broom. This incident finishes Bhola.

**12.** Hori drags on a weary and wretched existence. Gobar helps indirectly through his mother who failthfully serves the husband. A last time comes and he expires. Gobar gives him a gaudan.

Introduce – agricultural exhibitions, uplift, literary movement, sugar mills, co-operation.

In another place of the manuscript it is found to be written as follows:

Hori has two brothers-Shobha and Hira

Bhola has two sons- Kanta and Jangi. The daughter Jhunia who is a widow.

Hori has one son Gobar and two daughters- sona and Rupa.

His wife is Jhinki

Shoba is an idler. Hira hard working but rash and short tempered.

Readers of this outline must remember that Premchand changed the presentation, even the names of the charcaters at his will. This is not a summary of the novel but a mere outline or structure with which he started working on the novel. It vividly shows how he visualized scenes and created a final lay out and called a master craftsman of the art of fiction. He is often called " *Upanyas Samrat*" ( The emperor of the novel) and needless to say that his reading of world fiction in English and his zeal to be as good as the novels being written in Bangali paved the way of success.

He used to note down not only the plot structure of his novels but also of stories and you will be astonished to find that more often than not he wrote the outline a number of times. The following outline of the story *"Damul ka Kaidi"* is an example how Premchand wrote the outline two times and only then he wrote the story.

### *1. First Outline of the story* " **Damul Ka Kaidi"**

Sethji in a village-bridge construction, He kills a young boy to set the bridge piller erected. He is caught and sentenced for life. He returns after 14 years and moves towards his home. He finds the same boy as his son. He is awestruck. His whole fortune is ruined. His wife and child are living in obscurity and misery. Seth goes in quest of parents of the boy. They are nowhere to be found. He comes, his own house, is occupied with the building of the bridge. He is building the bridge. His son is caught and killed in a bridge construction. This turns him a wise man. He bows before the Lord with a true heart. He turns a new leaf of life. All desires vanish. He is no more a heretic.

### *2. The second outline is as follows:*

Sethji retuns high spirits, A big construction has been given to him. He departs to his work the same day. The pillers refuse to rise. A sacrifice is necessary. A young boy is caught secretly and sacrificed. The Seth is caught and sentenced for 14 years. He returns to find his house in the possession of othes. After a long serach he goes to the same bridge. It is being constructed. His wife recognizes him. She has a son. The Seth is awestruck. It is the same boy whom he had sacrified. What a change in the fortune! He now labours with his wife but is afraid of his son. One day he found his own son son sacrified in the construction. His wife already dead. His only source of life dried.

**An outline of an essay: Hindi Language and Rastra**

1. Hindi Hindustani and Urdu. The most popular form is Hindustani. The ideal of a language is its universality. Hindustani must be judged on this very test. A dictionary , common language readers,compulsory Hindustani in High School. Hindi Prachar in South India.
2. What are you giving to your own national literature?Much depends on one's gifts but guidance can do something and with this object lekhak sangh has been formed.
3. The chief aim of literature is to bring into play finer emotion to man-various aims- a villager's theory.

4. Literature is not imitation of life alone. It is like life but not life. it inspires at an improvement on god's creation. it rebels against unreason, false belief.
5. Discuss the theory of-
6. An all India board
7. Everything coming fresh from Europe is not sound- shocking thing in literature. Tendency to say striking things untrue things.

**Outlines of stories and novels never written:**

**Stories:**

**10-02-1936**

A social worker of position comes in contact with a crass widow. who is conducting a girls'school. They are attracted towards each other. Once while the gentleman goes to see her, he is taken to task by her husband. He takes offence and never goes to the lady.

Several years pass. Then he is invited by the lady to see her. He goes the lady gives him a lecture on the unreality of the world.

**11-02-1936**

1. A fairly wealthy man, with a good deal of weakness. He manages to secure a post in the diplomatic department and is appointed Ambassador in a court. There he happens to fall in love with the princess. He marries her.

But the princess soon defected. He is so vulgar and rough. She divorces him. This is the turning in his career.

He is depressed with. Then he joins a circus party, but soon leaves that job.

Then he becomes a waiter. But with unruffled making the best of bad bargain.

Novels never written: When we look at the manuscript of Karmbhumi we find an outline of a novel which was never written. This outline is as follows:

A youth punished for transportation in a political murder trail.

His betrothed and father are both transformed and when he returns he finds them ready to welcome him, all fear vanished.

The details should be worked out- 160 pages- Price- 12 aana

1st Chapter: The trial and punishment.

2nd Chapter: The betrothed girl was present at the court. She proposes to remain with the father of her fiancé. Her fiance's farewell latter.

3rd Chapter: The police threaten the father, but he is adamant. His temperament is quite revolutionized. The father subscribed secretly to the fund of the political party and is ready to help it in every way.

4th Chapter : The secret is divelged by one of the party. The police threaten the father but he is adamant. His daughter in law encourages him.

5th Chapter : The daughter in law attends a political meeting and is vociferously cheered. She is elected President of the Crogress committee.

6th Chapter : Lahore Congress. She attends and delivers a speech at Lahore. The resolution for independence. She supports it in an excellent speech.

7th Chapter : The ratification . Her effots to form a Lady worker's Union successful.

8th Chapter : Picketing by the lady and arrest.

9th Chapter :

There is another story idea written on a sheet of paper. You can not say if it is a story of a plot of a novel.

An old woman has an adopted daughter. She has brought up as her own daughter, found her as her own daughter, found her in a fair. She wanted to marry her to some decent youngman, but no body is forthcoming. Then she announcing a heavy dowry, she gives out that she has got some money buried in the house by her husband. No sooner the announcement is public hordes of youth come forward with offers of marriage. The old woman makes a selection and there are 7m elgible candidates. She decides to give away the daughter to the young man who can earn Rs. 100/ within a week.

The friends hold a meeting among themselves as to who should be the leader,how can they go on with their scheme without a leader? How could each of them earn Rs 100/ within a week ? They could all earn the amount together and then decide by lots as to who should be the bridegroom?

( But what are the qualifications of a leader ? He should be nimble of foot, he should be clever of tongue so that he may not be caught. He should be clever of tongue and he should be patient so that when in tight corner, he should not give out his identity.)

He should be clever with hand, clever wih foot, clever with tongue, and clever with sight.

He should be clever with tongue and when in tight corner he should be able to beat a hasty retreat.

How to decide who should be the leader?Why not give the leadership to one who was the best runner. They stand in a line, but it is difficult to wait for the final signal. Some of them in their impatience runs before the signal. When at last the signal problem is solved, the race begins. But the laggers play foul, by giving up one round and reach first. This scheme is unsuccessful, they then try single hand to hand fight. He who beats all the rest should be the leader. Ponga Nath is the best fighter and he is selected leader. All swear allegiance and perfect confidence in his leadership.

The leader now decides the scheme-

To earn Rs. 100 –by fair means was altogether out of question. Unless we could make fools of men, could hoodwink them, they couldn't earn anything. all those who had wealth knew how to turn the blindness and folly of others to their advantage. Our big Mahajans and Vakils and industrial magnates and scholars –what they all do – make fools- this is the universal law.

Then one of them puts on the appearance of a dancing girl, while three turn her Sazindas and begin singing and dancing in the streets. A crowd gathers. The remaining three men take to pick pocketing.

The leader has his two assistants standing a little apart from him and directed to come to his aid in case of emergency. The leader picks the pocket of a decent man and is caught red handed. He gets several slaps. Many men gather and begin to beat him. The two friends appointed to come to his aid in emergency take to their heels. The poor leader is belaboured and is made the laughing stock,made to ride on an ass with blackened face.

An outline of a story is found on the back of a letter received by Premchand as follows:

A poor girl, plain looking , gives the unlawful assembly and marches in procession in hand with flag.

A cloth dealer opens his foreign cloth-shop and creates a sensation in the congress camp. A number of volunteers at once run up but are arrested by the police.

There is a great commotion, congressmen volunteers are unnerved. At that time a girl comes forward- a plain looking slim figure.

Police come and arrest her, She returns after six months.

(2)

There are two plots:

A social worker of position comes in contact with a crass widow, who is conducting a girls' school. They are attracted towards each other. Once while the gentleman goes to see her, he is taken to task by her husband. He takes offence and never goes to the lady.

Several years pass. Then he is invited by the lady to see her. He goes, the lady then gives him a lecture on the reality of the world.

(3)

A fairly wealthy man, with a good deal of weakness. He manges to secure a post in the diplomatic deptt. And is appointed Ambassador in a court. There he happens to fall in love with the princess. He marries her.

But the princess is soon defected. He is so vulgar and rough. She divorces him. This is turning in his career.

He is depressed with. Then he joins a circus party, but soon leaves the job.

Then he becomes a waiter, but with unruffled making the best of bad bargain.

## Interview

When Indra Nath Madan was a student he sent a few questions to Premchand in English and Premchand replied him on 26-12-1934. The interview is worth reading to understand Premchand.

Madan: Which of your works do you consider as your best creative work?

Premchand: Rangbhoomi is, in my opinion, the best of my works.

Madan: Is it true that every novel of yours has an ideal character?

Premchand: Yes, I have in each of my novels an ideal character, with human failings as well as virtues, but essentially an ideal character. In "Premashram" there is Premshankar; in "Rangabhoomi" there is Surdas". Similarly in "Kayakalp" there is "Chakradhar", in "Karmabhoomi" it is Amarkant.

Madan: How many short stories in all have you written? Are there any unpublished stories?

Premchand: The total number of my stories reaches an approximate figure of 250. Unpublished stories I have got none.

Madan: Do you accept that some writers of the world have influenced you?

Premchand: Yes, I have been infmluenced by Tolstoy, Victor Hugo, and Romain Rolland. As regards the short stories I was inspired originally by Dr Rabindra Nath. Since then, I have evolved my own style.

Madan: Have you ever seriously tried to write dramas? If so, have you got any success of it?

Premchand: I never seriously attempted drama. I have conceived one or two plots which I thought might be better utilized in a drama. Drama loses its importance when not staged. Indian has not got a stage, particularly Hindi and Urdu. What passes for stage is the effect oft Parsi stage, for which I have a horror. Then I never came in touch with drama technique and stage craft. So my dramas were only meant as reading dramas. Why should I not stick to the novel where I have greater scope to reveal my characters, than I can possibly have in a drama? This is why I have preferred novel as a vehicle of my thought. I still hope to write one or two dramas. As far as financial success is concerned this commodity is rare in Hindi or Urdu. You may get notorious, but by no means financially independent. Our people have not the weakness for buying books. It is apathy, dullheadedness, and intellectual lethargy.

Madan: What are your expeciences of Cinema? Could a writer make a place for himself in the field of cinema?

Premchand: Cinema hass no place for a literary person. I came in this line as it offered some chances of getting independent financially, but now I see I was under a delusion and am going back to my literature. In fact I have never ceased contributing to literary work, which I regard as the aim of my life. Cinema is only what pleadership might have meant for me, only healthier.

Madan: Were you ever imprisoned during the freedom movement?

Premchand: I have never been to jail. I am not a man of action. My writings have several times offended the Powers, one or two of my books were proscribed.

Madan: Do you believe in bringing about social change through revolution?

Premchand: I believe in social evolution, our object being to educate public opinion. Revolution is the failure of saner methods. My ideal society is one giving equal opportunities to all. How is that stage to be reached except by evolution? It is the people's character that is the deciding factor. No social system can florish unless we are individually uplifted. What fate a revolution may lead us to is doubtful. It may lead us to worse forms of dictatorship denying all personal liberty. I do want to overhaul, but not destroy. If I had some prescience and knew that destruction would lead us to heaven, I would not mind destroying even.

Madan: What do you think of Divorce? Do you agree that divorce is a solution to marital problems?

Premchand: Divorce is common among the proletariat. It is only in the so called higher classes, where this problem has assumed a serious shape. Marriage even at its best is a sort of compromise and surrender. If a couple means to be happy, they must be ready to make allowances, while there are people who can never be happy even under the best of circumstances. In Europe and America, divorces are not uncommon, in spite of all courtship and free intercourse. One of the couple must be ready to bend, male or female it doesn't matter. I refuse that only males are to be blamed. There are cases where ladies create trouble and fancy grievances. When it is not a certainly and divoycies will cure out nuptial evils, I don't want want to fasten this on to society. Of course, there are cases when a divorce becomes a necessity. But "msfit" is in my opinion nothing but fastidiousness. Divorce without any provision for the poor wife-this demand is only made by morbid individualism. There is no place for it in a society based on equality.

Madan: Do you believe in the existence of some super power?

Premchand: Formerly I believed in a supreme diety, not as a result of thinking, but simply as a traditional belief. That belief is being shattered. Of course, there is some hand behind the universe, but I don't think it has anything to do with human affairs, just as it has nothing to do with the affairs of ants or flies or mosquitoes. The importance which we have given to our ownselves has no justification.

(Premchand ka Aprapya sahitya page 305-308)

**Letters**

Madhri Office

Lucknow

31-8-1928

My dear Kesho Ramji,

Many thanks for your most affectionate and encouraging letter. I was glad to know that "Mukti Marg" was well received and that Mr Sato is satisfied with " Mantra" . Yes, the Zamana version of the story was contributed after "Bishal Bharat", I read the story in a short story conference and naturally stopped dramatically. I felt I would be trying the patience of the audience with any further narration. I have just directed my publishers to send you the books marked on the margin. You will get them in due time. Yes, you may take only such stories as have some universal appeal.

Your name has been registered on the complimentary list of the "Madhuri". You may just scribble few lines at your leiusre on any aspect of Japanese thoughts and life. That would be highly welcome byour readers. A special annual number of "Madhuri" will be out by the 10th of September. You will continue to receive it from that issue.

The literary life in India is so discouraging. There is no public response. You may put your heart out, but your readers don't have. Hardly any of my works has seen the third edition. Some are still in the first. Our peasantry is poor and ignorant and intelligiancia go in for a ready sale but somehow my writng thought highly praised are hardly purchased.

You will find in our special a story from me. I would like to know what you think of it.

I am amused to learn you consider my style flowery. I write the simplest language in Hindi and this is one of my credentials. I shall, however, try to be simpler.

We have yet no rain in this province. The spectre of a famine is staring in the face. A successsion of bad harvests have made the situation worse.

Mahatma Gandhi reigns supreme our our hearts. We are proud of him. I don't know what Japanese people think of him. Just as present an All Parties Confereheld at Lucknow is being held to draw up a constitution for India to be presented before the Siman Commission. I hope you are in touch with Indian politics.

With best wishes,
Yours most sincerely,

**Dhanpat Rai**

3rd September, 1929

Madhuri Office
Lucknow

Dear Sabarwal,

You must be considering me so ungrateful to swallow all your kindnesses without writing to you even an acknowledgement. I have received copies of Japan Time regularly every month. The annual was particularly welcome being an encyclopedia of all about Japan. Let me thank you most sincerely for these considerations. I read The Times with much interest. It is so lively and informative. Its literary articles are of special interst to me. Don't you invite some noted Indians to contribute to Times as it would go a great deal towards better understanding between the two nations. One thing is regratable to me as an Indian. It is so indifferent about Indian and its struggle for freedom. India has every reason to be proud of Japan and naturally looks up to her for sympathy. The proud welcome Japan gave to Dr Tagore led one to believe that she has not totally lost its interest in India, but such instances are few and far between.

Did you like any of my recent stories printed in "Madhuri" and "Vishal Bharat"? You may not like their purchase, but India can never rise to the highest flights of Art, unless she is murmuring under a foreign yolk. This is where literature of a subject country is distinguishable from that of a free nation. Our social and political conditions force us to educate whenever we can and have an opportunity. The greater the feeling the more didactic the work. Young writers are greatest sinners in this respect. In their youthful zeal they forget the principles of art. Are they not excusable?

I have written two little novels recently- "Nirmala" and "Pratigya", none claim to be works of art and are more or less social evils expressed. Would you like to read them? Let me know please.

Rains have done havoc this year. Some provinces have been flooded. But if the rains don't keep up during September, the rains we have had till now would be of no good.

With my best wishes,

Yours Faithfully,
Dhanpat Rai
(Prem Chand)

An extract of the preface of the book *"Soz-i-Vatan"*

The literature of a nation reflects the march of time. The ideas which move it and the emotions that are echoed in their hearts are reflected in prose and verse, like your own image in mirror. Literature in the earlier phase of our life, when the people were steeped in ignorance, consisted of nothing but a few love songs and a few degenerate stories. The latter phase began when a life-and-death struggle took place between the new and the old ideas, and attention came to be devoted to plans for bringing about a reform in the social system. The stories of this phase largely revolve round the theme of social reform. The partition (of Bengal) has awakened ideas of revolt in the hearts of the people. These ideas cannot fail to influence literature. The few short stories presented here mark the beginning of this influence. It is hoped that, as our ideas take shape, literature of this type will also become increasingly popular. Such books are needed by the country badly in order to impress the imprint of patriotism on the coming generations. (1908)

# Chapter - 5

# Premchand and his contemporaries

Many scholars and Premchand readers ask a pertinent question, and we should be able to answer it ourselves too. When Premchand was such a fine writer, why did he not get or even considered for the coveted Nobel Prize for literature? Tagore could get it for his poetry but Premchand couldn't get it for his fiction. Can we say something? Yes, we can. Read what he wrote to Kesho Ram Sabberwal who lived in Japan and was instrumental in translating Premchand. He was very pleased to know that a few Japanese could read him in translation. How he longed to be read by those who knew English! Tagore made his work available in translation, Premchand couldn't. He couldn't attract and win the Western mind because he neither studied in the West nor understood the Western mind as Tagore and Mohammad Iqbal did. They frequently travelled abroad. Premchand didn't even go and meet Tagore. Therefore he was not able to communicate the West directly. Tagore got a few scholars to promote him but Premchand got none. We ourselves treat him as "the emperor among novelists" but he is still referred in the West for sociological study. Let us not only rediscover Premchand but also try to project him as a writer worthy of our time. Premchand is probably more representative of the nation and nationalism than Tagore who is considered a reprepresentative of internationalism and a writer for the Western audience. Premchand is way ahead of Allama Iqbal who wrote "Sare *Jahan se Accha Hindostan hamara*" but became one of the minds who proposed the idea of Pakistan to the gullible Muslims.

He may not be a Nobel Laureate but he is a *Novel Lauerate* for us in every sense of the term.

We have to read Premchand keeping in view his contemporaries to see how different he was from all of them. In the words of Francesca Orsini, Lecturer in Hindi at the University of Cambridge, "what an enormous stretch of ground he covered in his comparative short life, and how refreshingly able he was to pick up his pen and create characters who spoke and felt like human beings."

## Misunderestimating Premchand

As said earlier that Bal Krishna Bhatt wrote a review of Premchand's fiction and advised Hindi readers to avoid his type of work. But Bhatt was not prejudiced. Those were Premchand's early days when he was under the spell of Urdu fiction. You know, Premchand's book and stories were banned by the government and he had to change his name also. In the course of his literary pursuits, whenever he wrote something there were some disgruntled faces. As an editor of two journals Premchand had to write editorials which became controversial. Once he wrote an article and some of the Hindus called him a *"Convert from Hinduism"*. He was hated by some of the Brahmins because he repeatedly depicted them in poor light. Muslims too objected the theme of a few of his stories such as *Mandir aur Masjid*. He was asked to exercise restraint by his well-wishers. Premchand had to write to Banarsi Das Chaturvedi in reply, "...Hindi readers are so shallow and uncritical that they are always led to believe in the most nonsensical things dinned into their ears. One must tell them the truth. But I shall exercise greater control henceforth."

Ila Chandra Joshi said that while *Sevasadan* had placed new literary ideals before the Hindi readers, Premashram rendered no service to the cause of Hindi literature. Hazari Prasad Dwivedi was also of the similar view that Premashram lacked emotional ideals (*Bhavatmak aadarsh)*. Avadh Upadhyaya published a series of articles such as *"Premchand's originality: Parallelism in Premashram and Resurrection" and "Rangabhoomi and Vanity Fair"*. It was said that *Premashram* was a Hindi version of *Resurrection* and *Kayakalp* is of the *Eternal City.* Upadhyaya lived in Paris and from there he wanted to provoke and persuade Premchand to start a kind of critical analysis of his own work. After the death of Premchand he admitted "I wanted to persuade Premchand with the intention to provoking a controversy so that he could get a chance to reply to the criticism and thus set up conventions of healthy criticism in Hindi literatuture."

Thakur Shrinath Singh, joint editor of *Saraswati*, wrote an article entitled *"My Literary Pilgrimage to Calcutta,"* in which he ridiculed a number of renowned writers including Premchand. Premchand called this *"Literary Goodnaism"* and wrote an editorial in *Hans*. Saraswati magazine very promptly wrote back in the most insulting manner, "We have respected Premchand because at one time he was a tolerably good writer .... But we have never admired his trash and have at times exposed the market-place nature of some of his works." Premchand was dubbed as a *"Preacher of Hatred".* Shrinath Singh was apprehensive about the image of Hindus and more specifically of Brahmins of India who, according to him, were being portrayed by Premchand as the most tyrannical, selfish, hypocritical and hateful beings on earth.

Some said that Premchand first wrote a few stories and gave them to his wife to get them printed in the form of a book in her name as the author and Mrs Shivrani Devi was no author at all.

It was also alleged that Premchand drew heavily from European literature and attempted to transplant something that could not strike roots in the Indian soil. He was alleged of plagiarism too. Premchand answered all these allegations with great calm and composure. He said that he did not model Sophia on Vanity Fair's Amellia and her idea had been taken from the personality of Miss Annie Besant. While Vanity Fair's theme is 'social', Rangabhoomi is 'political'. "On the one hand, we see the wrongdoings of the Hindu pandits and priests, on the other; we see exposed the communalism of the Muslim mullahs. Both are victims of selfishness. If some people do not like it, what can I do?" Premchand once replied. In fact he wanted to follow the true religion. According to him, "religion is what shows the way to a drop of water to find its way to the ocean. It guides the individual to merge themselves into the wider circle of humanity. If our religion teaches us that humanity, sysmpathy, and fraternity are for only those of the same religion then I would not like to be religious and would stay out of it."

In a letter to Banarsi Das Chaturvedi Premchand advised him and gave a vent to his feelings too as follows: Who has not got Cavillers? I myself am surrounded by detractors who would not miss an opportunity to hit me? Unfortunately our literary workers have not got the breath of views and the spirit of fellowship. There is a class of men who delight in ruining the reputation; others have taken years to build up. But what about that? We have to keep our conscience clear and it is all that matters. You seem to take the humorous touches rather too seriously...The matter goes serious when when imputes motives. This would never be tolerated in any case. Innocent flings you need not mind. If you are so touchy, you will give an impetus to detractors to prick your back, face them with a smile upon your face. There was a time when an unfriendly cut kept me awake nights before.but that stage has passed and I know myself much better now.

## Premchand and others

Premchand lived in the age of realism. That was the time when Idealism and Romanticism both existed side by side. In poetry, Sumitra Nandan Pant, Jai Shankar Prasad, and Surya Kant Tripathi Nirala were the representative poets of *Chayavad* as Gandhi and his Congress represented the masses. Premchand took idealism, realism and romanticism in parts. The time was such that no one could be a complete idealist or a realist. Premchand lived in the age when Quit India movement of 1942 was in the womb of uncertainty and Congress was busy in Khadi and Charkha. There were humble attempts of resistance before the overpowering might of the British Empire. It was nothing in comparison with the Russian Revolution which produced Gorki, Tolstoy and Dostoevsky.

These novelists are so great that the great English novelist E. M. Forster in his book "*Aspects of the Novel*" (1927: 19) mentions that "no English novelist is as great as Tolstoy-that is to say- has given so complete a picture of man's life, both on its domestic and heroic side and no English novelist has explored man's soul as deeply as Dostoevsky." Though great in their own right, these three great writers were not the true representatives of their age and time as Premchand was.

Maxim Gorki was a sort of vagabond who cared little about the revolution; Premchand didn't write anything without a purpose. Premchand wanted to attend a meeting organized to mourn the death of Gorki and during his conversation he told his wife, "when literacy spreads in India, Gorky's name will become a household word in every Indian home, and he will be worshipped like Surdas and Kabir." Premchand was all praise for him. Premchand is a step ahead of Gorki. Gorki's novel "Mother" and "Rangbhumi" are similar in sentimentality but the touch of Premchand is different. Gorki depicts only, Premchand preaches too. The character of Kale Khan in Karmbhumi looks like a character form Gorki's stable. Gorki emphasized the strategy of revolution, Premchand preferred a peaceful evolution. Gorki's stage was the marketplace and the factory; Premchand's was the village.

Tolstoy was a practicing Christian who was busy in experimenting with truth like Gandhi; Premchand was a secular and liberal *Arya Samaji* (nearly an atheist) who penned the vain confrontation of two religious communities and wanted to see them reason. Professor Kedar Nath, writing on Premchand's "mind and art", credited Premchand with rescuing "literature from the utter chaos of catchpenny romanticism, diffuseness and verbosity", and compared him to Tolstoy. But the breadth and variety of *War and Peace* is beyond Premchand. Tolstoy wrote with poise and detachment of an artist; Premchand was a labourer with the hammer and tongs. He was a *kalam ka sipahi*, not an artist who portrayed pen-pictures with elan.

Dostoevsky was more interested in writing about criminals, murderers, and mentally abnormal characters and it will be an insult to Premchand if we even try to compare them. Dostoevsky was neither a revolutionary nor a writer with substance; Premchand was the voice of the comman man. He makes it clear in a statement on the craft of story-writing that "climax" and "psychological insight" are the heart of a story, but the heart cannot function without "a touch of humanity and poetic nuance. This nuance makes a story. Everything else fails." Premchand does not want psychological insight divorced from current events.

There are a number of Indian novelists and we are generally tempted to compare each one of them with Premchand. For Instance, we compare Premchand and Sarat Chandra. But they are poles apart. Sarat Chandra, as coined by Vishnu Prabhakar, is an *"Awara Messiah"* who used to show us what an unfulfilled desire and hazy sentimentality might result into. Premchand had no business with the emotion what man call "love". He was the voice of the oppressed, farmers, labourers, and women. His aim was to convey their anguish and the anguish of the people who were fed up with the oppressive regime and their antics. But there is a point in comparison. We compare him with his contemporaries because it gives us a wider perspective and understanding of the greatness of Premchand. Premchand's contemporary novelists in Hindi Ramnarayan Pathak and Sanat Vir or the Marathi writers P. Deshpande and Mama Varerkar and Sindhi novelist M. V. Malkani in their novels Avati Kal (1937), Krantine Kinare (1937), Vishal Jivan (1939) and Sipahi Vaiko, Batai (1937) respectively reflect the change of mood and tenor. Theme of exploitation is a recurring one and all these writers including Premchand seem to be loosely Socialists. Therefore Premchand.

## Tagore and Premchand

Yes, Premchand and Tagore (1861-1941) are contemporaries. Premchand was persuaded by his friends and admirers to meet Tagore but somehow they couldn't meet. It was decided too to visit Shantiniketan but it was postponed and the *Yatra* could never take place. Somehow Premchand avoided travelling without proper reason and planning.

Premchand liked Tagore's fiction and stories but was not very fond of his sentimental feminine poetry. "I wish to see literature masculine and do not like feminity in literature, no matter in what form. It is for this reason that I do not like most of Tagore's poems." Once he wrote to his friend Taj and similarly once when he was in conversation with Jainendra Kumar he admitted that his dislike was due to Tagore's strong feminine characterization and sentimentalism. (The contrast between Yeats's praise of his work in I912 'These lyrics... display in their thought a world I have dreamed of all my lifelong', 'the work of a supreme culture' and his denunciation in I935 'Damn Tagore' echo similar sentiments.)

In a thought provoking work *"Tagore's nationalism – and Premchand's : A complementary Comparison" (2017)* Harish Trivedi underlines the fact that Tagore's resolute opposition to Nationalism is widely known but it is not often widely acknowledged that in contrast most of his contemporary writers including Premchand were passionate supporters of Gandhiji and the freedom movement. Tagore used to utter such words as, "What is *Swaraj*! It is *Maya*; it is like a mist that will vanish, leaving no stain on the radiance of the Eternal" (Qtd in Trivedi 1995, p. 55). It is high time that we should not treat Tagore as Arnold treated Shakespeare. "Others abide our question, though art free!" This kind of hero worship is not scholarly. In this connection Girish Karnad coins a new word "Tagorolatry" (2009) and advises us to leave chauvinist perspective of reading books and authors.

Georg Lukacs found Tagore's novel "*Ghare Baire*" (The Home and The World) to be "a petit bourgeois yarn of the shoddiest kind", "at the intellectual service of the British police", and "a contemptible caricature of Gandhi". In the novel Nikhil is keen on social reform including women's liberation. But he is not very much inclined towards nationalism. So he gradually loses the respect and regard of his strong-willed wife, Bimala. Bimala becomes fascinated with Nikhil's nationalist friend Sandip who speaks intensely and acts with patriotic fervour, and she falls in love with him. In spite of this development Nikhil refuses to change his views: I am willing to serve my country; but my worship I reserve for Right which is far greater than my country. To worship my country as a god is to bring a curse upon it.

This is quintessential Tagore.

On the other hand, Premchand was a freedom fighter through and through and he wanted to contribute his might by writing fiction and to inspire the readers for the sake of his country. In a letter to Keshoram Sabarwal he wrote, "There is a divergence of opinion in the matter; moderate opinion is not prepared to go to the extreme-independence-but the younger politicians will not hear anything short of that. Dominion status, in my view; is a camouflage and independence is the only fitting reply to the arrogant imperialists of England." "My aspirations," he wrote to B. D. Chaturvedi, "are few, and foremost among them is that we should be successful in our struggle for independence." Premchand's articles and editorial used to be on the subjects like *"The role of literature in the struggle for independence," "Dominion status and swaraj," "The duty of the youth," "Get ready for the struggle for independence," "Machine-gun and peace," "Need for propaganda in villages," "The big stick," "Simon Report," "Boycott of the Round Table Conference."*

This is ideal Premchand.

Tagore's flirtation with Mussolini are also well known. In fact, Premchand is probably more representative of the nation and nationalism than Tagore as Tagore is more representative of international and internationalism than Premchand. It is argued that Tagore renounced his knighthood as a protest against Jallianwala Bagh Massacre ("I for my part want to stand, shorn of all special distinctions, by the side of those of my countrymen who for their so-called insignificance are liable to suffer a degradation not fit for human beings" Tagore). But Premchand had nothing to renounce as he was taking his B. A. examination then and his anger, indignation and revolt that simmered within him for quiet a long time got its expression in the form of a novel called *Premashram.*

Premchand took time but on 15 February 1921, a week after he had heard Gandhi address a public meeting in Gorakhpur to promote Non-Cooperation movement, he resigned the comfortable government job, which he had held for twenty-two years. It was a turning point in his career as he could liberate himself from *moha* to write ceaselessly to help the nation attain what Tagore termed a mirage. It must also be added that Premchand lived on, whereas Tagore's luminosity diminished as commented by Graham Greene in just after a year of Premchand's death. "As for Rabindranath Tagore, I cannot believe that anyone but Mr Yeats can still take his poems very seriously." (1937)

## Gandhi and Premchand

> Gandhi is also a human being. Everyone can become Gandhi through efforts. He has powers. He was not born Mahatma. He became so through his own efforts. Nobody made him a Mahatma.... I also do my work, so does Gandhiji. He also faces many problems, but does he worry about them? This is the meaning of life. (Premchand Ghar Mein, P. 120)

Shivrani Devi asked her husband if he wanted to be like Gandhiji. Premchand replied as quoted above. He was of the opinion that to be like Gandhi was no big deal. But to remain like him is an expensive deal. That is why he wanted to be his follower with a difference. He picked up what suited him the most about him and ignored the rest. Premchand was influenced by Bal Gangadhar Tilak first and his ideology but later he became a moderate. It is exemplified by the character of Premshankar in Premashram who got influenced by revolutionary ideals first but later became a satyagrahi. Sisir Kumar Das and several other historians say that it was Gandhi who changed Premchand's course of life.

Premchand was already there when Gandhi arrived after experimenting in South Africa and started his campaign for an independent India. *Kalam Ka Sipahi* was already ready at the frontline and writing to inspire the masses when Gandhi arrived and made his mark. There is a trend in Hindi literary criticism to label Premchand as *Gandhivadi* or a follower of Gandhiism. There are others who associate him with Maxism as in his last days he chaired the first session of the Progresive Writers' Association and spoke favourably about them. But I would like to say that we should read him with an open mind and then decide. It is of no use to associate him with any "*ism*". "A writer is influenced by his environment; whenever there is an upsurge in the country, it is impossible for a writer to bc unmoved" wrote Premchand in Hans ( April 1932, p.40). Yes, he was very much influenced by Gandhi and his ideals but he was not a Gandhian in the strict sense of the term. In his writings there is an influence of Gandhi. He once himself said in a jocular way that he was a natural disciple of Gandhi (*kudrati chela),*but as his thinking matured he started writing differently. As early as in 1919 he told the leaders of the Congress "There is no reason for the public to prefer your governance to that of foreign rulers" and in *Karmabhumi,* he had stated that the transfer of power from one group to another did not, in itself, constitute liberation. In another novel Gaban, a character named Devideen tells a congress leader, "After independence, you will get big salaries. You will live in bungalows like the English men now live. When the regime is not yours, you renounce the delicacies and luxuries, but you wull crush the poor when you get the power in your hands."

In a way showing disagreement with the policies of congress party was indicative of showing disagreement with Gandhi. On the other hand, in his personal capacity he resigned from government service to obey the command of Mahatma Gandhi. He was pleased to know that his wife did her little bit for the sake of freedom struggle and went to prison for it. In a way Premchand liked Gandhi, believed in him, bowed his head before him but did not get overpowered by him.

> "Are you not a Gandhian?" he was asked. "Even though I believe in the Mahatma's philosophy of change of heart, I am not really Gandhian. His philosophy can bring the zamindari system to an end. Anyhow, land shall one day belong to the peasant who tills it." (Quoted in Gopal, 1964, 450)

But there is no doubt that he was very much influenced by Gandhi's persona. He was an epitome of goodness and repository of great social power. The reason of Gandhi's mass appeal was his affinity with the tradition and moral as well as ethical values of yesterday-years. He experimented with the truth and the public took him as a harbinger of Ram Rajya. He became an *Avatar* of Satya Narayana for the masses. His coinage of the word "*Harijan*" was akin to the concept of *Daridr Narayan*. Gandhi spoke about non-violence, truth, no-cooperation, brotherhood, and his mass appeal was mesmerizing. Premchand's Surdas in *Rangbhoomi* is Ganndhi incarnate. Premchand tries to inculcate in him everything Gandhi stands for.

Premchand, like Gandhi, did not want a war between classes and appealed to the landlords to prevent this from happening:

> If the landlords would not stain themselves so much with their injustices that their existence is disgusting in the eyes of others they would for ages remain the chiefs, the leaders and the protectors of the peasants. After independence, of course, land rents will be somewhat reduced-the peasants will not accept less than fifty per cent-and along with that the landlord's wealth will be reduced but will self-rule be so empty of justice and righteousness that it will snatch away the proper rights of any group? That is not possible. (*Vividh Prasang* page 111)

Devleena Das opined that "from early portrayal of Gandhian solutions to all peasant problems, he gradually moved to a point where the logic of his fiction demanded violent and radical social change." Godan is not Gandhian in approach. There he argues like a communist, "Nobody has a right to fatten upon the labour of others. Such a social order, in which a small part of society leads a comfortable life, whereas a large one writhes under the fell clutch of hardships, has no right to exist." Premchand's literary reach was wider than Gandhi as he was able to not only challenge the oppressor as a ruler but also making his readers aware of the enemies within. He was a social reformer who could challenge the powers of feudalism and imperialism at the same time. Premchand wanted to free Indians from not only political bondage but also economic, religious, mental and social bondage. He is not a follower of politicians including Gandhiji. He was a torch-bearer who marched ahead and showed us the path of truth, justice, brotherhood, amity and freedom.

In *Mangalsutra* he says, """If a poor peasant steals a few sheaves of corn, he is arrested and punished. On the other hand, the rich who rob the people in broad daylight are honoured by society and awarded titles. People armed with all sorts of weapons come down upon the workers and peasants, enslave them and rob them in the name of taxes, levies, and so on and so forth. And they all draw huge salaries, have all the comforts and pleasures and indulge in licentiousness. Is this the world created by God? Is this justice?" Madan Gopal rightly comments after quoting a long passage from Mangalsutra and his tongue in cheek comment is not far from truth, "The Gandhi in him, as one would have said, had either gone asleep or the image of the Mahatma had been dislodged from the inner temple of his heart."

Gandhi was a religious man. To be precise, he was a devout Hindu. The last words he uttered were "Hey Ram!" (See the premonition uttered by Premchand about this ill-fated end in his incomplete veiled autobiographical novel *Mangalsutra* "There always have been, and will always be, pious people who claim that the world is based on religion and moral law. They sacrifice their own lives and quit the world...) For Gandhi, religion and politics were indivisible. He wanted to present a blend of politics and religious values enshrined in the Gita and the Upanishadas and the various other scriptures. For him religion and politics can be seen as together because their aim is the same "the welfare of the whole world". For him *Satya* (Truth), *Ahimsa* (Non-violence), *Satyagraha* (no-cooperation) are the means sanctioned by religion and can be used to change the heart of the oppressor. He had an innovative way of doing things. He started calling untouchables as *"Harijan"* (the People of God) as if the change of name would bring change in their lives. Gandhi was an out and out religious man, whereas Premchand was an atheist. He was a materialist. "God is the ghost of the heart that weakens the man. He who is self-reliant is the master of the world. Religion is the vortex of superstituion, the way to cheat the fool." (Premchand Ghar Mein, 1956, 91) Premchand proclaimed vehemently in Mahajani Sabhyata also "Neither am I a Hindu nor a Muslim. In a religion in which one can not drink the water touched by others there is no room for me."This was the ultimate Dalit Vimarsh from Premchand's pen which acted like a syringe. On his death-bed when he was in conversation with Jainendra Kumar his feeble voice mumbled his awakened truth:

"In this condition, Jainendra, people think of God," said Premchand, uttering the words with difficulty. "I also have been advised to do likewise, but I haven't yet been able to persuade myself to bother Him."

No doubt, he remained with Gandhi for long time. The socialism and Marxism did not suit his temperament also. But Premchand's son and biographer thought that ultimately he became a Marxist and socialist. " ...Therefore if anyone studies Premchand's novels and stories in chronological order of their publication, one can very easily come to the conclusion without reading them microscopicly that he was slowly but surely going in the direction of socialism." (*Yug-Pratinidhi Kalakar Premchand.* 1976, 11) In fact, after 1930 , Premchand changed his ideological stance and started behaving as a communist or socialist. In "*Mahajani Sabhyata*" (Bourgeois Culture) he remarked: "The sun of the new culture is rising from the remote corner of thc West (Soviet Union) which has uprooted this capitalism." K. P. Singh in his research paper "Premchand and Gandhism" (1980) also concludes that each and every work of Premchand enshrines an intention to undo the injustice and exploitation and to bridge the gap between the haves and have-nots. Premchand is an authentic writer of the masses before whom the liberation of the people is the foremost aim. Gandhi and Premchand were thus poles apart in the totality of their thought.

Eminent Hindi writer Dr Kamal Kishore Goenka (He is a devoted anti-left scholar who was conferred with prestigious 24th Vyaas Samman for the year 2014 in recognition of his work '*Premchand ki Kahaniyon ka Kaal Kramanusaar Adhyayan*'- a critical analysis of Hindi literature's doyen Munshi Premchand) is of the opinion that Premchand was neither a poor man nor a leftist or Marxist. Descriptions of his bank accounts reveal that Premchand's last days were not spent in penury. Premchand had no sympathy for the Bolshevik Revolution and it was just a matter of chance that he attended the Progressive Writer's Association's conference in the last months of his mortal life. But it should be understood that Premchand was an atheist and was also attracted towards Arya Samaj, so it will be too much to think him as an aficionado of the saffron brigade and Hindutva agenda.

Prabhakar Machwe, in *'Gandhi, Marx and Premchand'* (1981) in Dr Nagendra (Ed), *Premchand: An Anthology* said that "there was a renewed curiosity amongst literary historians about the ideological framework within which Premchand wrote. His rather paradoxical inclinations towards both Gandhian and Socialist ideas were reassessed and his ideological makeup and writings were classified into stages. Initially inspired by Arya Samajist reformism which marked his transition from an Urdu to a Hindi writer, he read up Swami Vivekanand and Annie Besant. In the period between writing *Sevasadan* and *Karambhumi* he was inspired by Gandhi. In the third stage, socialist ideas influenced him. While not abandoning his Gandhian admiration, in 1934, he scripted a film called Mil Ke Mazdoor. In 1936, he launched the Progressive Writers' Association at Lucknow."

Premchand is a text and like all texts it is open from all the sides to be read by each one of us in the way we like and with the type of glasses we put on.

In other words Premchand is Gandhi, Marx, Vivekananda, Dayananda and Sarat Chandra rolled into one. Gulzar who brought Premchand and his world alive on Doordarshan said,

> "As a child I used to see my mother baking crisp tandoori rotis in a particular way. When I read Premchand I felt he had written about my mother. Later, after entering college I read Premchand's writing in English and got an insight into the zamindari system and the gap between the rich and the poor. While making films, I could feel that Premchand was extremely observant and even described animal movements and characters in great detail" (The Hindu, 3-5-2014)

Rakhshanda Jalil who is so fond of Premchand, and her fondness is our fondness too, wises to meet him.

> "When Premchand died he was only 56. I have often wished that he had lived longer. For I was destined to meet him in more ways

than one. At that time, of course, I was just two and lived in Dina, a distant town of Punjab province, which now falls in Pakistan."

This is the way scholars and lovers of his writing remember him. Translating Premchand is also a kind of tribute and reading of the text called Premchand.

## Senapati and Premchand

Premchand was not alone in recording the realism for posterity in the form called literature. There were scores of scholars uninstinctively goading the mind with the sickle of their stylus. For instance long before Premchand, Fakir Mohan Senapati wrote a novel "*Chha Mana Atha Guntha*" (Six Acres and a Third) in 1899 and we assume that Premchand was unaware of this masterpiece. He could read Gorki and Galsworthy; he could not read Senapati and Tripathi. They were not available in translation then. All of them were busy in projecting the realistic scene of their part of India. They were not portraying for art's sake. Their agenda was to produce the literature of resistance by giving voice to the oppressed and marginalized. That is why it is necessary to study Premchand along with others to get the whole story. In a way *Godan* and *Chha Mana* are complementary to each other. What was left there could be found here. In his 1995 novel, *The Moor's Last Sigh*; Salman Rushdie introduces a character named Aurora Zogoiby. She is the protagonist's artist mother and is a fictionalized colleague and friend of Manto, Premchand, Ismat Chughtai and Mulk Raj Anand during pre-independence days. In place of idealistic imagination these writers present realistic imagination and that is why they pass the test of time with distinction. A person who can be a bosom friend of Manto, Premchand, Chugtai, and Anand at the same time can better understand them in one go.

## Chha Mana Atha Guntha (1899) and Godan (1936)

The novel Godan must be placed and should be studied in comparison with other novels of the age and it will not be an exercise in futility if we look at the other texts such as "*Chha Mana Atha Guntha*" by Fakir Mohan Senapati (1843-1918). Perhaps it is the first revolutionary and remarkable Indian novel to deal with the exploitation of landless peasants by a feudal lord. Reading from Nawalpuri's 1959 Hindi translation of the novel or from an English Language translation by the University of California Press (2005) the reader gets a kind of original Oriya feel the words can't express (*Is it Senapati's "oriyanising" spirit?).* This is a masterpiece. Long before the advent of Foucault who discussed the strange relationship between power and knowledge here was a novelist in a so-called vernacular language of India who showed us how power corrupts and absolute power corrupts absolutely. When the age of Premchand started, Senapathi was no more. In his autobiography (published posthumously in 1927) Fakir Mohan Senapati defined himself not only against the British but against the hegemony of the Bengali language. He was a late-flowering writer who wrote almost nothing before he retired from the administrative service. But as pointed out by Namvar Singh in *"Bhartiya Samaj aur Premchand"* that *Chha Mana* is the very first Indian novel. Its creator gave the novel such an insight that the foundation of the growth of novel was laid. Manager Pandey begins his essay *"Bhartiya Upanyas aur Premchand"* with a statement about Fakir Mohan Senapati with the words, "After Fakir Mohan Senapati, Premchand developed the tradition and art of realistic portrayal of the life of peasants in Indian novel (Upanyas aur Loktantra, 2013: 119). Though the first novel to be published in Oriya is said to be *Padmamali* (1888) by Umesh Chandra Sarkar (1857-1914), this novel, states Rabi Shankar Mishra, is the first major statement in Oriya novelistic discourse in which Senapati defines a modern temper that is critical and secular which also demonstrates, at the same time, what Partha Chaterjee has called "our *maya* for the past".

According to Mishra this *maya* for the past is narrated through the silences of a woman who is called Saantani. She speaks only two sentences of five words each in the entire novel but her abundant generosity speaks volumes. On the other hand Hori's wife Dhaniya puts a meager amount into the hand of the Brahmin and says: "Maharaj, there is no cow in the house, not even a she-calf. Accept these twenty annas; there is nothing left in the house. This then is his gaudan." She faints. Hori dies. She talks, expresses and speaks her mind now and then. She intervenes and interrupts.

Unlike Senapati's Oriya novel where the main witness is an Englishman and everything is Englished, an interesting aspect of Premchand's approach in this novel is the almost complete absence of any British colonial presence, despite being set in pre-independence times. *Six Acres* provides "a detailed and accurate picture of colonial Indian society from the rural perspective" but Godan provides a detailed and accurate picture of rural India in comparison with the urban society. Premchand describes the rural world but Senapati analyses it thoroughly. That is why Premchand's realistic portrayal is conventional and naturalistic; Senapati's is realistic in deeper sense of the term.

This six acres and thirty two decimals of land is described by the novelist as a destroyer of family similar to the pining for a cow in "Godan". Senapati has a childless weaver couple named Bhagia and Saria and Premchand presents Hori and Dhaniya. While Senapati weaves an allegory of the Raj, Premchand is here to tell a tale of the oppressed. "Godan presents a moving human document and social panorama but Six Acres considerably deepens the "referential" function of its own discourse by rewriting reference as "epistemic access" to the structures of domination. The novel of a tyrant and of a tyrannical system thus becomes the product of a complicit social ideology and discourse, encouraging scepticism about what is given. It problematises the real so that the rules of this world can be rewritten, unlike Godaan, which settles for the familiar reality of psychodrama" opines Himansu S. Mohapatra in his oft quoted celebrated essay" Two classic tales of Village India"( 2008).

It is interesting and hilarious to read what Senapati has to say about this piece of land addressed as *Six acres and thirty two decimals*:

> It is said that the world famous jewel, Kohinoor, destroyed every family that took passion of it. The fate of Kings from Allauddin to Ranjeet Singh is a brilliant proof of the above saying. And yet, since the day this jewel had adorned the crown of our highly

revered, greatly honoured, Empress of India who dewells in the white island and who is manifest like our goddess Kamala, the face and power of England have spread all over the globe. The poison that kills everyone else glows around the neck of Lord Mahadeva, the God of Gods, and express His supreme divinity. The point of this is that anything in its right place is never the cause of trouble. Forget about big things. Consider our small plot of land measuring six acres and thirty two decimals. People said that in the whole Govindapur it would be hard to come by such a fertile plot. But this piece of land was a destroyer of families. It destroyed the Bhagasingha's, it caused Saria's death and every one knows what happened to Mangaraj's family even before six months and six fortnights passes since he took possession of this plot of land...

On the other hand Premchand describes Hori's village:

There was not a man whose face was unlined by grief, as if sorrow, not life, was manipulating them like so many puppets. They would walk, work, suffer and be crushed because misery and oppression was their fate. Life held out to them no hope or excitement. It was as if the very springs of their lives had run dry.

Both the texts collectively present and re-present what is now called a colonial perspective by the colonized. But *Chha Mana* is a novel before its age; whereas *Godan* is the product of the time. It will be more appropriate to compare the novel with *Rag Darbari* of Shri Lal Shukla or Salman Rushdie's *Midnight's Children*. Satya P. Mohanty, Professor of English at Cornell University in an interview says that Fakir Mohan Senapati's novel Chha Mana Atha Guntha written in colonial India in the later 1890s is written in an allusive, parodic mode called post modernism, but underneath that mode- and indeed through those very subversive narrative conventions- Senapati develops a rich descriptive and analytical account of colonial Indian society and culture. So he is a (philosophical) realist writng in a mode that has post modernist characteristics – and this is 60 to 70 years before the advent of the postmodernist novel in the West! Premchand is a (literary) realist who wants to depict the society for the sake of experimenting with the truth of life.

## Tarashakar and Premchand

Tarashankar Bandhopadhya was at a better pedestal than Premchand was. Tarashankar Bandhopadhya (1898- 1971) wrote about 65 novels, 53 story collections, 12 plays, 4 essay books, 4 volulmes of autobiography, 2 travelogues etc. In short his output is immense in comparison with Premchand's.

Premchand, Tarashankar and in a way Phanishwar Nath Renu (1921-1978) make a triangle for depicting the village of their neighborhood. In fact, Tarashankar is entirely for a region like Renu and unlike Premchand. Sukumar Sen in the *History of Bengali Literature* (1960) says "Banerji is happiest in his regional stories and novels. He knows quite well the man and the nature of the part of the country he belongs to (Birbhum district in West Bengal) and his stories are always interesting." Renu's *Maila Anchal* which was published in 1954 and is called an anchlik upanyas or a regional novel can also be placed with these two novels just to make the point. (K. M. George has translated "anchalik" as "regional". However Suvaas Kumar in his book *"Anchalikta, Yatharthavad Aur Phanishwarnath Renu* (1992) disagrees as "regional" does not communicate the connotations of "anchalik" adequately. I feel that in such a novel the region is also a potent character.)

Tarashankar mentions about the decaying condition in his autobiography. "The village is dovoid of all strength, it is waiting for death...No amount of whipping can revive it...But the dead body is being guarded by the state...You have to remove both the state and the decayed village life simultaneously." (Tarashankarer *Smritikatha* Vol. 1, 1928, p. 139) Simlilarly in the novel *Ganadevta* a frustrated political prisoner named Jatin bemoans, "Dynasty after dynasty tumbles down, revolution succeeds revolution! Hindu, Pathan, Mogul, Sikh, English, become masters one after another, but the village community remains the same." This is the pain and anguish Tarashankar carries when he pens the novel *Ganadevta*.

## Ganadevta (1942) and Godan (1936)

There is a hiatus of a few years between these two novels. The distance of time between the two is very significant because in the history of Indian freedom movement the time Premchand was writing was before the second world war and after that the village didn't remain as before. The coming events started casting their shadows and the novelist in *Ganadevata* realized that the impeding future was imminent to arrive. Godan and Ganadevta are also *anchlik* in their own ways. I wish to place these two novels side by side as both the novels try to underline the fighting spirit of man in the wake of human weaknesses (*Pallir pratiti ghar jeern shri heen, manushguli durbal, se shiksau nai, se dikhau nai, se drastic nai. A sab manush aar aik jater manusya. Aar aik dhater manush. Manusher name amanush – Ganadevta. The future of the peasant is dark; he sees no way out; all his senses are dead and dulled. Before his house, there are heaps of refuse and waste which stink, but his sense of smell is gone. His eyes are without a beam- Godan*). They tell a combined tale in which Hori and Patu are similar. If you read *Godan* first and *Ganadevta* next, you will find that Godan's Hori, Datadeen, Malati are Patu, Chiru and Durga respectively.

Hori is the hero of Godan and Patu is the central character of Ganadevta. Both are being exploited. Datadeen is a novice before the evil Chiru pal. He is evil incarnate. Premchand was writing to give voice to the wretched of the earth who can seldom speak out. For him Indian peasant is in the centre of the narration. Tarashankar's canvas is bigger than Premchand's. He is there to project the whole village- Indian village. For Premchand a farmer represents the village, for Tarashankar the village and its entire populace represents the scenario. One thing that Premchand couldn't visualize then was the advent of machines and their devastating effect on the handicrafts and employment of the people. Machine is the enemy of the village and villagers. Gandhiji's Charkha was helpless before it. Man is leaving the village and going towards city because there are machines and factories. Slowly and surely Hori is dying in the village and his son Gobar is going to the city. People are leaving agriculture and are eager to be laborer in the cities. Gobar represents the new generation. He takes to the ways of the town life-a Western style hair-cut, smoking of cigarettes and chewing of pan, putting on a thin dhoti and using pump shoes. "Why should I suffer for the misdeeds of my father?"

he tells his wife. "He didn't consult me before taking the loan, nor did he take it for my sake. Why should I pay it?" When Gobar goes to the city and takes up a job of a labourer in a sugar mill, he takes to drinking, his son dies and he starts beating his wife in frustration. The novelist of Ganadevta starts the novel with this kind of description when a man is going to the city leaving his village behind. Man is going to the city leaving his village to die in the smoke of the mill leaving the fresh air of the fields. He has chosen to accept disease and pain instead of natural health. He is leaving his fields to work as a labourer. Hori is dying and in his place Gobar is rushing to earn his lielihood *(jaikhane manus duto paisas pave, sekhanai jave).*

It is repeatedly said and admitted that women played a very crucial part in the development of the novel as a genre and also as Icon and representative of the *matr shakti*. Her shape and figure was differently depicted by the novelist but the spirit is the same. There is an attempt also to underscore woman in distress as the nation in distress. For instance, Durga in Ganadevta is like Malati of Godan. She is even one step forward than Malati. Malati is called a butterfly from outside and a bee with sting from inside. Durga is what she is because of her circumstances. The ideal face of Malati shines when she gives a helping hand to Mehta and Durga gives herself to Anirudha and thus shines with her conduct. She is considered a beloved of Chiru and Dev both but how different she is. She is encircled by so many dark hearted people but remains a *devi.*

Premchand is portraying his age. Tarashankar too does the same but his time is different. He stands at the cross-road where he is able to see and show the change in future. In Premchand's time mills were not as ferocious as in Tarashankar's. So there is not only a generation gap but the total environment and scene is changed. Premchand has only a dream to see India free from the British tyrant. Tarashankar is able to see beyond it when the ruler will be replaced but rule will remain. It's a challenge of life where no godan can do the miracle. He wishes to see preservation of values and Indian village ethos even after devastation in tune with Premchand who says in Godan- "There is no hope in this life. We ask neither for a kingdom, nor for a throne, not even for comforts. We want to have coarse meals and coarse clothes -and to live with our honour intact. But even that is denied to us." Premchand and Tarashankar both try to underline the new realism and expose the value of social and economic factor in human development. Premashram's Premshankar and Ganadevta's Debu evolve slowly but surely and there is no doubt that the characters created by their respective creators speak their language. One can say that both Premchand and Tarashankar are writing to present their point of view and perspective and not necessarily of the oppressed and deprived section of the society. They pushed realism and the projection of *Jeevan ki sacchaiyan* to its limit at the time of colonial hoopla.

## Saratchandra and Premchand

It is an interesting exercise to place Premchand (1880-1936) and Saratchand (1876-1938) side by side. They are not only different from each other, but they are also complementary also in more ways than one. Both are loved and liked by the readers and we never ever thought that what we have been reading is translation and Saratchandra is a novelist of another language. Both are contemporaries. They lived at the same turbulent days when the nation was reeling under the colonial masters and Indian masses started agitating under the leadership of Gandhiji. Premchand was under the influence of the national movement and used to call himself a natural disciple of Mahatma Gandhi. He resigned from the post when Gandhi asked everyone to do so. He inspired his wife to take active part in the freedom movement. In fact she went to jail also. But Premchand's contribution was more or less literary and he was a *kalam ka sipahi* not a *morche ka sipahi*. On the other hand Sarat took an active part in the movement. He was an active member of the Congress party. He was once elected the chairman of the Howrah Congress Committee. He used to address the masses during party gatherings. Both wanted to get freedom from the British Imperialists. The difference was in their approach.

Sarat is busy in portraying Bengali Bhadralok and their domestic challenges; Premchand is more concerned about the underdogs and oppressed. Sharat is more concerned about women and their powerful attraction, Premchand is not limited to love, sex and marriage. For him, conflict between people, their problems and social awakening are the issues. When we read Sarat we get to know the basic challenges being faced by the people of Bangal. The characters he portrayed and the novels he wrote are the mirror of the people and their struggle to get rid of the social barriers. "Man is born free but everywhere he is in chains" said a great French thinker and it was very true in the case of the people of Bengal as depicted by him. When we read Premchand we are face to face which the problems, mainly social problems of the people of the North or North India but when we read Sarat we are able to feel the inner commotion in the heart of the people. Premchand takes the society as a person, for Sarat, an individual is the focal point and in his liberation is the liberation of the society and the country. Therefore Premchand is expansive but Sarat is inclusive. For instance, except in Godan, Premchand presents a problem and tries to offer its solution also, but Sarat is an expert in delineating and portraying and leaves the solution on the good sense of the reader. Premchand asks questions but is unable to provide answers in a convincing manner. That is why he requires an ending in which some miracle should happen. In Godan, there is no surprise but in most of his novels and even in stories Premchand relies on change of heart or any such thing. Sarat is different. He is not only an expert in weaving his characters to perfection, but also gives us a glimpse of their inner self.

His female characters are more artistically presented than Premchand's. Sarat's characters try to oppose social system but fail to muster courage to break the system. For instance, the character of Rama is very revolutionary indeed. She does the kind of work a man of that time would find difficult to accomplish. But in the end the novelist sends her to Kashi because at that time that was the only place considered appropriate for a widow. The novelist doesn't have the courage to let the widow remarry. Premchand is also not able to let the two hearts meet in the play *"Prem Ki Vedi"* and Yograj dies because the girl he loved and wanted to marry after his wife's death was a Christian. Premchand and Sarat both try to project themselves feminist but they are the kind of feminists who belong to their age. Woman in Premchand and Sarat are similar but Sarat's women are more tender and soft. Premchand couldn't enter the inner core of the female characters with the deftness with which Sarad could. Premchand's women are Malati of *Godan*, Devpriya of *Kayakalp*, and Gayatri of *Premashram*. Sarat's women are Kamal of *Shesh Prashan*, Rajalaxmi of *Srikanta*, Bharati of *Pather Dabi*, Kiranmoyi of *Charitraheen* and Chandramuki and Paro of *Devdas*. In Chandramukhi he created a prostitute with dignity and poise. In Srikant Rajlaxmi is not only a child widow but also a baiji.

The society Premchand depicts is generally lower middle class and the oppressed people. He tries to see their problems and desires in relation to society. But Sarat is basically a family man who looks at the characters who belong to a family first and the society next. Therefore the problem of a character in Premchand is the problem of the entire society, whereas Sarat has no such class conflict. He is a master story teller in whose novels the personal pains and pines are projected in various ways. For instance, in "Pather Dabi" Apoorb and Bharati cannot meet and live happily ever after because of their different religions and thinking process. They love each other but do not marry because Bharti has given her life for the service of the nation and she doesn't want any pleasure and satisfaction in her personal life. In short, Premchand is a portrayer of the outer world and the conflict of an individual in the outer world which is basically full of contradictions, superstitions, inequalities, and dissatisfaction, Sarat is a portrayer of the inner self in which the character is at war with self. The power to win the inner self is projected in a way that the person comes out in a very lively manner. Sarat himself says, "We cannot measure the depth of the hearts by simply putting forth a number of events and incidents in a parallel line" (Shrikant III, Parv, p 90). Premchand considers the novel "a mirror of man's character" and Sarat considers it "a medium of liberated description of man's aspirations". Premchand thinks that the object of a writer is not only to entertain the reader as a clown or a juggler does. He is our guide and a person who takes us to the path of righteousness. Sarat does not write about the economic tragedy of Indians during the British Raj but Premchand is all about it. Sarat has not discussed the economic policy of the government at the time when the whole country was under the oppression of the worst kind, he was busy in discussing love, jilted lovers, star-crossed lovers and so on. Both write about love. Premchand wants love according to the social norms, Sarat is a little revolutionary.

Once Sarat Chandra wrote the following lines in an essay *Narir Mulya* (1922) (The Value of Women) and compared them with the most valuable thing in the world.

> Jewels and gems are considered priceless since they are rare. It follows from this that the value of woman is not much because she is not scarce. Water is a daily necessity yet it doesn't cost anything. If someday it were to become extremely scarce even the greatest of kings would not hesitate to exchange the finest jewel of his crown for a few drops of water. Similarly God forbid, if someday women were to become scarce only on that day-not today- the dispute regarding her real worth would be finally decided fro today she is not in short supply...

In "*Premchand ki Upanyas Kala*" (p 154) Janardanprasad jha Dwij compares the art of Premchand with the art of Sarat Chandara and says that in Sarat's art the element of feminine is prominent, in Premchand the element of masculinity is predominant. So the former is a messenger of tenderness and the latter is of fervour. Therefore Sarat's fiction is the depiction of commotion of the heart; Premchand's fiction is the delineation of the battle of life. Sisir Kumar Das very succinctly puts the art of Saratchandra as follows, "Saratchandra brings out the tensions and trepidations, the charms and the excitement, the moments of bliss and the agony of unfulfilled love with power. But his challenges against the social authority, though remarkable in the context of his time, are always frought with hesitations. (340-341)

## Dickens and Premchand

Premchand has been compared with Thomas Hardy, Gorky, Galsworthy and Charles Dickens. We take pride in calling Kalidas, the Shakespeare of Sanskrit. This is a kind of complex that even Janardan Prasad Jha 'Dwij' who wrote "*Premchand ki Upanyas kala*"and presented the first copy to Premchand, couldn't escape following. There were others who during his life-time tried to tarnish his image by accusing him of literary theft of ideas. In post-colonial studies we find that this has been the nature of the West to demean the Eastern literary pursuits since beginning. Edward Lane informed readers in notes to his popular translation of *The Thousand and One Nights (1859)* that the Arabs were far more gullible than educated European readers and did not make the same clear distinction between the rational and the fictitious. Edward Fitzgerald in "*The Rubaiyat of Omar Khayyam*" accused the Persians of artistic incompetence and suggested that their poetry became art only when translated into English. Every one knows how Thomas Babbinton Macaulay treated us in his infamous minutes (1835). J. C. Ghosh, who was one of the first Indians to obtain a D. Phil. in English from Oxford, wrote the following in 1932:

> The bulk of it [i.e., Bengali literature] was monotonous, platitudinous, convention-ridden, and devoid of substance, variety and virility. [...] [C]ontact with English literature has given it substance and variety, intellectuality and modernity. It has [...] become a fit medium for adult and civilized consciousness. More important than anything else, it has become humanized. [...] The Bengali writer need no longer live in the darkness and isolation of his native medievalism; he is a citizen of the entire modern world.

They forget that "it was India which first exercised a literary influence on the West, an equation that was utterly reversed later through colonial intervention" (Trivedi 2007). Sisir Kumar Das, in his History of Indian Literature, very adroitly speaks not only of "Western Impact" but equally of "Indian Response" in the following lines:

> What makes this period (1800-1910) unique in our literary history is its continuous conflict between the indigenous and the alien ideals, values and sensibilities. It was not a contact between two authors or two texts; it was a contact between two civilizations in an unfortunate historical circumstance. [...] This love and hate relationship with the West made the literary contact tortuous and complex. (1991:331)

Bharat Bhushan Agarwal, a Hindi poet and novelist and once a senior administrator in the Sahitya Akademi produced a doctoral thesis on *"Hindi Upanyas par Pashchatya Prabhav"* (Western Influence on the Hindi Novel-1971) in which he explored Western influence on about a dozen modern Hindi novelists after Premchand. Hindi writers are often subjected to a close interrogation regarding their possible Western sources. Indian Council for Cultural Relations invited Dr. Siegfried A. Schulz to deliver Azad Memorial Lecture in 1981 (23 February, 1981) and in his lecture *"Premchand: A Western Appraisal"* the German scholar spoke on *Godan* and admitted that none of his novels have ever been translated into German and Premchand's existence in Western learned handbooks and literary lexica are relegated to "phantom existence." Schulz spoke, "In reply to an enquiry. Premchand wrote in late December 1934, just at the time when Godan had gone to the press, that he had been influenced by Leo Tostoy, Victor Hugo, Romain Rolland, Maxim Gorki, and Rabindranath Tagore. He does not mention any of the English writers whom he had to study laboriously in his high school and some of whom he had translated into Hindi e.g. Charles Dickens, George Eliot, Galsworthy." Is it a crime to mention just a few and not all?

Schulz analyzes Godan and asserts that the presence of structural and other feautures in Godan indicates that Premchand is influenced by Dickens. In Premchand's *Godan* two sets of characters are presented in clear-cut opposition, the masters and servants or workers, very much like those of Dickens' novel *Hard Times*. Dickens attacks the injustice of the divorce laws and the oppression of the poor by the rich; Premchand questions the deeply ingrained concept of Dharma ad the oppression of the poor by the rich. He mentions the desirability of a new divorce law in passing. Like Dickens, Premchand links his characters with one another at the end rather than at the beginning as Tolstoy does, when toward the end, villagers and townspeople meet in a scence as unconvincing (Miss Malti gives the village mothers a lesson on how to real the babies!) as that of Hard times (where Louisa and her "class" approach the dying Stephen and his girl Rachael).

Schulz claimed that Premchand borrowed and transplanted from Dickens even more than just structural elements. He took events and characters, even sets of characters, which he inverted and then adapted with great ingenuity to the Indian scene. The dismal Coketown of Hard Times, in an industrialized country , becomes the poverty- stricken village of Belari, a prime example of the rural blight exhibited in Godan. The main characters of Dickens' novel, Gradgrind's comfortable family and the worker Stephen with Rachael ( who remain unmarried) appear in Godan on the opposite side of the social scale : Hori, his wife and three children, some of whose experiences resemble those of the Grandgrind family, but on a different level; and Mehta and Malti from the city who also remain unmarried , wedded only to their respective causes, and become honest champions of social justice, and thus irritants to their anglicized group, as do Stephen and Rachael, the Martyr and his beloved, to their workers... Siliya sounds very much like Ceciliya of Hard Times. There are many other unobtrusive details which give valuable clues to an alert reader of both these Hindi and English novels (Cf. S. A. Schulz, *"Premchand's novel Godan: Echoes of Charles Dickens in an Indian Setting* 1992). Though the speaker finds no deceitful plagiarism involved, he is of the opinion that it is an inspired and ingenious borrowing. I think that this lecture was just a kind of hair splitting similar to the research work cited earlier. One can very easily see that Premchand is not making fun of the poor and the oppreseed as does Dickens. He has profound love and concern for the under-dogs.

It is worth mentioning that Dickens died at the age of 58 and Premchand at 56. Both were poor. Both wrote for money. Many writers write for money and for Dickens – whose indigent father, John, was imprisoned for debt in the Marshalsea – solvency and riches were in a very real sense the Holy Grail. His childhood and early adolescence were marked by a descent into ever less-genteel poverty. It was poverty that denied him an education and shamefully sent him instead to work in a blacking factory by Hungerford Bridge when he was 12. Similar is the case with Premchand. He was also hand to mouth and his first marriage and education remained in doldrums. As both aged their earning power increased. They didn't die in penury. According to the standard of living at that time both lived well. The story of Dickens's marriage and his long affair with the young actress Nelly Ternan is similar to Premchand's love life. Dickens, aged 45, fell for Ellen Ternan when she was 18. Premchand also revealed certain things to his wife. Dickens had long been unhappy in his marriage, Premchand also was not happy with his first marriage. Dickens died in 1870 from a cerebral haemorrhage, aged 58, with his last novel, *The Mystery of Edwin Drood,* unfinished. Premchand died in 1936, with his last novel, *Mangalsutra,* unfinished.

I would like to conclude with a solemn note. Premchand is writing for upholding values so dear to all Indians. He uses *"Marjad"* 49 times in the novel and *"Dharma"* more than 100 times to say that we Indians since the days of Rama and Krishna value our traditions. We live with these and die for these. Ram Swarup Chaturvedi concludes his history of Hindi literarture *"Hindi Sahitya aur Samvedna Ka vikas"* with the premise that our great writers including Premchand are great because they uphold and keep the values of a family intact by protecting what is called Marjad or Maryada. (Ram is Ram because he is Maryada Purushottam). Godan is not only a story of this *maryada* but also it is a modern epic to uphold Dharma. [Premchand himself showed a number of times that he was very careful about self-esteem. In the incidents when he didn't get up to salute an English officer and when he spoke resolutely before the magistrate, we saw Premchand similar to Manohar of Premashram and not timid like Hori of Godan (*Apni marjad ki raksha karna mardo ka kaam hai)].* Godan revolves around *"Dharma"* and *"marjad".* Hori lives and dies for it. With the death of Hori the life of one who struggled to keep *Dharma* and *marjad* was over, but in his death he gave all a lesson of life. Surdas too dies in Rangbhumi. What remains is dharma. Premchand shows maturity and ripeness in Godan.

Premchand can be called a man of Dharma or Dharmatma. For him all the "isms"were there to be used to attain Dharma and to understand the essence of his deep rooted Indian sensibility we must associate his works with his expereiments with Dharma. Such motifs as humanity, Dharma, an ideal village, and dedication are more clearly reflected in his short stories and novels than the Arya Samaj movement or Gandhism [Doi 1967: 15). His boundless confidence in human nature is more palpable than his acceptance of Socialism or Communism as an ideology. Therefore, Premchand is in line with the great classical writers like Valmiki, Vedvyasa and Kalidasa. Premchand gave a new direction to Hindi fiction and inaugurated a new age of Hindi literature and he continued the tradition set by his forerunners also.

## Chapter - 6

# Wrapping up

I want to keep this concluding chapter very short. Only a very short conclusion can tell you that the text of Premchand is so wide and deep that not even an omnibus edition can embrace all and everything of him. He is an ocean, an Indian Ocean in which all rivers fall.

I am unbelievably and immensely grateful to the texts of Premchand for exciting and inciting me since my childhood when I first read "*Premchand ki Shreshth Kahaniyan*". I have been reading him since then. Recently someone asked me to translate a few of his stories in which policemen such as *Namak ka Daroga* were characters of some consequence. This study is an off-shoot of that venture. This book is written in Arba Minch University, Ethiopia (Africa) and in a way for *swantah sukhaya*. We can read Premchand on internet as he is in public domain now. Premchand is our *Bade Bhai Saheb* who sums up his fears and implied hopes with regard to his readers in the following concluding lines of the story of the similar title.

One becomes wise not by reading books but by seeing the world. Our mother never went to school and our father perhaps didn't go beyond class five. We might accumulate all the knowledge in the world, yet they will always retain the right to admonish and correct us. Not because they have given us life but because they have, will always have a far greater experience of the world... I won't let you to tread the wrong path. And if you don't listen I would even use my hand.

I capitulated to this new stratagem. I really became aware of my smallness, and I began to look upon him with reverence. With tearful eyes, I said: Not at all. Whatever you have said is true, and you have every right to say it.

I am indebted to one and all. Let me run behind him and fly the kite now! Please do join us.

# Appendix - I

# The Nature and Purpose of Literature

*Presidential Address of Munshi Premchand, delivered at the First All India Progressive Writers' Conference, held at Lucknow on 9-10 April 1936( Sahitya ka Uddeshya in Premchand kuch vichar, Allahabad, Sarasvati Press, pp. 5-25.)*

This conference is a memorable occasion in the history of our literature. Hitherto we had been content to discuss language and its problems; the existing critical literature of Urdu and Hindi has dealt with the construction and the structure of the language alone. This was doubtless an important and necessary work. And the pioneers of our literature have supplied this preliminary need and performed their task admirably. But language is a means, not an end; a stage, not the journey's end. Its purpose is to mould our thoughts and emotions, and to give them the right direction. We have now to concern ourselves with the meaning of things, and to find the means of fulfilling the purpose for which language has been constructed. This is the main purpose of this conference.

Literature properly so-called is not only realistic, true to life, but is also an expression of our experiences and of the life that surrounds us. It employs easy and refined language which alike affects our intellect and our sentiments. Literature assumes these qualities only when it deals with the realities and experiences of life. Fairy tales and romantic stories of princely lovers may have impressed us in olden days, but they mean very little to us today. Unless literature deals with reality it has no appeal for us.

Literature can best be defined as a criticism of life. The literature of our immediate past had nothing to do with actuality; our writers were living in a world of dreams and were writing things like Fasanai Ajaib or Chandra Kanta tales told only for entertainment, or to satisfy our sense of wonder. Life and literature were considered to be two different things which bore no relation to each other. Literature reflects the age. In the past days of decad ence the main function of literature was to entertain the parasitic class. In this literature the dominant notes were sex or mysticism, pessimism or fatalism. It was devoid of vigour, originality, and even the power of observation.

But our literary taste is undergoing a rapid transformation. It is coming more and more to grips with the realities of life; it interests itself with society or man as a social unit. It is not satisfied now with the singing of frustrated love; or with writing to satisfy only our sense of wonder; it concerns itself with the problems of our life; and such themes as have a social value. The literature which does not arouse in us a critical spirit, or satisfy our spiritual and intellectual needs, which is not 'force-giving' and dynamic, which does not awaken our sense of beauty, which does not make us face the grim realities of life in a spirit of determination, has no use for us today. It cannot even be termed as literature.

In the past, religion had taken upon itself the task of striving after man's spiritual and moral guidance; it used fear and cajolery, reward and retribution as its chief instruments in this work. Today, however, literature has undertaken a new task, and its instrument is our inherent sense of beauty; it tries to achieve its aim by arousing this sense of beauty in us. The more a writer develops this sense through his observation of nature, the more effect ive will his writing become. All that is ugly or detestable, all that is inhuman, becomes intolerable to such a writer. He becomes the standard bearer of humanity, of moral uprightness, of nobility. It becomes his duty to help all those who are downtrodden, oppressed and exploited - individuals or groups - and to advocate their cause. And his judge is society itself - it is before society that he brings his plaint. He knows that the more realistic his story is, the more full of expression and movement his picture, the more intimate his observation of human nature, human psychology, the greater the effect he will produce. It is not even enough that from a psychological point of view, his characters resemble human beings; we must further be satisfied that they are real human beings of bones and flesh. We do not believe in an imaginary man; his acts and his thoughts do not impress us.

The question may be asked, but what is beauty? Why does a waterfall, the sunset, and other such natural scenes and phenomena affect us? Because, there is a certain harmony of colour or sound in them. We ourselves are created by a harmony of elements, and our spirit always seeks the same bal ance and harmony in everything else. It is the harmony which creates beauty. Nature demands that this harmony should exist everywhere, and, the more art keeps in touch with nature and with reality, the better it will be.

In this sense, the name 'progressive writer' is defective - an artist or a writer is by his very nature progressive. But perhaps it is necessary to use this qualifying word because progress has a different meaning for different people. For us 'progressive' is that which creates in us the power to act; which makes us examine those subjective and objective causes that have brought us to such a pass of sterility and degeneration; and finally which helps us to overcome and remove those causes, and become men once again. We have no use today for those poetical fancies which overwhelm us with their insist ence on the ephemeral nature of this world and whose only effect is to fill our hearts with despondency and indifference. We must, resolutely, give up writ ing those love romances with which our periodicals are flooded. We have no time to waste over sentimental art. The only art which has value for us today is that which is dynamic and leads to action.

According to us, subjective art is that which drags us down to inaction and passivity; and such an art is good neither for the individual nor for the society. I have no hesitation in saying that I judge art from the point of view of its utility. Undoubtedly, the aim of art is to satisfy our sense of beauty; and it is the key to our spiritual happiness. But happiness itself is a thing of 'utility'. The same object from this point of view, may stir in us feelings of joy or sorrow.

But beauty like everything else is not absolute; it too has relative value. The same thing which gives happiness to one, causes pain to another. A rich man sitting in his beautiful garden and listening to the song of the birds thinks of paradise; to a poor but intelligent human being who regards this pomp of wealth as being tainted with the blood of workers, it is the most hateful thing.

Brotherhood and equality, from the dawn of human culture and civililization have been the golden dream of the idealists. Religious leaders have made separated attempts to realize their dreams by creating religious, moral and spiritual senctions. But they have not succeeded. Buddha, Christ, Mohammed, all the prophets, tried withut success to lay the foundation of their equality on moral precepts without any success. Today the distinction between high and low, rich and poor, is manifesting itself with a brutality which has never been surpassed before. There is a saying amongst us that to try that which has already been tried is a sign of stupidity – we shall fail again if we attempt to attain our goal with the help of religion or ethics.

Are we then to give up our ideals? If that were so, the human race might as well perish. The ideal which we have cherished since the dawn of civilization; for which man has made God knows how many sacrifices; which gave birth to religion- the history of human society is a history of the struggle for the fulfilment of this ideal- we too have to place that ideal before over selves; we have to accept it as an unalterable reality and then see the vulgar pride, ostentation and lack of sensibility in the one, the strength of modesty, faith and endeavour in the other. And our art will notice those things only when our artistic vision takes the entire universe within its purview; when the entire humanity will form its subject matter; then it will no longer be tied to the apron strings of a particular class. Then we shall no longer tolerate a social system under which a single individual can tyrannise over thousands of human beings; then our self respecting humanity will rise the standard of revolt against capitalism, militarism, and imperialism; and we shall not sit quiet and inane after doing a little bit of creative work on pieces of paper, but shall actively participate in building that new order which is not opposed to beauty.good taste and self respect. The role of literature is not simply to provide us with amusement, or recreation; it does not follw, but is, on the contrary, a torch –bearer to all the progressive movements in society.

We sometimes complain that literary men are not given an honourable place in society, that is to say, in Indian society. In other civilized countries, literary men are placed very high on the ladder of social esteem. The highest place people in the land consider it an honour to meet and to know these men; but, then, India still in many ways living under medieval conditions. If our writers have played the sycophant to the rich to earn their livelihood by flattery, if they are unaware of the dynamic forces working in modern society, if they choose to shut themselves up in ivory towers, completely oblivious of their surroundings, it is not surprising that they find themselves as a class more and more discarded by society. It is true that the writers are born and not made, but we would not forget that rigorous intellectual, moral spiritual and emotional discipline which Aristotle prescribed to them. With us a simple inclination to write is considered sufficient reason for a man to taken to the profession of writing. He need not equip himself for it, he neeen have no knowledge of politics, economics, or psychology; and still he will be a writer. This should not be so, for it is a sign of stagnation.

The ideal which we want to put before literature today is not that of subjectivism or individualism, for literature does not see the individual as something apart from society, but considers him as a social unit; because his existence is dependent on the society as a whole. Taken apart from society he is a mere cypher and non-entity. It follows, therefore, that those of us who have the good fortune to be educated and who have been endowed with a trained intellect, have certain obligations towards society. Just as we consider the capitalist to be an usurper and an oppressor, because he lives on the labour of others, in the same way we should strongly condemn the 'intellectual capitalist', who, after having received the best education uses it for his own private ends. It is the duty of our intellectuals to serve society in every possible way. They should acquire not only the art of writing well, but should also acquaint themselves with the general condition of society. If we read the reports of International

Writers' Conferences we find that there is hardly a subject concerning life, literature, economic problems, historical contro versies, philosophy, which is not discussed there. When we compare our selves with these people, we really feel ashamed of our ignorance. We must, therefore, raise the cultural level of our writers. I know it is difficult under the present economic system, but let us at least strive after this. If we do not reach the top of the mountain, we shall at least raise ourselves from the sur face of the earth to a higher place. With love to guide our activities, and with service of humanity as the outward manifestation of this love, there is no difficulty which we cannot overcome. For those who are after wealth and riches, there is no place in the temple of love. If we place our services at the disposal of the masses of this country, we shall have done our duty. The happiness which we get from serving humanity will be our reward. We stand or fall with society, and as true artists we should disdain self advancement and cheap exhibitionism.

Such are the objects which have led to the formation of the Indian Progressive Writers' Association. It wants literature to bear the message of efforts and action. It is not concerned with problems of language as such. With a correct ideology, language will become simpler and better. So long as the content of our writing is on the right lines, we need not worry about the form. The literature which is patronised by the privileged classes will adopt their forms of expression; the literature which is of the masses will speak their language. Our object is to create such an atmosphere in this country as would help the growth of progressive literature. We want to establish bran ches of our Association in all the literary centres of India; we want to organise the creative literary life in those centres, by reading papers, by discussions and by criticism. It is in this way that our literary renaissance will take place. We want a branch of the Association in every province and in every linguistic zone, so that we can carry our message to all parts of the country. For some time past, Indian writers have been feeling the necessity for such an organi sation. At various places some steps have already been taken in this direction. Our object is to help all such progressive tendencies in our literary world. We writers suffer from one great defect, and that is the absence of action in our lives. It is a bitter reality; we cannot shut our eyes to it. Indeed, this absence of an active life was considered to be a virtue by our writers, for it was agreed, an active life leads to intolerance and narrow-mindedness. A puritan, enforcing his doctrine on others, is certainly a greater nuisance than a libertine; the latter may save himself, whereas there is no hope for an arrogant puritan. So long as the object of literature was mere entertainment, so long as it was a means of escape from life, when it demanded a mere shedding of tears over life and its sorrows, an active participation in the social struggles was not required from a literary man. We, however, have a different conception of literature and the duties of a writer. We shall consider only that literature as progressive which is thoughtful, which awakens in us the spirit of freedom and of beauty; which is creative; which is luminous with the realities of life; which moves us; which leads us to action and which does not set on us as a narcotic; which does not produce in us a state of intellectual somnolence for, if we continue to remain in that state it can only mean that we are no longer alive.

# Appendix - II

# A Hole in Premchand's Shoe (Premchand ke Phate Joote)

## Hari Shankar Parsai (1922-1995)

One of Prem Chand's photos is in front of me. He is seated beside his wife. He is wearing a cap made of some thick cloth, a kurta and dhoti. The sideburns seem pasted, the cheekbones are prominent, but a thick moustache fills up his face.

He is wearing canvass shoes, with the laces tied haphazardly. If you tie the laces carelessly the aglets come off and it becomes difficult to string the laces through the eyelets. Then tying laces becomes a hit-and-miss affair.

The shoe on the right foot is in good shape, but there is a big hole in the left shoe through which one of the toes is peeping out.

My eyes have latched on to this shoe. I begin to wonder: If this is his dress for posing for a photograph, what does he wear on ordinary occasions. No, this man would not have clothes for special occasions. He doesn't have the knack to change dresses. He poses for a photograph just as he is.

I look at his face. O my literary ancestor, do you know that there is a hole in your shoe and one of the toes is peeping out? Are you aware of this? Doesn't this embarrass you? Don't you realize that by lowering a part of your dhoti a bit you could cover up this peeping toe? In spite of all this, you look so nonchalant and self-assured! On the photographer's 'ready please' command, you must have tried to feign a smile, drawing it gradually out of the deep well of pain; and the photographer would have 'clicked' and said 'thank you'. This half-hearted smile is laced with sarcasm.

What kind of a man is this? Wearing a holed shoe himself, he has the cheek to mock at some one!

If you were going to get yourself photographed, you could have worn a decent pair of shoes. And, where was the need to get yourself photographed? You could have avoided it. May be it was your wife who urged upon you, and you said 'all right' and sat down for it. It is really tragic that a man should have no proper shoes for a photograph. By looking at this photograph I sense your miserable lot and almost break down, but the painful and sardonic smile on your face stops me.

You just can't appreciate the importance of getting yourself photographed. Had it been so, you would have borrowed shoes from someone. People show off their sons for match-making in borrowed jackets. And ride in borrowed cars for marriages. People even borrow wives to get themselves photographed, and you couldn't borrow even shoes! You really don't know. People go to the extent of perfuming themselves so that the photograph itself becomes fragrant. The photograph of even the uncleanest man smells sweet.

One could buy a cap for just five annas, but shoes not for less than five rupees. Shoes have always been more expensive than caps. Now-a-days shoes have become still more expensive and dozens of caps can be bought for the price of one pair of shoes. You were also a victim of this gap between the price of a cap and that of a pair of shoes. This anomaly didn't hurt me so much before as today after I have seen the hole in your shoe. You were called a great story writer, an emperor among novelists, a pioneer and what not; but your shoe has a hole in it.

My shoe is also not in good shape but it looks good from outside. The toe doesn't peep out, but the sole under the toe is worn out and the toe often rubs against the ground and becomes bloody when it rubs against a rough surface. The sole would crack and the sole of my foot get hurt, yet the toe won't show. Your toe shows but your foot is very safe. My toe is invisible but my foot is getting worn out. You do not know the importance of hiding behind a curtain, and we love to conceal so much.

You are wearing your holed shoe with great elan. I can't do this. And I would never get myself photographed in this manner, even if I have to remain unphotographed for life.

Your mocking smile unsettles me altogether. What does it convey? What kind of a smile is this?

Did Hori succeed in donating a cow?

Did pigs eat up Halku's crop on that bitterly cold night?

Did Sujan Bhagat's son die, because the doctor sitting in the club refused to attend on him?

No. It seems Madho drank away the charity money given for his dead wife's coffin. You seem to be smiling at this.

I look at your shoe once again. How did this hole come about, my people's writer?

Did you keep wandering?

Did you walk many a mile to avoid the demands from your bania creditor?

The shoe wears out if you keep walking, but it does not get a hole. Kumbh Das's shoe was also worn out because of his many trips to Fatehpur Sikri. He was filled with remorse:

*My shoe wore out through coming and going, and I forgot to remember God.*

And for such generous givers he said*: One is forced to salute those whose very look causes pain.*

The shoe only wears out from walking; it does not get a hole. How did your shoe get a hole?

It seems you have been hitting against something very hard. Something that has accumulated centuries of crust, and you have torn your shoe hitting against it. You tried your shoe against a mound that had blocked your way.

You could have ignored it and bypassed it. One can strike a compromise with obstacles. All the rivers don't break through the mountains. They change their course and go round.

You could not make such compromises. Did you also have the same kind of weakness that ruined Hori – a call of Dharma? Hori was chained to this call. But the way you are smiling it looks Dharma was not a chain for you but liberation.

This toe peeping out of your foot seems to point out at something. You seem to be pointing out with your toe, not your finger, towards something that you hate.

Are you pointing out towards that something against which you have been kicking with your foot and have torn your shoe?

I understand. I know the direction in which your toe is pointing and also the sarcastic smile on your face.

You are laughing at me and all those who are concealing their toe and walking with their worn out shoes, those who are skirting round that mound. You are saying: 'I have torn my shoe hitting against that mound, that my toe is out but my foot is safe and I have kept on walking. But you in your anxiety to conceal your toe have been ruining your feet. How shall you continue walking?'

I know. I understand the story of your torn shoe. I understand what your toe is pointing at. I know what that sarcastic smile is about.

*Prem Chand ke Phate Joote (Satiric Essays) edited by Gyanranjan, Bhartiya Gyanpeeth 2012 ghai-tc.blogspot.com/2013/12/prem-chand-ke-phate-joote.html. Accessed on 17-07-2017*

# Select References


Asaduddin, M. (ed. 2016) Premchand in World Languages: Translation, reception and cinematic representations. India: Routledge.

Bailey, T. G. (2008) A History of Urdu Literature (repr.). [1928], Delhi: OUP.

Brueck Laura, R. (2014) Writing Resistance. Columbia: CUP.

Das, Sisir Kumar (1995), A History of Indian Literature 1911-1956: Struggle for Freedom; Triumph and Tragedy, Delhi: Sahitya Akademi.

Devi Shiv Rani (1944) Premchand: Ghar mein. Banaras: Saraswati Press.

Ghouri Hassam-ud-Din Khan (1937) Prem Sog . Hyderabad : Maktaba-i-Ibrahimiya.

Gopal, Madan. ( 1964). Munshi Premchand: A Literary Biography. Delhi: APH.

Gopal, Madan. (1965). Kalam ka Mazdoor: Premchand. Delhi: Rajkamal Prakashan

Gulzar. (2005) "Living with Munshi Premchand." Indian Literature XLIX.2 119-25.

Gupta, Prakash Chandra (1968). Prem Chand. Delhi: Sahitya Akademi.

Nagendra (ed) (1981), Premchand: An Anthology, Delhi: Bansal and Co.

Orsini, Francesca. (2004). The Oxford India Premchand (Introduction) Delhi: OUP.

Premchand (1962) Vividh Prasang, Amrit Rai, ed., Allahabad: Saraswati.

Rai, Alok, Hindi Nationalism, Delhi: Orient Longman.

RAI, Amrit. (1982) Premchand: A Life, tr. Harish Trivedi, New Delhi: People's Publishing House.

Rai Amrit, Trivedi Harish (1991). Premchand: his life and times. Delhi: OUP.

RAZA, J. (1983) Premchand: Urdu-Hindi Kathakar, Allahabad: Saeaswati.

Rubin, David. (1969): The World of Premchand: Selected Short Stories. Delhi: OUP

Rushdie, Salman. (1995) The Moor's Last Sigh. New York: Vintage.

Sadiq, M. (1995) A History of Urdu Literature, Delhi: Oxford University Press.

Schulz, Siegfried A. (1981). Premchand: a Western appraisal, Delhi: ICCR

Senapati, Fakir Mohan. (2006) Six Acres and a Third (Chha Mana Atha Guntha). Trans. Rabi

Shankar Mishra, Satya P. Mohanty, Jatindra K. Nayak, Paul St. Pierre. New Delhi: Penguin.

Shukla, R. (1940) Hindi Sahitya ka Itihas, Kashi: Lokbharati Prakashan.

Sigi, Rekha (2006). Munshi Prem Chand. Delhi: Diamond.

Vanita, Ruth (2008). The Co-wife and other Stories. India: Penguin.

Zide, Norman H. (1965) A Premchand reader Honolulu: East-West Center Press.

# Index

**A**

Abdul Halim, 64
Acadia University, 79
Acharya Chatursen Shashtri, 163
Acharya Ram Chandra Shukla, 63, 70
Adh khila phool, 63
Advaita Malla Burman, 61
Afsana Kuhan, 32
Ajaib Lal, 20
Ajanta Cinetone, 38
Akira Takahashi, 134
Alaler Gharer Dulal, 62
Alif-Laila, 171
All India Progressive Writer's Assocaition, 134
All-India Progressive Writers' Conference, 69
Allahabad, 21, 26, 27, 32, 34, 67, 93, 119, 137, 151, 182
Allahabad Training College, 157
Allahabad University, 185
Alok Rai, 16, 43, 90, 112
Amar Nath, 93
Amardeep Singh, 105
Amarkant, 97
Amartya Sen, 73, 76
Amina Azfar, 75
Aminabad, 30
Amitabh Bachchan, 48
Amrik Kalsi, 62
Amrit Rai, 33, 77, 110, 112
Anandi Devi, 20
Andhra Pradesh, 57
Anmol Ratan, 31
Anti-Dalit, 136
Anuj Kushwaha, 143
Arabian culture, 64
Arabic and Persian words, 28
Arba Minch University, Ethiopia, 239
Arya Samaj, 26, 65, 71, 221
Arya Samaj movement, 237
Arya Samajist, 93
Aryavarta, 156
Asian Studies University, 162
Asrar-i-Maabid, 67
Assam, 59
Assamese students, 59
Assistant Master, 34
Aurangzeb, 58
Aurora Zogoiby, 223
Avati Kal, 214
Azamgarh, 21

**B**

Babu Gadadhar Singh, 61
Babu Radha Krishna Das, 62

Badalganj, 21
Bade Ghar ki Beti, 33, 111, 119
Bal Gangadhar Tilak, 152
Bal Krishna Bhatt, 61, 210
Banaras, 38, 86
Banarsi Das Chaturvedi, 29, 153, 187, 210
Banda, 21
Bangali language, 171
Bankim Babu, 78
Bankim Chandra, 58, 61, 72
Bankim Chandra Chatterji, 78
Bankim Chandra Chattopadhyaya, 58
Basant Kumar, 93
Basti, 21
Bazaar-e-Husn, 33, 68, 75
Benaras, 23, 36
Bengali and Marathi translators, 66
Bengali Bhadralok, 230
Bengali language, 224
Bengali novels, 59
Bengali writer, 58, 105
Berkeley, 75
Betaab, 30
Bhagat Singh, 153
Bhagat Singh and his comrades, 96
Bhagavad-Gita, 172
Bhagia and Sharia, 58
Bhai Vir Singh, 57
Bharat Bhushan Agarwal, 235
Bharatendu Harishchandra, 89
Bharatiya Hindu Shuddhi Sabha, 160
Bhargava Book Depot of Benaras, 112
Bhartendu Harishchandra, 61
Bibhuti Bandhopadhyaya, 65
Bihar Virasat Vikash Samiti, 135
Birbhum district, 227
Blind beggar Surdas, 83
Brahmin priestly classes, 112
Brahmin temple priests, 28
Brahmin village elders, 98
Braj Bhasha, 165
Brij Nandan Sahay, 34
British Empire, 54, 212
British government, 81, 199, 129, 186
British India, 93
British Raj, 115
British Resident, 84
British rule, 36
British yolk, 17
Buddhi Lal, 34

**C**

Calcutta, 60, 77
Celebration of vigilance, 63
Central Training College, Allahabad, 26
Champa Lal Johari, 60
Chand Press, 93, 112
Chander Shekhar Ajad, 153
Chandrakanta, 63
Chandrakanta Santati, 62, 66
Chandramukhi, 232
Chandraprabha, 89
Chandu Menon, 56
Charitraheen, 72
Charles Dickens, 53, 176, 185, 235
Charles Wilkins, 172
Charlotte Bronte's, 54
Chetan Bhagat, 176
Chha Mana Atha Guntha, 226
Child widowhood, 110
Choudhury Itarat Ali, 154
Chunagarh, 67
Civil Service trainees, 63

Colegiate High School, 23
College administration, 37
Colonial Difference, 49
Colonial India, 226
Colonial rule, 55
Colonialism, 110
Commercial environment, 38
Condition of farmers, 128
Convert from Hinduism, 210
Cornell University, 226
Corrupt landlords, 98
Corruption, 110
Courtesans' Quarter, 75
Cultures and Linguistics, 133

D

D. A. V. School, 34
Dakshin Bharat Prachar, 155
Dalit characters, 134
Dalit Chetna, 141
Dalit Consciousness, 138
Dalit intellectuals, 146
Dalit Literature, 138, 141
Dalit Writer, 134, 140, 144
Dalit writer-activists, 140
Dalmandi, 74
Dan Nath, 93
Daniel Defoe's Robinson Crusoe, 55
Daroga Daftar, 63
Darul Ashayat of Lahore, 170
David Rubin, 90
Daya Narain Nigam, 27, 30
Daya Shankar, 80
Dayananda, 153
Delhi University, 164, 185
Department of English Brandeis University, 48
Dev Kumar, 40
Devaki Nandan Khatri, 62
Devasthan Rahasya in Hindi, 28
Devki Nandan Khatri, 63, 68
Devkinandan Khatri, 63
Devleena Ghosh, 105
Dhanpatrai, 67
Dilfareb and Dilfigar, 117
District School at Kanpur, 27
District School in Pratapgarh, 26
Dominion status and swaraj, 216
Dowry, 37
Dowry system, 152
Dr Grierson, 63
Dr Harivansha Rai Bachchan, 48
Dr Hazari Prasad Dwivedi, 16, 79
Dr Kamal Kishore Goenka, 221
Dr Priy Nath, 80
Dr Totaram Gautam, 123
Dr. Bharat Singh, 147
Dr. Indernath Madan, 148
Dr. Nazir Ahmed, 64
Dularelal Bhargava, 112
Durga Sahae Suroor, 67
Durga Sahai "Saroor", 185

E

E. M. Forster's lectures, 52
Easter holidays, 26
Eastern Pennsylvania, 105
Edward Fitzgerald, 234
Edward Lane, 234
Emperor among Novelists, 18
English Education, 159
English fiction, 63
English Literature, 66, 185
English novel, 52

Essays on Premchand, 114
European fiction, 109
Extraordinary intelligence, 63

**F**

Faizabad, 77
Fakir Mohan Senapati, 58, 223, 224
Family Instructor, 64
Farmers, 89
Fasana-e-Mubtala, 72
Fasana-i-Azad, 25
Fatehpur, 29
Deudal system, 110
Frances W. Pritchett, 114
Francesca Orsini, 210
Dreedom movement, 228, 230
French thinker, 231

**G**

G. P. Srivastava, 60
Gandhi and his non-violent movement, 71
Gandhi and Premchand, 217
Gandhi arrived, 217
Gandhi became Mahatma, 48
Gandhian era, 18
Ganga and Yamuna, 98
Geetanjali Pandey, 163
George Eliot, 79, 235
Ghats of Benares, 100
Godaan, 16, 40
Goddess of Beauty, 117
Gopal Krishna Gokhale, 27, 152
Gopal Krishna Maniktala, 161
Gopal Ram Gahmari, 63, 68
Gopinath Mohanty, 58
Gorakhpur, 21, 23, 32, 34, 35, 36, 80
Gordon C Roadarmel, 106, 113
Govind Narayan Sharma, 79
Graham Greene, 217
Gramophone record, 43
Great epics, 55
Gujarat, 66
Gujarati, 65
Gulistan and Bostan, 171
Gullli Danda, 21
Gyan Shankar, 78, 80

**H**

Hadi Ruswa, 65
Half-Hindu and half-Muslim, 48
Hamida Begam, 114
Hans Raj, 51
Hans Raj Rahbar, 173
Hardoi, 23
Hari Narayan Apte, 56
Harish Trivedi, 28, 33, 90, 172
Harishchandra, 66
Hassan Nizami, 130
Hazari Prasad Dwivedi, 210
Hazrat Hussain, 131
Helen Hunt Jackson, 54
Helpless Hindu, 62
Hey Ram, 220
Himanshu Roy, 38
Himansu S. Mohapatra, 225
Hind Pustak Agency Calcutta, 109
Hindi and Urdu writers, 155
Hindi Kalidasa, 66
Hindi Language and Rastra, 197
Hindi literature, 62, 63
Hindi novel, 52
Hindi Pustak Agency, 37, 77
Hindi Sahitya Parishad, 184
Hindi Sahitya Sammelan, 137

Hindi Sahitya Sammelan Calcutta, 59
Hindi Urdu polarization, 162
Hindu girl, 88
Hindu Muslim unity, 155, 160
Hindu Rajput patriotic fervor, 28
Hindu- Muslim unity, 87
Hindu-Muslim question, 163
Hindu-Muslim tussles, 88
Hindu-Muslim unity, 71, 131, 163
Hindus, 89
Historical drama, 130
Historical novel Manomati, 59
History of Bengali Literature, 227
History of Indian Literature, 55
Holi ki Chhutti, 25
Holy Grail, 236
Honhar Birvan ke Chikne Chikne Pat., 23
Hori and his wife Dhaniya, 99
Howrah Congress Committee, 230
Hubbe Vatan, 31, 119
Hungerford Bridge, 236

**I**

Ideal woman, 148
Imtiaz Ali Taj, 185
Indian Council for Cultural Relations, 235
Indian farmer, 100
Indian National Congress, 27, 152
Indian National Congress at Kakinada, 160
Indian peasant, 100
Indian Penal Code, 182
Indian rural society, 65
India's freedom movement, 110
Indirabai (Kannada), 60
Indulekha (Malayalam), 60
Industrialist John Sevak, 83
Interesting Story of Pathetic Greatness, 62
Irfan Ali, 80, 82
Ishq-e-Duniya, 31, 119

**J**

Jageshwar Nath Verma, 30
Jai Ram Das Gupt, 63
Jai Ratan, 173
Jainendra Kumar, 39, 220
Jainendra Kumar Jain, 41
Jallianwala Bagh Massacre, 77, 216
Jalva-i-Isar, 161
Jamnia, 23
Jawahar Lal Nehru, 161
Jhinguri Singh, 103
John Steinbeck, 105
Joseph Conrad, 55
Journalist Premchand, 179
Jungle Book, 54
Jwala Singh, 80, 81, 82

**K**

K. K. Goenka, 77
Kalam ka sipahi, 19
Kali, 58
Kamal Kishore Goenka, 98, 110, 112, 138, 185
Kamala, 33
Kamla Devi, 60
Kamlacharan, 76
Kamlaprasad, 93
Kanchan Singh, 129
Kandukuri Viresalingam, 57
Kanhiya Lal Manik, 48
Kannada magazine, 57

Kanpur, 21, 34, 37, 41, 67, 185
Karachi (Pakistan), 75
Karl Marx, 153
Karmabhoomi begins, 158
Kashi Nath, 37
Kathakram Samman Samaroh, 144
Kathanjali, 57
Kayakalp, 87
Kayakalp: an outline, 189
Kayashths in North India, 48
Kayastha zamindar, 29
Kerala, 56
Kesho Ram Sabarwal, 172
Khilafat movement, 160
Khwaja Hasan Nizami, 163
Khwaja Saheb, 88
Kishna, 31, 67
Kishori Lal Goswami, 34, 68
Kishorilal Goswami, 63
Kite flying, 21
Krantine Kinare, 214
Kuldeep Kumar, 164
Kutcha mohalla, 73

**L**

Lakhanpur, 80
Lal Fita (Red Tape), 35
Lalit Srivastava, 96
Lalpur near Lamhi, 21
Leadership of Gandhiji, 230
Lehigh University, 105
Leo Tolstoy, 235
Literary critic Nobat Rai, 31
Lokmanya Bal Gangadhar Tilak, 27
Longest Hindi Novel, 68
Lord Krishna, 130
Love, sex and marriage, 45
Lucknow, 21, 30, 37, 69, 80, 99, 182
Lucknow hospital, 169

**M**

Machine-gun and peace, 181
Madan Gopal, 33, 90, 145, 153, 170, 173, 220
Madhumati, 62
Madhuri magazine, 37
Madurai, 100
Mahabharata and the Ramayana, 163
Mahadev Prasad Verma, 30
Mahajani Sabhyata, 220
Maharastra, 66
Mahatma Gandhi, 29, 35, 160, 206, 218, 230
Mahendra Bhatnagar, 69
Mahendra V. Desai, 98
Mahoba, 32
Mahtabrai (Chhutak), 23
Makarand Paranjape, 65
Malabar, 56
Malayalam, 56
Malayalam fiction, 61
Malyalam, 65
Manik Bandhopadhyaya, 65, 105
Manju Ghosha, 56
Manju Jain, 86
Mannan Dwivedi, 44, 109
Mantra, 205
Marathi, 65
Marathi and Bengali languages, 56
Marathi and Gujarati translators, 66
Marwari School, 37
Marwari Vidyalaya, 41
Marx and a Gandhi, 135
Marx and Marxism, 65

Mathematics book, 25
Matthew Arnold, 79
Maulana Sharar, 23
Maulana Zafrul Mulk, 43
Maulvi Mohammed Ali, 23
Maxim Gorki, 235
Maya Shankar, 80
Mazdoor, 222
Medical Hall Press of Benares, 30
Meenakshi Mukherjee, 52, 55
Meerut Conspiracy Case, 94
Mehta and Malti, 236
Mehta Lazza Ram Sharma, 34
Men and women, 89
Mental slavery, 76, 184
Michael Denning, 70
Milan Kundera, 17
Militant woman, 29
Minu Mumtaj, 183
Mirza Mohammed Hassan, 43
Mirza Mohammed Hassan Askari, 43
Mirza Muhamed Hadi Rusva, 64
Mirza Rusva, 23
Miss Malti, 101
Misunderestimating Premchand, 210
Modern Hindi novel, 62
Modern History, 24
Modern South Asian Studies, 73
Mohammadan History, 114
Mohammed Ali, 160
Mohan Bhawnani, 38
Mohan Dikshit, 170
Mohan Roy, 153
Montagu- Chelmsford, 152
Motilal Nehru, 161
Mrs Shivrani Devi, 24
Mrs Shivrani Premchand, 30
Muir Central College Allahabad, 41
Mukti Marg, 114, 205
Municipal Board, 73
Muslim army, 117
Muslim zamindar, 154
Muslims, 89
My Elder Brother, 114

**N**

Nakaam, 78
Namvar Singh, 65, 98
Naro Sadashiv Rishud, 56
Nath Madan, 37
Nationalist movement, 153
Naurange Khayal, 113
Navabrai Allahabadi, 67
Nawab Rai, 28
Nayar tradition, 56
Nazin Ahmad, 72
Nikhil Govind, 151
Nirmala, 91
Nobel Prize for literature, 209
Non-co-operation movement, 35, 112, 152
Normal High School, 34
North India, 70

**O**

Oka Oori Katha, 183
Om Prakash Valmiki, 140
Om Puri, 137
Omar Khayyam, 234
Opportunist intellectuals, 98
Oriya novelistic discourse, 224
Osaka University, 134
Osmania University Hyderabad, 48

## P

P. Lal, 173
Paap ka agnikund, 111
Panch Pameshwar, 111
Panchtantra and Kadambari, 55
Pandey Bechan, 60
Pandit Banarsidas Chaturvedi, 37
Pandit Mannan Dwivedi Gajapuri, 67
Pandit Ratan Nath Sarshar, 23
Panna Lal Patel, 58
Panna Patel, 65
Pariksha Guru, 62
Partha Chaterjee, 224
Path of Ahimsa, 82
Patna, 135
Paul Giffard-Foret, 146
People of the North or North India, 231
Phanishwar Nath Renu, 227
Phulmoni, 59
Poet Balakrishna Sharma, 41
Political bankruptcy, 160
Poor arithmetic skills, 24
Poor Dalit woman, 144
Poor peasantry and Harijans, 112
Poos ki raat, 114, 136
Potheri Kunjambu, 60
Poverty, 110, 152
Prakash Chand Gupta, 153
Prakash Chandra Gupta, 28, 31
Pratapgarh, 67, 77
Pratigya, 37
Prem-Pratima, 37
Prema, 67
Premashram, 37
Premchand and Language, 70
Premchand's Progeny, 42
Priestly Brahmin class, 182
Priy Nath, 82
Priyamvada Gopal, 70
Prof. Francesca Orsini, 133
Prof. K. R. Srinivas, 61
Prof. Ramdas Gaur, 78
Prof. Ravi Ranjan, 115
Professor at IIT (Delhi), 43
Professor Mehta, 101
Professor Sisir Kumar Das, 65
Progressive Writers' Association, 40, 104, 217, 222
Prophet and his son in law, 161
Prostitution, 110
Pt. Bal Krishna Bhatt, 34
Pt. Govind Vallabh Pant, 97
Pt. Ram Shankar Vyas, 62
Pt. Vihnu Chandra Sharma, 59
Pt. Vishnu Sharma, 51
Public domain, 18
Punjab, 57
Pyare chand Mitra, 62

## Q

Queen Dilfareb, 117

## R

R. K. Narayan's masterpiece, 77
R. Krishnamurthy, 57
Rabi Shankar Mishra, 224
Rabindranath Tagore, 58, 235
Radha Charan Goswami, 61, 62
Radhakrishan Das, 61, 62
Rae Bareili, 77
Raghupati Sahai, 41
Rahbar, 51
Rai Kamlanand, 80

Rajani Palm Dutt, 100
Rajput sacrifices, 118
Rakhshanda Jalil, 49
Ram Chandra Shukla, 72
Ram Raj, 80
Ram Rajya, 218
Ram Vilas Sharma, 79
Ramashankar Ray, 58
Ramayana, 66
Ramchandra Mangaraj, 58
Ramrakh Singh Sahgal, 151
Ramvriksha Benipuri, 41
Rangabhoomi, 83, 84, 211
Rangbhoomi or Karmabhoomi, 16
Rashmi Sadana, 70
Ratan Nath Dar, 64
Ratn Nath Sarshar, 67
Regional novel, 227
Revolutionary and rebels, 100
Rich and poor, 89
River Yamuna, 98
Robert Oscar Swan, 173
Rokeya Hossein, 60
Romain Rolland, 235
Rosa Lambert, 64
Round Table Conference, 181, 216
Rudra Narayan Aggarwal, 169
Rudyard Kipling, 54
Russia, 17
Russian Revolution, 212

**S**

S. K. Pottekat, 65
Sadan (house), 73
Sadgati, 183
Sadhna, 183
Sadhu Baba, 129
Sahitya Akademi, 235
Sahitya Martand Rabindra Babu, 68
Salman Rushdie, 223
Salt Satyagraha, 61
Samual Richardson, 53
Samuel Beckett, 17
Samuel Vedanayakam, 57
Sangram, 37
Sanskrit and English, 56
Sanskrit literary masterpieces, 63
Sanskrit prose style, 55
Sant Kumar, 107
Sapt-Saroj, 37
Saraswati magazine, 32, 119, 181
Saraswati Press, 38, 77, 110
Sarat Chandra, 61, 72, 214
Sarat Chandra Chattopadhyaya, 58
Satyajit Ray, 137, 183
School of Languages, 133
Senapati, 65
Senapati and Premchand, 223
Sensual pleasures, 62
Seva (service), 73
Seva-Sadan, 37, 66, 68
Seven Lotuses, 67
Sex-workers, 74
Sexual activities, 28
Sexual exploitation of poor women, 28
Sexually harassed, 144
Shadi ki Vajah, 44
Shaivya, 40
Shakespeare of Sanskrit, 233
Shakespearean tale, 79
Shankar Nasim, 67
Shankars of Kashi (Benaras), 78
Shantanu Mukherji, 154

Sharan Kumar Limbale, 141
Sharar and Sarshar, 64
Shaukat Ali, 160
Sheikh-i-Makhmoor, 28, 31, 119
Shiv Ram Karant, 65
Shiv Ram Karant in Kannada, 65
Shivpujan Sahai, 41
Shivrani Devi, 19, 29, 32, 35
Shrinath Singh, 137
Shripat Rai, 110
Shruti Jain, 143
Shyam Sunder Das, 72
Sila-i-Maatam, 31, 119
Simon Report, 181, 216
Sipahi Vaiko, 214
Sisir Kumar Das, 55, 110, 234
Snehal Shingavi, 70, 75
Social texture of Varanasi, 73
Socialism and Communism, 65
Somerset Maugham, 100
Somvati Amavas, 25
Soordas, 86
South Africa, 217
South Asia Section, 133
South Asian Literature, 133
South India, 56
Soviet Union, 221
Soz-i-Vatan, 119
Sri Lankan, 99
Sri Lankan scholar, 147
Srikant Rajlaxmi, 232
Srinivas Das of Delhi, 62
Stephen and Rachael, 236
Sub Deputy Inspector of Schools, 158
Subhas Sharma, 135
Sudha Chauhan, 43
Sugar mill, 101
Sultana's Dream, 60
Sumit Sarkar, 33
Sunil Dutt, 183
Surdas and Kabir, 213
Sursagar, 66
Susan Bassnett, 172
Swami Dayanand, 71
Swami Gajanand, 74
Swami Vivekananda, 65, 77, 152
Swarn Lata, 62
Syed Akbar Hyder, 162

**T**

T. Graham Bailey, 166
T. Shivshankar Pillai, 65
Tabatun Nusooh, 64
Tagore and Mohammad Iqbal, 209
Tagore and Tolstoy into Urdu, 171
Taimur, 114
Taj Mahal, 100
Takazhi Shivshankar Pillai, 58
Tamil novel, 57
Tarashankar Bandhopadhyaya, 65, 227
Television soaps, 63
Telugu language film, 183
Temple of Nagari, 67
Thakur ka kua, 136
Thakur Shrinath Singh, 211
The outline of "Godan", 194
The Queen of Heart, 114
The Shroud, 133
Theth Hindi ka Thath, 63
Thomas Babbinton Macaulay, 234
Tilism-e-Hoshruba, 23
Titash Ekti Nadir Naam, 61

Tragic tale of a young girl, 71
Travancore, 100
Treasure Island, 54
Turkish woman, 114
Turks, 114
Twelfth Night, 185

U

Umesh Chandra Sarkar, 224
Umrao Jan Ada, 64, 72
United States, 156
University of California, 73, 75
University of California Press, 224
University of Cambridge, 62, 210
Upanyas Bahar, 63
Upanyas Lahri, 63
Upper caste landowner, 144
Urdu and Persian, 21
Urdu literature, 67
Urdu magazine of Lahore, 113
Urdu novel Jalva-i-Isar, 76
Urdu novelists, 64
Urdu panorama, 109
Urdu tradition, 28
Urdu translations of Bankim Chandra, 25
Urdu weekly Awaz-e-Khalk, 28
Urdu- Hindi tradition, 69
Urdu-Hindi fiction, 67
Uttar Pradesh, 96

V

Varanasi (Banaras), 20
Varnashram Swarajya Sangh, 138
Vasudha Dalmia, 166
Venktesh Nagulkar, 65
Victor Hugo, 235
Victorian, 79
Victorian novels, 99
Vijay Bahadur, 25
Village and city life, 128
Virasat Vikash Samiti, 135
Virpal Singh, 84
Vishal Jivan, 214
Vivekananda, 153
Vividh Prasang, 111
Vladimir Nabokov, 17
Voice of God, 133

W

Walter Scott, 53, 185
Warren Hastings, 172
Wealth and woman, 129
West Bengal, 227
Western impact on Indian novelists, 55
Western mind, 209
Western Models, 52
Western techniques, 73
Western Universities, 177
William Shakespeare, 127, 185
Winter's Tale, 133

Y

Yehi Mera Vatan Hai, 31, 119
Yodhya Singh Upadhaya, 63
Young Hindu widows, 28
Younger Krishna, 91, 92

Z

Zamana, 33
Zamana of February, 160
Zamindari exploitation, 152
Zamindari system, 82, 112, 159, 218, 222
Zamindars, 79, 89, 96
Zulekha, 118